Voices of Guinness

Voices of Guinness

An Oral History of
the Park Royal Brewery

Tim Strangleman

OXFORD
UNIVERSITY PRESS

OXFORD
UNIVERSITY PRESS

Oxford University Press is a department of the University of Oxford. It furthers
the University's objective of excellence in research, scholarship, and education
by publishing worldwide. Oxford is a registered trade mark of Oxford University
Press in the UK and certain other countries.

Published in the United States of America by Oxford University Press
198 Madison Avenue, New York, NY 10016, United States of America

Library of Congress Cataloging-in-Publication Data
Names: Strangleman, Tim, 1967– author.
Title: Voices of Guinness : an oral history of the Park Royal Brewery /
Tim Strangleman
Description: New York, NY : Oxford University Press, [2019] |
Includes bibliographical references and index.
Identifiers: LCCN 2018035700| ISBN 9780190645090 (hardback : alk. paper) |
ISBN 9780190645113 (epub) | ISBN 9780190937294 (online component)
Subjects: LCSH: Guinness (Firm) | Beer industry—Ireland—History. |
Brewery workers—England—London—History. |
Breweries—England—London—History.
Classification: LCC HD9397.I74 G8577 2019 |
DDC 338.7/6634209417—dc23
LC record available at https://lccn.loc.gov/2018035700

9 8 7 6 5 4 3 2 1

Printed by Sheridan Books, Inc., United States of America

Contents

Acknowledgments

This book has been a long time in the making, and I have incurred so many debts in the process. I began thinking about what would eventually become "the Guinness book" in 2004, and gradually over the years, it has developed into what follows. I feel very privileged to have been allowed the time and space to develop the ideas during this extended period. Most academics now have to work on very much shorter deadlines than I have here, but this is a better book for that time. Much earlier in my career I was lucky enough to meet John Russo and Sherry Linkon at a conference in Belgium, connecting with them through a shared love for Bruce Springsteen and his song "Youngstown." This was the introduction to the field of working-class studies and a group of fantastically supportive people. Sherry has read the entire manuscript and given so much support and encouragement. Through "Youngstown" I also met Jack Metzgar, who has been with me all the way on this project. Through hours of hotel conversations—including a stay at the Bates Motel in Kalamazoo—and talk in bars that I never wanted to end, Jack has sharpened my thoughts and ideas immeasurably over the years. This has not always been a comfortable process, but Jack is a phenomenal writer, thinker, and friend. I like to think I've at least achieved mediocrity here.

Richard Jenkins has been a valuable and supportive critic of the book and has read every word. Thanks, too, to George Revill, Charles Watkins, Greg Bamber, Ian Glendon, Bridget Henderson, Susan Halford, Tracey Warren, Bob Carter, and Patrick Wright. My colleagues at Kent, Julia Twigg and especially Iain Wilkinson, have provided immensely helpful comments and encouragement along the way. Thanks also to Dawn Lyon, David Nettleingham, Luke Shoveller, Sophie Rowlands, Emma Pleasant, and Paul Cook. Over the years I have taught my Sociology of Work module to hundreds of students, and many of them have contributed to my ideas. Jane Alderson-Rice has been wonderfully supportive in a number of ways, in trying to find out more about one of the Guinness photographers, and then in proofreading the manuscript. Thanks are due to Jeff Cowie, Steven High, and Jeff Torlina.

I have given presentations about this research at a number of universities, including Dublin, Humboldt University Berlin, Central European University in Budapest, Ghent University, Youngstown State, Georgetown, Cornell, Stony

Brook, Glasgow, Strathclyde, Newcastle, Durham, Manchester, Warwick, Essex, City, Southampton, Cardiff, Bristol, and Exeter. I am grateful for the many comments and ideas people have given me along the way.

I would like to thank Rob Perks, the series editor at Oxford University Press, for first approaching me about publishing the book with the oral history series and to Nancy Toff and her colleagues in Oxford's New York offices. Nancy has been a wonderful editor, and I apologize for my passive voice; it's an English thing.

I would like to thank all of the Guinness workers at Park Royal and those I have subsequently caught up with. They have been so kind and generous with their time. I would especially like to thank Terry Aldridge not only for his interview but also for his support and advice. Thanks, too, to Mike Thomas and Henry Dawson. David Hughes was a great interviewee as well as very helpful in putting me in contact with other Guinness employees and managers, including Tony Purcell and Edward Guinness. I am very grateful to the archivists at the Diageo archives in Scotland and in Dublin, including Deirdre McParland, Eibhlin Roche, and Joanne McKerchar. I would like to gratefully acknowledge the British Academy Small Grant (SG-54093) that funded the archival work on which this study is based.

I am very grateful to David McCairley for his help with the project and the use of his photographic material. Thanks to Adrian Sturgess both for his interview with me and for sharing his photographic material so generously. I am grateful to cartoonist Louis Hellman for his kind permission to use one of his illustrations and to Gavin Stamp for his insights into the work of Giles Gilbert Scott.

Thanks to Ted and Sean, my oldest friends, and to John and Sue for being great neighbors. This book is dedicated to Max, Maddy, and Claudia. Max was born when I started the research, and all three of them have had to put up with me going on about a brewery they have never seen. My love to all three; this is for you.

INTRODUCTION: THE IMAGINED GARDEN

In the late summer of 2005, a series of posters sprang up on billboards all over southeastern England. Produced by the multinational beverage firm Diageo, the advertisements featured the world-famous Guinness toucan, and, though each was distinct, the text was the same: "Guinness: Now shipped from Dublin." For the casual observer, these huge images probably meant very little. But the workers who had just lost their jobs at the now-defunct Guinness Park Royal Brewery in West London, which had closed at the end of June that year, regarded the glossy retro advertising with mixed emotions. The posters were eye-catching and colorful and drew on an image that had been associated with the brand since the 1930s.[1] In their way, these ads both announced great change and also occluded it, informing its audience that the Guinness they drank would be more "authentic" from now on while passing over the fact that for seven decades much of the stout consumed on the mainland United Kingdom had been brewed not in Dublin but in a corner of West London. These posters were telling of how a corporate body engages with its past; the images evoked ideas of history and heritage, of tradition and nostalgia. They spoke to notions of authenticity, permanence, and rootedness. But they also told a different narrative, even in the silences and absences that surrounded them, stories about a large modern brewery built because of Anglo-Irish political and economic tensions, of the premier architect of his day who designed the buildings with loving care, marrying harmoniously tradition and modernity in the interwar battle of the styles. What is also hidden from view the complex workplace culture of an important place of employment that sheds new light on a far wider story of work in the twentieth century. This book attempts to tell that story.

Guinness opened its English brewery at Park Royal in early 1936, and it went on to supply most of the company's stout consumed in Britain for the next seven decades. The factory at its peak employed some 1,500 people in what was for a time a workforce that was almost entirely vertically integrated, including brewers, transport workers, coopers, coppersmiths, electricians, clerical staff, groundskeepers, farmhands, bricklayers and scaffolders, cleaners, waiters, and laundry staff. The brewery diversified its product range to include draught stout and later lighter lager beer. From the 1980s, the workforce was progressively reduced as the brewing process became more automated and productivity increased. However, by the turn of the twenty-first century, with falling sales of Guinness and overcapacity in its European operation, Diageo, the owner of the brand, decided to close its operations at Park Royal and concentrate production in Dublin at its historic St. James's Gate brewery.[2]

In 2004, I found myself at the Guinness brewery at Park Royal. I was leading a project that sought to understand the experience of older men in the contemporary workplace and wider labor market. The brewery was a good place to do this research as successive waves of restructuring had restricted recruitment over the years, and therefore, with the passage of time, most of the vastly reduced production crew fit the age range I sought. The closure of the brewery had been announced some time before, and it was obvious that it preoccupied all of those employed on the site. During a project meeting, I suggested to the manager we were dealing with that Diageo, the owner of the Guinness brand, might like to fund a small piece of research to record the last six months of production and the subsequent closure in words and pictures. I had been inspired to do this by Bill Bamberger and Cathy Davidson's *Closing*, a beautifully poignant book combining photographs and oral histories from the last six months of a North Carolina furniture factory.[3] The idea was that I would work with a photographer who would try to capture visually the spirit of the people who worked on the site as well as the built environment and material culture found there. My task was to record oral history interviews with as many workers as I could in the time we had before closure the following summer. The immediate output was to produce a DVD, which was to combine a selection of the images with brief passages from the longer oral accounts; it was to act as a family album for those losing their jobs after, in some cases, four decades of employment. In discussions with workers it became apparent just how much history haunted the site itself, and one worker suggested that we visit the archive in Scotland where the records, including photography, of Park Royal were kept.

I will never forget the day when the incredibly helpful archivist welcomed me into the wood-paneled front room of the Diageo archive at Menstrie, some ten miles outside Stirling in central Scotland. Housed in the former manager's house of a whisky distillery owned by Diageo, the building contained archives belonging to the various brands subsumed into the wider Diageo group.[4] Apologetically, she hoped that we had not wasted our time, as there were *only* four archive boxes of Park Royal photographic material. Opening the lid of the first box revealed an amazing visual record of this one site from its beginnings in the 1930s. In just those initial hours in the archive, it became apparent that there was a far larger project to be done, a much richer and more complex story to be told.

This small collection was simply the tip of an enormous iceberg. On later visits, I discovered that there were not four archive boxes of images but fifty-nine, masses of material taken for all sorts of reasons over the years to record different types of brewery history for a range of audiences. Through a doorway off the ground floor, the archivist led me to a vast subterranean vault holding the bulk of the archive. The space reminded me of a Bond villain's lair, the type of place that housed the submarine/spaceship that will ultimately be destroyed in the film's denouement. In the racks was a complete three-decade run of the brewery's staff magazine, *Guinness Time*, begun in 1947. There were masses of other material, including written documents of various shapes and sizes, oral histories carried out by the company over the years, and film and videos of the site—as well as a fish on a bicycle, which is a different anecdote.

Of course, the ideas for this project did not arrive out of the blue. I have spent much of my career researching, writing, and teaching about work, industrial decline, closure, and deindustrialization. Leaving school in the early 1980s at age sixteen, in the midst of a deep recession and an era marked by high unemployment, I began my working life on the London Underground. London Transport taught me a lot in a very short time about workplace culture and the employment relationship and would stand me in good stead when I became a sociologist of work. Railway employment also gave me access to cheap travel around London as well as the rest of Britain. With workmates, I would set out on journeys around a rapidly changing country in the middle of the Thatcher era. Visiting places such as Liverpool, Manchester, Newcastle, Sheffield, Scotland's central belt, South Wales, and the Midlands made a profound and lasting impression on me. It made me curious about both the process of decline and closure and the industries in their heydays.

Later, when undertaking my doctoral research, I studied the railway industry, and issues of loss and decline played an important role in framing my work, particularly around questions of the erosion of workplace identity and culture.[5] As a postdoctoral researcher, I worked on a project on the impact of closure in the former coalfield communities of South Wales, the North West, the North East, and the East Midlands. I was struck here by the continuing legacy of occupational and industrial identities long after the pits had closed. As I interviewed scores of miners and their families, they reflected on their lives, their homes, and the meaning of coal mining and compared it with their current employment. Many expressed the wish to go back to the pits "tomorrow," not because they enjoyed their former work—they often despised it—but because they missed the banter, humor, and camaraderie of their former jobs.[6] To varying degrees, this positive evaluation of work was replicated in many of the other industries I have studied, such as engineering, construction, ship repair, and papermaking.

Throughout all this research, I have been fascinated by the idea of the sedimentation of value in the past, in what is often hard, sometimes dangerous, often boring work. Are these workers simply viewing their collective and individual pasts through rose-tinted spectacles, were they engaging in what Jeff Cowie has called "smokestack nostalgia," and what would it mean if they were?[7]

But these isolated and individual stories and reflections of work are replicated on a far wider scale on regional and even national levels. There is a widespread disquiet about deindustrialization and a set of existential questions has been raised about the nature of work now and in the past.[8] One way to think of deindustrialization is to see it as what the ethnomethodologist and sociologist Harold Garfinkel called a "breaching experiment," an event or action that disrupts taken-for-granted, almost unconscious action and, in the process, exposes social structure, norms, and values. Decline, closure, and the process of deindustrialization can tell us much about the experience of work, and not just in these periods of eclipse; perhaps the contemporary absence of industrial work says even more about work in the past, its meanings and values.[9]

A long and sustained examination of the deindustrialization process in the United States and Europe began with Bluestone and Harrison's 1982 foundational text *The Deindustrialization of America*.[10] Its real value is its focus on the combined impact of industrial restructuring, linking the social, economic, and political factors associated with the process. Since the early 1980s, many books and articles have emerged from countless studies. The field remains a growing and vibrant one that has opened up many new approaches and questions about the nature and meaning of industrial shutdown.[11] There are dozens of volumes devoted to individual plant closures, and they pose many vital and important questions.[12] There are also numerous studies of plants in their heyday; indeed, the golden age of industrial sociology coincided precisely, and not accidentally, with the era of the long boom.[13] What both these approaches lack, however, is a sense of how these stories intertwine with and inform each other. How does the founding and creation of an industrial enterprise create a trajectory that shapes understandings of work and organization from before the cradle to after the grave?

It seems to me that the current generation of scholars of work and industrial decline *themselves* occupy a privileged occasion; they stand at the confluence of a number of particular moments in the development of capitalism. We have much scholarship on the employment of the industrial age from sociologists, historians, anthropologists, and others. We also work in an era when the process of contemporary deindustrialization itself has been ongoing for four decades. But this timing is also important in terms of the oral sources upon which we draw. The youngest of those who experienced work in the long boom would now be well into their fifties, and the majority would be much older. It is possible, therefore, to begin to make historical sense of this process precisely because we are not so close up to it; emerging patterns and meanings begin to be revealed with the passage of time, given what Sherry Linkon has described as the "half-life of deindustrialization."[14] This phrase allows us to conceptualize the process of industrial decline as just that, a process that has its antecedents long before the point of actual closure and creates multiple social, economic, political, and structural legacies thereafter, generation after generation.

Those studying work do so at a fascinating juncture where the old certainties of the modern Fordist state, the three decades after 1945, have been eroded and with it the stability of the "job for life." This has led some writers to talk about the "end of work" or less dramatically a decline in the ability of people to draw a real sense of their own identity from what they do. Others have used terms such as the "corrosion of character," the "fissuring of the workplace," or "precarity" to describe how contemporary capitalism restricts workers' ability to embed themselves in what they do and in the process forge meaningful bonds with co-workers and employers alike. Increasingly, individualized workers have to focus on their own curriculum vitae and their whole outlook on the world becomes narrower, undermining their ability to put down roots and become active in social life; their relationships become fugitive.[15]

Another element of this story of contemporary work is the growing interest in inequality and how this contrasts with the era of growing affluence in the wake of World War II—the long boom, or what French historians have labeled the Glorious Thirty, the years from 1945 to 1975.[16] As this period recedes from view, debate rages about its role and meaning and how it should be remembered. Does it represent a period to aspire to, or to look back on fondly, even nostalgically, as providing a model to return to? Is this the period we should see as being as good as it gets for working people? More profoundly, those thirty years, some have argued, represent a period of exception, a time against the grain of capitalism's long run.[17] Finally, there has also been a trend to reach back in to that same thirty-year period and characterize the work that went on there as meaningless, that workers then were simply specialized functional cogs in a machine. The experience of those employed in that period is hollowed out and flattened, the implication being that if they took any pleasure in their work, it was a product of their own false consciousness.[18]

So it is important that I locate myself in this study. When entering the Guinness plant for the first time, I was not a blank slate. I carried around a set of interests, understandings, and prejudices about industrial work. My ability to research at Guinness, its closure as well as its active life, was not accidental. Equally, when visiting the archives, I was able to read them in a particular way in order to tell a particular story. The book I want to write, then, aims to draw all of these strands together through the story of one plant, from before the cradle to after the grave. I want to argue that the Guinness brewery allows us to think about these questions in new and important ways, and that further it offers some answers to them. For in the story of Park Royal, we can see many themes that have animated work sociology and politics more generally played out.

This book tells the story of Park Royal and also contextualizes it historically, illustrating the relationship between what happens there with far wider trends regionally, nationally, and internationally. Park Royal was born out of the pressures of an international trade war in the middle of the Depression. Its design embodies the tensions within contemporary architecture and is a statement of corporate values and commitment at a time of uncertainty. In the postwar period, we can eavesdrop on conversations about the nature of work at a time first of austerity, then of growing affluence. What was the role and meaning of work, and what should be the right and proper role of the firm in underpinning this? Like many companies at this time, Guinness aimed, and succeeded, at almost complete vertical integration of its workforce at the brewery, simultaneously expressing the wish to create "Guinness citizens."

This concern opens up into a wider discussion about the relationship among work, leisure, and identity in the long boom: How would profits be shared between capital and labor, and what was the extent of corporate responsibility toward both its workers and wider society? The Guinness story allows us to chart the way the long boom was experienced and thought about from its expansionary stages in the 1940s and 1950s through its decline and eclipse in the 1970s. Here we begin to see a process of retrenchment in the postwar settlement as the organization distances itself from a more expansive notion of corporate welfare.

During the 1980s, Guinness was one of the high-profile players in corporate expansion and for a time was embroiled in a financial scandal resulting in the jailing of its managing director. During the 1990s, the company, like many others, increasingly sought to outsource even key parts of its production process, breaking down the prized vertical integration of the previous era At the same time, Guinness became one brand among many others as the company transformed itself into a multinational beverage conglomerate with an immense global reach. This process reached its peak with the decision to close Park Royal in 2005, reflecting wider trends of plant closure and deindustrialization. Finally, as the plant lay empty and eventually was demolished, it still offered insights into the contemporary nature of capitalism. Its buildings were invaded by urban explorers, as heritage groups sought to save the brewery from demolition. Simultaneously, the firm planned to replace its brewery buildings, designed to last "a century or two," with contemporary factory units. Each moment of this story, then, represents a privileged occasion to understand the wider whole through a fragment or detail.

METHODS, SOURCES, AND APPROACHES TO IMAGINING WORK

The size, scale, and quality of the Guinness brewery's historical record is one of the features that makes this story so special. Park Royal's history is marked by a series of privileged occasions from which to make sense of the wider story of work in the twentieth century. This is partly accidental and partly the product of a conscious corporate and individual desire and effort to remember. This was an active process of remembering and forgetting, which at times were in conflict— the skipped document no longer of official value is, moments later, rescued by the amateur worker-historian reading meaning into the discarded artifact, and then donating it to the archive.[19]

Over the years, the brewery sought to record itself in a variety of ways. My initial project in 2004–2005, at the time of closure, was one such example. I collected a number of oral histories with staff then employed there. Subsequently, I have recorded further interviews both with former members of staff and management and others involved in some way or another with the brewery. In turn, I discovered in the archives, both in Scotland and Dublin, a number of other oral history projects undertaken at various times with staff from the shop floor to brewery board.[20] This wealth of material is enriched by numerous instances of biographical and autobiographical writing by and about people and the history of the plant. This can be seen most obviously in Edward Guinness, who began his career at the brewery in 1945 and two years later became the founding editor of the Park Royal staff magazine *Guinness Time*. In 2014, Edward Guinness published his autobiography, *A Brewer's Tale*, which gives a wonderful contextual insight into brewery and corporate life across seven decades. Earlier he had edited *The Guinness Book of Guinness* to mark the sixtieth anniversary of Park Royal, and much of this material was gleaned from *Guinness Time*.[21]

Over the past few decades, business and management scholars have been expanding the range of material they examine, including staff magazines, in trying to understand the organizations they study. In part, this marks a new desire to explore questions of organizational culture and identity.[22] Labor scholars, too, have taken to using staff magazines to ask a series of questions about work meaning and the construction of the workforce.[23] Like all the material considered here, we must always ask a series of critical questions: Who produced these texts, what was their motive in doing so, who were their intended audiences, and finally how can we read them now? Such publications, at their best, provide a rich vein of material that reflects the hopes, fears, and fantasies of those producing them. But we cannot simply "read off" in some crude sense "reality" from such works. Rather, we have to see them as constructions, as reflections. Often they distort, shield, and mask, or, like any memory store, they occlude altogether the uncomfortable and the undesired parts of a story.

Guinness Time represents an extraordinarily insightful account of its subject. The publication ran from 1947 through 1975, beautifully capturing perhaps accidentally, perhaps by design, the period of the long postwar boom. From the beginning, what distinguished this publication were its high production standards and the sheer range of material it covered. Each number began with a two-page editorial piece that covered a huge number of topics concerned with brewery life, community, and work itself. Editorials were followed by a photo essay on a particular aspect of brewing process labor; over the years, these essays reflected those directly involved in production as well as cleaners, catering staff, transport drivers, chauffeurs, airline pilots, builders, and payroll clerks. Indeed, by the end of its run, the magazine had covered all of the jobs on the site. The remainder of each quarterly issue was devoted to births, deaths, and marriages. It also reflected the numerous sports and social activities, as one would expect, and in doing so, *Guinness Time* acted as a kind of village magazine for the plant. Alongside this was a continual and deliberative reflection on history and the importance of recording and archiving contemporary experience for posterity. One editorial notes the relative paucity of historical material in the archives before the launch of the magazine: "One of the primary purposes of *Guinness Time* has been to remedy this position, to act indeed as a mirror of activities as they take place within the company so that each of us may gain some perspective of the part he or she plays in the ultimate aim of providing each customer, here or overseas, with a perfect Guinness."[24]

There is, then, a wonderfully rich historical sensibility and reflexivity to *Guinness Time* that sets it apart. In part, this quality lies in its willingness to ask big philosophical, indeed existential, questions about work and the way it was to be practiced, in the process elevating what could be a mundane if charming staff magazine into something more valuable and important for those interested in the period. The Park Royal archive also contained tens of boxes of staff and brewery records allowing insight into the minutiae of an industrial workplace—the correspondence between plants and the number of pastry chiefs employed by Guinness in the 1970s, to name but two.[25]

If memory embedded in the written and oral archive is one pillar of this book and its approach, then the visual is the other. The visual in its multiple guises keeps appearing, bubbling up and generally impinging on the story of Park Royal. It was present when I first visited the site in 2004 through my own ethnographer's eye; it was there again in the initial project, which combined words and pictures. Images make their presence felt most especially in the archive with such an abundance and volume of sources. This range of visual material is not just present in photographs taken by and for the company down the years. Engineers and contractors took pictures to record progress and to place particular aspects of the brewery's construction. Other photographs were lodged in the archive by and for workers, amateur historians eager to see *their* history preserved. During one session in the archive, I discovered a bundle of almost abstract images of bare steelwork marking the skeletal progress in the brewery's construction in the 1930s. Wrapped around the parcel was a short text explaining what the images recorded. There was no name signed, but the author understood the importance of what he had done. Even in his self-imposed anonymity, he wanted *his* history to count.

And what of the official photographers themselves: How do we understand their work? The most impressive images in the collection date from the late 1940s and early 1950s. Beautifully composed and richly evocative, these are images influenced by what later became known as the "New Look" in industrial photography and were taken by A R Tanner. Tanner had cut his teeth in the interwar years on the magazine *Picture Post*. During the war, he served in the Army

Photography Unit recording the Allies' progress across Europe after D-Day. He helped to record the liberation of the Nazi death camps at the end of the conflict. What, one wonders, was Tanner thinking about when he took his skillful pictures at Park Royal just half a decade later?[26]

Photographs represent the bulk of the visual material, but these are joined by a wide range of other image types. Oil paintings commissioned by the Guinness Company of the site and importantly the labor that went on there include studies by John Gilroy and the leading industrial artist Terrance Cuneo. There are also a number of films and later videos of various aspects of Park Royal made by professionals and amateurs across the years, including a short silent film of the last apprentice cooper and his "graduation ceremony."[27]

The social sciences and humanities are far more receptive to visual imagery now than even in the relatively recent past. Indeed, it could now be seen as part of the mainstream of many disciplines.[28] There remains, though, a lingering suspicion that such material lacks credibility, and perhaps my own subdiscipline of work sociology remains one of the most resistant—a reviewer once commented that I should write about "real" workers rather than "pictures" of them.[29] The visual is used here in a number of ways. It is used to show the act of visual historical witness—a deliberative and deliberate recording of events, things, and people. In doing so, the book reflects on the framing and editing of what is included and what is excluded in such an act. I am interested in the ways an organization comes to know itself through the visual, how it reflects on its past when images are recycled and rediscovered. It follows that the intention here is to examine the role visual material plays in how we know the past *now* and how we have known the past *in the past*. As social historian Raphael Samuel noted: "The art of memory, as it was practiced in the ancient world, was a pictorial art, focusing not on words but on images. It treated sight as primary."[30]

I have also used the visual in another way. In various interviews, for instance, I used images of Park Royal to elicit memories of place and persons. Images help to stimulate and provoke. They allow us to ask questions in slightly different ways and they play a democratizing role in the interview process—the interviewee becomes the expert, the interviewer the eager listener. Through such photo-elicitation techniques, we learn more about what is present and what is excluded in narratives.[31]

We could see the rise in popularity of visual material within academic study as marking a wider process, what Samuel, drawing on Freud, has called "scopophilia"—the desire to see.[32] This desire reflects a sense of loss, especially in the context of this book, the loss of industry and the industrial structure of feeling associated with it. As Samuel suggests, "Under this optic old photographs could be seen as a play on the irrecoverability of the past, the impossibility of bringing the dead to life. The keeping of the photograph here is a grasping after shadows; it is a closing of the stable door after the horse has bolted."[33]

In looking at all the material collected for this book, visual and nonvisual, we are confronted with a disparate set of resources, and the question begged is: How do we make sense of them? The evidence presented here can be read as images of different kinds, both the literal images, such as the photographs, and the written and oral sources. Here I am drawing on the ideas of Humphrey Jennings. In *Pandaemonium*, Jennings sought to collect hundreds of fragments of writing—reportage, diary entries, and creative work—by people who had lived through and witnessed the Industrial Revolution in Britain in the seventeenth and nineteenth centuries.[34] *Pandaemonium* is important in both form and content. The collection and structuring of the material illustrates Jennings's own surrealist sensibility—the juxtaposition of differing images that allow us to look anew upon the process and events of industrialization. While interested in differing views of industrial transition, his collection seeks to capture a poetic sensibility of that change. He described these passages as "images," and his intention was to create what he called an *imaginative history*. In explaining his method, he wrote in the introduction to *Pandaemonium*:

> I do not claim that they represent the truth—they are too varied, even contradictory, for that. But they represent human experience. They are the record of mental events. Events of the heart. They are facts (the historian's kind of facts) which have been passed through the feelings and the mind of an individual and have forced him to write. And what he wrote is a picture—a coloured picture of them. His personality has coloured them and selected and altered and pruned and enlarged and minimised and exaggerated. Admitted. But he himself is part, was part of the period, even part of the event itself—he was an actor, a spectator in it.[35]

We could, therefore, see the types of material with which we collectively render working life in this way, as images of life and labor. These images allow us a glimpse, albeit a fleeting one, of a life lived from the perspective of those who experienced it. We understand from these images what motivates people, what they see as important, what they choose to highlight and ignore, how they choose to start their story and how it is ended, how they coped with and understood their triumphs and setbacks, slights and victories. We get, then, what the late American oral historian Studs Terkel described as the opening of "sluice gates of dammed-up hurts and dreams."[36]

What does all this mean, and what are the implications for this study of working life and, ultimately, deindustrialization? I think the power of what Jennings was trying to do lies in his attempt to capture different aspects of life, and especially the lived experience of working life, often but not exclusively working-class life. It was his surrealism, his poetic and filmic sensibility that allowed him to tap into these feelings and affective responses around industrial change in *Pandaemonium* and his films.[37] Jennings recognizes the complexity of these processes, and as a result we have to seek approaches and methods that allow us access to these complexities. His art captured fragments of identity and meaning, in the doing, the waiting, the listening, and the rhythms of work. He captured in minute fragments the richness of work and in the process evokes an industrial structure of feeling.

I use the words *image* and *imagination* to examine the different forms of thinking about the past, present, and future of both Guinness and the wider world of work and organizations. The story of Park Royal is, in microcosm, the story of work in the twentieth century more broadly. Those who worked at Park Royal conceived of work at various points in time in particular ways. These were shaped powerfully by experience inside and outside the workplace. At the same time, they were in all their different ways imagining and reimagining work in the past, present, and future. As a Guinness regional manager noted of the status of his own memory and history:

> Each person lives in his own world. Each person interprets and records his experiences in the light of previously recorded experience. Memory is only the difference between how you recorded something at the time and what you allow yourself to extract from the record now. If no two people see the same event in the same way, does it matter if their ability or willingness to remember it later varies? This is why it is always interesting to cover the same ground, historically speaking, as seen by more than one person. You obtain interest, but not accuracy. When a majority agree in their description of an event, it is taken to represent the truth of the matter. Such is reality![38]

This echoes what Samuel and Thompson called the myths we live by, where "memory is inherently revisionist, an exercise in selective amnesia. What is forgotten may be as important as what is remembered."[39] Within oral history theory, this is an accepted strength of the approach, as Italian oral historian Alessandro Portelli notes: "The oral sources used in this essay are not always fully reliable in point of fact. Rather than being a weakness, this is, however, their strength: errors, invention and myths lead us through and beyond facts to their meanings."[40]

The competing images produced as part of the Guinness story afford us a different sort of insight into the truth of events. The Guinness material shows the ways that staff were confronting problems and finding solutions within a fluid social and economic dynamic. Park Royal was imagined as a rational efficient factory, as an architectural design that successfully married modern and traditional sensibilities. This was a building that was imagined as lasting a "century or two," a wonderfully vague yet simultaneously confident statement of purpose, of faith in history and progress. Guinness was nearly two centuries old by the time it built its London brewery but managed to mix paternalism with its progressive labor regimes. It was a site where industrial citizenry would be forged, creating "Guinness citizens." Before it was opened, rumors circulated that the buildings were to house a bicycle factory or an armaments plant making explosives from potatoes. Park Royal was also imagined as a garden, an "estate in factoryland," a village, a family. The site across its life was imagined as an arena of play and fantasy—it hosted events for the 1948 London Olympics, it was the backdrop for the 1960s police drama *Z Cars*, and it was invaded by alien Cybermen for the BBC's *Doctor Who* children's sci-fi classic. Later still, developers reimagined the area as a site of conflict, as a landscape of neoliberalism and ultimately as a terrain of demolition, destruction, and deindustrialization. And before it closed, urban explorers reimagined it as an abandoned ruin to be spurlunked, photographed, and fetishized. The brewery was used as a backdrop for the films *Basic Instinct 2* and *Batman Returns* and the TV play *Friends and Crocodiles*. As the buildings at Park Royal were about to be demolished, the preservation community, in particular the Twentieth Century Society, imagined the site as one of the finest examples of intact industrial architecture in the country, while the owners reimagined it as populated by newly built modern industrial buildings.

This book is an attempt to understand work through this kaleidoscope of images—oral, written, material, and visual. As such, it is an argument *for* and an example *of* a new way of thinking about work sociologically—in other words, an imaginative history of work.

1

THE MACHINE
IN THE GARDEN

In the autumn of 1933, J. B. Priestley set out on what was to become the subject of his book *English Journey*, a long, looping meander through a troubled and changing landscape. Priestley began his travels from London by catching a motor coach that drove out of the capital along the Great West Road on his way to Southampton. After some reflections on the democracy of his chosen mode of transport—this was his first trip in a motor coach—he fell to musing about the scene that he passed by:

> After the familiar muddle of West London, the Great West Road looked very odd. Being new, it did not look English. We might have suddenly rolled into California. Or, for that matter, into one of the main avenues of the old exhibitions, like the Franco-British Exhibition of my boyhood. It was the line of new factories on each side that suggested the exhibition, for years of the West Riding have fixed for ever my idea of what a proper factory looks like; a grim blackened rectangle with a tall chimney at one corner. These decorative little buildings, all glass and concrete and chromium plate, seem to my barbaric mind to be merely playing at being factories.[1]

Priestley refused to see these new factories as authentic, as he continued: "You could go up to any one of these charming little fellows, I feel, and safely order an ice-cream or select a few picture post-cards. But as for industry, real industry with double entry and bills of lading, I cannot believe them capable of it."[2] To Priestley their cosmetic appeal and prominent positioning on a main arterial road symbolized the shift of industry from the "old" North to the "new" South. But his concern with authenticity does not end with the new architecture in which they are self-consciously wrapped, for these new places of work produced not tangible heavy industrial products but rather "potato crisps, scents, tooth pastes, bathing costumes, fire extinguishers." These sites of industry, the work that goes on in them and the products made there, had a certain weightlessness about them; they were somehow trivial, insubstantial, and inauthentic. As Priestley noted, "if we could all get a living out of them, what a pleasanter country this would be, like a permanent exhibition ground, all glass and chromium plate and nice painted signs and coloured lights."[3] Priestley sensed a "catch," that somehow this new landscape of industry and labor was too good to be true and that real value was being created elsewhere.[4]

Priestley was not alone in his unease about the English, or about the wider British, economy in the 1930s. Fellow essayist George Orwell made a similar but more narrowly defined trip in 1936, to Yorkshire and Lancashire in the industrial North and Northwest to discover the fate of authentic workers and their old industries. Early on in *Road to Wigan Pier*, he reminded his readers of the centrality of industrial labor, especially that of the coal miner:

> Our civilization . . . is founded on coal, more completely than one realizes until one stops to think about it. The machines that keep us alive, and the machines that make the machines, are all directly or indirectly dependent upon coal. In the metabolism of the Western world the coal miner is second in importance only to the man who ploughs the soil. He is a sort of grimy caryatid upon whose shoulders nearly everything that is *not* grimy is supported.[5]

Like Priestley, Orwell set out to discover the *real* and *authentic* condition of England and of the sources of wealth on which industrialism is based; both read value in the grime of the old and are suspicious of the cleanliness of the new. This lionizing of heroic work and workers was a common trope in the interwar period and especially the 1930s. The left-leaning Documentary Film Movement self-consciously sought out workers in traditional industries as subjects for their films of the period. Influenced by European socialist realism, the group attempted to capture the "dignified labour" of steelworkers, shipbuilders, and coalminers. Paul Swann, in his fascinating account of the movement, quotes Edgar Anstey, an influential member of this group, on his attitude to the representation of manual labor: "The workingman can only be a heroic figure. If he's not heroic, he can't be a workingman almost."[6]

These and other contemporaneous accounts of the period invoke a series of dichotomies: male/female, masculine/effeminate, grimy/clean, heavy/weightless, tradition/new, authentic/inauthentic, decline/expansion, and finally North/South. Britain was a country of difference during this period when three million unemployed were largely, although by no means exclusively, confined to the old industrial North and the Celtic fringe while new industries in the South expanded, defining the imaginative geography of the nation.[7]

These distressed areas, and the distressed people who populated them, made a stark contrast to the greenfield sites slated as "industrial locations and primed as a new field for Fordism, ready with all the modern things: connectivity, technology and marketability."[8] In a 1934 parliamentary debate a member of Parliament contrasted the fates of old and new industrial regions and their relative attractions:

> It is, I think—and many industrialists agree with me—a real barrier to the establishment of firms in depressed areas to be faced with the ruins of industries. You

cannot expect the birth of new industries in the rather unkempt graveyards of the old. There is not one prospective employer, looking for a site for a factory, who, taken first to the Great West Road, with its neatness, tidiness and newness, with all the signs of growth and progress, and then to one of the derelict areas with the relics of past industry all around, would not be influenced in favour of the first and against the second.[9]

This relative attraction of the South and the repulsion from the North was not simply a case of competing aesthetics. What was often left unsaid was that the older industrial areas were heavily unionized and were bastions of the Labour Party. The attraction of southern England for many investors seeking to build anew lay in the fact that they could recruit a "green" workforce from the ranks of women, the youth, and men from more deferential backgrounds, unused to industry and unlikely to have trade union experience.[10]

Labor in the new industrial areas was imagined as a tabula rasa, a blank slate, being without character or tradition. The sense of a new type of work and a new type of worker emerging at this time found resonance more abstractly in landmark caricatures of industrial labor in popular culture during the interwar period. Films such as Fritz Lang's *Metropolis* (1927) and Charlie Chaplin's *Modern Times* (1937), and novels like Huxley's (1932) *Brave New World*,[11] portrayed workers engaged in mind-numbing routines—factories producing mass products *and* simultaneously mass undifferentiated workers. The lack of differentiation and absence of character in this new mass becomes an object of fear. In this dystopian vision, the new masses are read as mindless unthinking workers easily manipulated by those who might seek to control them.

The 1930s was a pivotal decade in British history. Rather than being a dead space sandwiched between two world wars, it was a period of contrast and contradiction, an era marked by tradition and inertia as well as upheaval and change. For subsequent generations, the 1930s has become a totemic decade against which subsequent eras have reacted and from which they have set themselves apart. The postwar era of the "long boom" or the Glorious Thirty cannot be fully understood without appreciating the lasting legacy of the 1930s. In Britain, at least, the Depression era acted as a lodestone, powerfully shaping a collective set of postwar political, economic, and social assumptions—a consensus that was only really challenged from the 1970s onward.[12]

At around the same time that Priestley sped along the Great West Road in his motor coach, senior members of the Guinness Company were scrambling through a corrugated iron fence on Western Avenue, another parallel arterial road close by. They were engaged in a secretive cloak-and-dagger search for a site for their new English brewery and had decided on an old exhibition site at Park Royal. The story of the conception, planning, building, and eventual opening of the Guinness brewery throws new light on work and industry during this time and how it was imagined.

BUILDING AN ENGLISH BREWERY

Why did Guinness decide to build its English brewery? The company founded its Dublin brewery at St. James's Gate, to the west of the city center, in 1759. The site, on which Guinness obtained a nine-thousand-year lease, grew over the years but was hemmed in by urban sprawl. This brewery at first produced a lighter type of ale before turning to the production of the darker, heavier, and stronger porter beer, which had its origins in London's East End.[13] Guinness increased its market share in both Dublin and then the whole of Ireland. It began exporting beer to the British mainland through the west-coast ports of Bristol and Liverpool in the early nineteenth century. In 1886, Guinness became the first major brewer to be traded on the London Stock Exchange. The company was by then the largest brewer in the United Kingdom, producing more than a million barrels annually for domestic and export consumption.[14] The new undertaking was known as Arthur Guinness, Sons & Company, and the floatation consisted of 250,000 ordinary shares at £10.00; 200,000 6 percent cumulative preferred shares at £10.00; and a further 150,000 5 percent debenture shares, redeemable at the company's option after twenty years. One-third of the ordinary shares were reserved for Edward Cecil Guinness, at a stroke making him the wealthiest man in Ireland and one of the richest in the United Kingdom. Significantly, the headquarters of the new organization would be in London rather than Dublin.[15]

Over the years Guinness had considered creating a production base in England, and indeed had purchased land in Manchester in the Northwest. Plans were even drawn up for the design of the putative brewery, but these were put on hold at the outbreak of the Great War in 1914. These drawings were periodically updated over the years but were not developed, to a large extent because the St. James's Gate facility was more than able to supply the existing demand. The decision to build in the end came down to politics.

The Guinness family were Protestants in a largely Catholic country but had been sympathetic supporters of Catholic emancipation and were known as fair and generous paternalistic employers.[16] Ireland was an unstable place even before the Great War, with Protestant unrest in the North, in Ulster, and after 1916, following the nationalist Easter Rising centered in Dublin, in the rest of the country. Throughout this period the company continued to brew in Ireland and distribute its stout on both sides of the Irish Sea with little interruption.[17] There was, however, growing concern for the firm's longer-term prospects, after the creation of the Irish Free State in 1921 and with the labor troubles the company experienced during the first half of that decade. Guinness was in a vulnerable position, being a London-registered company brewing in Dublin while reliant on the mainland for some of its raw material and much of its market— by the early 1930s, two-thirds of St. James's Gate's production was exported to England.[18] In 1931, economic crisis hit the United Kingdom, bringing down the

Labour government and creating impetus for protectionist measures in the new budget.[19] Excise duty was raised on a standard barrel of beer from 103 to 134 shillings. The company predicted that this would reduce their sales by one-fifth. Then, in February 1932, the Fianna Fáil Party led by Eamon de Valera was elected to power in Ireland on a platform of repudiating agreements on land annuities dating back to the setting up of the Free State a decade before.[20] Throughout 1932, Anglo-Irish governmental relations worsened, with an "economic war" breaking out and duties placed on certain exports. However, the company predicted that creating a second base in Manchester would hit profits, when transport and distribution costs were taken into account. The real tipping point came when the British government, through Secretary of State for the Dominions J. H. Thomas, gave a stark warning to the company that unless Guinness undertook to build a brewery in England the UK government would impose an import duty on beer from Ireland.[21]

The timing of the actual decision to create the English brewery is difficult to determine as this was disguised within the board's minutes, but several sources speculate that it was probably made November 9, 1932, when a minute of the board meeting rather prosaically recorded: "The chairman then gave the meeting his views on various matters connected with our trade, and discussed the way in which future developments might affect the policy of the Brewery."[22]

This same wording was used to record subsequent board discussions about the new English brewery in order to maintain secrecy during planning and early building stages.[23] Why was there so much secrecy about the new development? Reading through the archive and the secondary material written about Park Royal over the years, I feel less like an academic and more like a consumer of spy fiction, for Guinness, at least for the initial stages of the planning and building, engaged in a level of subterfuge that befits a Cold War novel rather than a company history.

The reasons for this opacity, often referred to subsequently by those involved at the time as "cloak-and-dagger" maneuvers, were numerous. First, the board members were genuinely concerned about the reaction of the Irish government to the news of building in England. Guinness was the biggest exporter from the Free State and its largest company. It was a big employer in Dublin, producing 80 percent of the beer consumed in Ireland. One consideration, therefore, was that the Irish government might have retaliated against the company in some way, possibly nationalizing the Dublin plant. Second, the board wanted to maintain cover for as long as possible so as not to inflate land prices in whichever area it chose to build. Third, Guinness was concerned that consumers would be wary of the product if they knew it was brewed in the United Kingdom rather than Ireland. Guinness was eager to sustain the mystique surrounding its product and the supposed superiority of River Liffey water, from which it was assumed it was made. Finally, the company was in a vulnerable position in the United

Kingdom, because they sold their product through the retail trade of the UK brewers. In the United Kingdom most beer was sold in so-called tied premises—publicans had to sell the beer produced by the brewery that owned their pub. While at that time ownership was fairly diverse, Guinness needed the goodwill of these brewers in order to sell its stout, as it owned no retail trade estate of its own. Guinness at that time was sold in bottles at a premium. This suited brewers and publicans, who enjoyed a healthy profit margin on Guinness in excess of that on their own beer. The members of the Guinness board were therefore concerned about the reaction of these brewers at the news of the construction of a new brewery in their own backyard, which might have been interpreted as a hostile move.

In August 1932, before the board had been informed of the development, T. B. Case, the managing director of Guinness, visited the London offices of the company's legal advisor, Owen Bulmer Howell. Howell's firm had had previous dealings with Guinness and their business interests in the United Kingdom. Case made the trip from Dublin in order to engage Howell as Guinness's agent to search for a suitable location for the new brewery. Case informed Howell that the company was now ruling out its site at Trafford Park, Manchester, and concentrating instead on southern England in order to be closer to their main London market. The Trafford Park site was still useful, however, as it was used to deflect interest in the firm's new intentions. The company also hired the services of consulting engineers Sir Alexander Gibb and Partners.[24] One of first contacts they made was with one of the firm's partners, Hugh Beaver. Meetings between the consulting engineers and the Guinness firm were subject to great secrecy, with brewery staff adopting pseudonyms:

> At the Monday meeting it was decided not to invent a name for the company, but to call Mr. Case "Mr. Wood," Mr. Deanesly "Mr. Russell" and Mr. Cawthra, Senior Engineer, "Mr. Herbert," all three becoming from then on fairly frequent visitors to Queen Anne's Gate and Watling Street and sometimes accompanying Mr. Beaver and Mr. Howell on expeditions in search of a site.[25]

This search initially focused on East London, but lack of affordable land suitable for a brewery ruled this option out. The new brewery site needed a combination of a large area of land, a plentiful supply of good-quality water (five hundred thousand gallons per day), as well as adequate effluent disposal (roughly the same figure), good transport and distribution links, and available housing for what was to become a sizable labor force. Beaver, then working for Alexander Gibb but later to be managing director at Park Royal, described the challenges they faced:

> One rather attractive area North west of London was in our minds for quite a time, until we discovered that the owner was a rabid teetotaller. Once we spent some

hours explaining to the Twickenham Urban District Council how fortunate they would be to have us (as indeed they would) without, however, being able to disclose to them who we were or what sort of a works we were going to build.[26]

In March 1933, Howell identified a potential site at Park Royal, writing to Case:

> I also enclose print of a plan of a site at Park Royal which seems admirable in every way except that it appears to be just outside the West Middlesex Sewerage Scheme. It is, however, a highly developed industrial estate, and we are ascertaining what arrangements are there for effluent disposal. It consists of between sixty and seventy acres bounded by the red lines and they are asking £1,000 an acre.[27]

To put this price in context, Guinness had been considering a site in East London where land prices were ten times this per acre. One hundred thirty-four acres were eventually purchased, at a total cost of £132,000. The purchase was made through Howell and this remained the case until the creation of two companies—Park Royal Development Company (for the general development) and Associated Agricultural Processes Limited (for the building of the brewery).[28] Beaver described what they had bought:

> And then we found this spot, the old site of the Royal Agricultural Show, an ordnance depot in the first world war, later the home of the Queen's Park Rangers and when we came the abode of gipsies, ponies and still a few rabbits. There was a tall corrugated iron fence around it and the key of the gate was kept by the owner's solicitor in London. So on the early visits of inspection we used the gipsies' entrance which meant wriggling more or less on one's stomach or back under the fence. The Chairman was very successful in negotiating it and, as he first discovered it, it used to be called the Chairman's Hole; but alas, it defeated his brother Ernest, then Vice-Chairman, who was lame.[29]

Even before Guinness made the final decision to build at Park Royal, there was tremendous speculation in the press about the construction of an English brewery. A rash of articles on November 10 speculated about the move. The *Daily Express* ran the headline "Guinness's to brew in England," followed by the subheadings "Water as good as the Liffey" and "Tariff War causes bold move."[30] The *Dublin Evening Mail* was less sure of its story, running the headline "Guinness For Britain?"[31] Guinness released a short statement denying the rumors, reiterating that the company did own a site in Manchester. In much of the press coverage variations on the same theme emerged. The journalists were correct in reporting the plans for a new brewery and that the "economic war" between London and Dublin was the main driver of this move. However, Guinness was remarkably successful at deflecting attention from the story for long enough that the building was well under construction before its purpose was publicly known.

Internally this secrecy was maintained rigorously with a very small number of brewery staff being told of the plans. Mark Plumpton, an engineer in Dublin, explained in a later piece reflecting on the era:

> For some two years, I had been working with the late H. Cawthra on designs for the "English Brewery"—as it was known in those days. I later learnt to my astonishment that this had been on the Project Enquiry List for many years previously. I well remember the Head Engineer asking, at the beginning of 1933, for block plans and estimates for a four, six or perhaps eight kieve brewery,[32] but as this had been happening from time to time for the previous twenty years it did not cause much excitement.[33]

But then Plumpton was let in on the secret:

> Then one day in early 1933 "The Dean" [head engineer H. Deansley] sent for Cawthra and me, and we made our way to his office, little knowing what lay ahead of us. After carefully locking the door of his office and extracting our promise of secrecy we were going to hear, we were told, that the company had decided to build a brewery at Park Royal London. It was not to be made public until construction was well advanced.[34]

Plumpton went on to describe the extent of the charade, the adoption of noms de plume, the constant locking of doors and desk drawers as well as having to smuggle senior members of brewery staff out of Dublin to London without alerting other curious members of Guinness staff:

> A real problem then arose, and that was to arrange for H. Cawthra to be wafted to London without arousing curiosity and speculation at St. James's Gate. It was decided that he would simply pack up everything and cross over to London without giving any explanation whatsoever to anyone in the Brewery or, in fact in Dublin. This decision once made, the plan was set in motion. It was surprising the number of small things that had to be taken care of, for example Cawthra had to remove his name from all his technical books, files and such things as slide-rules. The great day came one Saturday in June, 1933, when after lingering behind at our Brewery luncheon, we smuggled two large boxes into the back of my car, but not before we had run into one of the Dublin Engineers, Rawdon Green who, greatly to his credit, just smiled and asked no inconvenient questions. I often wonder what he thought. The same night I took "Mr. Herbert" [Cawthra], down to the B. & I. boat at the North Wall and hoped that we had covered our tracks satisfactorily.[35]

Cawthra walked out of Guinness and Dublin so completely that friends, acquaintances, and most of his colleagues at St. James's Gate had no idea where he had disappeared to. Plumpton's account, echoed by others involved, is replete with descriptions such as "whodunit atmosphere," "conspiratorial," and "anxieties" and relates endless precautions taken to avoid leaking information to anyone outside a magic circle of those "in the know."

BUILDING PARK ROYAL

Beaver had estimated that the new brewery at Park Royal could be completed within just eighteen months of contracts being let in the autumn of 1933, but in the end, it was finished by January 1936. The first brick laid in July 1934, without ceremony, again due to the need for secrecy. The basic design of the buildings and the brewery equipment was subject to long-standing plans drawn up internally by Guinness engineers and other staff. However, consulting engineers from Gibb's firm were central to the building's construction, and it was they who recommended and approached Sir Giles Gilbert Scott as an architectural consultant for the buildings. This phrase "architectural consultant" was important, as there was debate as to how much actual involvement Scott had in the buildings. What is clear is that initially he had little or no knowledge as to the function of the buildings. In the letter of appointment from Gibb dated October 30, 1933, Guinness was described as "our clients, Messrs Associated Agricultural Processes Limited." Scott's role was set out as follows:

> Technical and engineering considerations fix the siting, orientation, size and height of the buildings. Within these limits Sir Giles Gilbert Scott would advise on the architectural treatment of the complete range of buildings, materials to be used, colour, emphasis, ornament, etc. He would deal with the front elevations of all the main buildings in the front line. . . . Sir Giles Gilbert Scott will supply small scale drawings of the whole elevation, and such detail drawings on a larger scale as are necessary to show the actual treatment of the various parts.[36]

The fee suggested, and agreed upon, for the work was 1,000 guineas,[37] and Scott was asked to be "prepared to undertake the work forthwith." In the same correspondence Scott was invited to meet "one of the principals of our clients' firm [who] will be in England about the 8th November, and would like, if possible, to be in a position to give him some indication of the treatment that you favour."[38] It is reasonable to suppose that at that meeting Scott would have been told the ultimate purpose of the building he was helping to create.

In later years Guinness officials were immensely proud to draw attention to their buildings and their architect. Writing in his 1960 obituary for Scott, Beaver recorded:

> When the new brewery was being planned for Park Royal nearly thirty years ago, the Board decided that it would wish to have a building that would outlive the taste of the moment, something that would not attempt to hitch on to the latest mode or to set a new pattern, that would not try to seem anything else than a large and efficient factory; built firmly and solidly to last a century or two as the company

itself had already lasted. There is no doubt they got just what they wanted in Sir Giles Gilbert Scott's design.[39]

Scott was a central figure in British architecture when Guinness, through its intermediaries, approached him. Born in the 1880s to an architectural dynasty, Scott was by 1933 the president of the Royal Institute of British Architects (RIBA) and had, by this time, a large number of the landmark buildings of the twentieth century to his name. He is best remembered today as the designer of Liverpool's Anglican cathedral and the Battersea and Bankside Power stations in London, as well as the iconic "K2" red telephone box. Scott combined both tradition and modern styles in a thoroughly pragmatic way, unafraid to use Gothic in his ecclesiastical commissions while adopting new trends for his industrial designs of the machine age. In 1930, the *Architect & Building News* praised Scott's middle way, noting that "his work is never startling in its novelty, and he is quite free from the modernist's vice of cleverness for its own sake. Yet his work is completely satisfying, full of life, originality and interest. In truth he belongs partly to both parties, and wholly to neither."[40]

Scott had a lucrative practice, which included the design or "tidying up" of many industrial buildings of the era, but again, he did not take machine worship too far. In his RIBA presidential address in 1933 he said, "I see crowds marching on the factories, breaking up the machines, many being electrocuted or scalded to death in the wide orgy of destruction."[41]

Scott was to design a building that became a futurist icon, his Battersea Power Station. His work for Guinness at Park Royal was an excellent example of his compromise between styles, combining traditional building materials—brick—without attempting to disguise it as anything other than a large set of modern factory buildings. The result was described as "a slightly asymmetrical grouping of big blocks in the Battersea style, with none of the flashy overdone Deco detail which brought the new factories along the Great West Road into rapid professional disrepute."[42] The *Architect & Building News* for January 1936 noted the contrast with Wallis, Gilbert and Partners' Hoover Factory on Western Avenue, completed in 1935: "[After Hoover] it needed a great architect to destylise the factory and identify architecture with the contemned tradition of simplicity, fitness and order."[43]

Scott believed that some of the contemporary modern designs, while striking, were undermined by the poor quality of their finish and the materials from which they were constructed. By contrast, material such as brick, while superficially "traditional," would last. The steel frames of the brewery buildings were clad in brick, which was "2⅜" Wellington facings, beautifully laid and jointed with Scott's favoured yellow-tinted mortar. The block are characteristic of his use of cut and angled brickwork, set vertically in bands as cornices and raised in strips for occasional and unifying decorative relief."[44]

Beaver would recall his relationship with Scott during the building of Park Royal in the short obituary he wrote for the architect in *Guinness Time*:

> Sir Giles conformed to all our needs and requirements in engineering and production; he did not attempt to twist the plan so as to suit some preconceived architectural objective. He was severely practical. I remember suggesting to him that he should bring in some relief to the long wall of the Vathouse, but he said that a simple wall of good brickwork needed no relief. The only concession he made was in the casing in brickwork of the 127 concrete silos of the Malt Store; and in the end it was this south front of the Malt Store which he considered the best feature of the whole brewery.[45]

A little later in the same obituary Beaver reflected on the buildings and Scott's skill as a designer:

> We have grown so used to them that perhaps we no longer observe with a seeing eye the architecture of the buildings in which we spend so much of our lives—the placing of the windows with their narrow cathedral-like lighting; the delicate ornamentation along the tops of the buildings; the different colouring of bricks used and the special bonding; the ribbed concrete course; and inside the panelling in different unusual timbers of the main rooms in the central offices.[46]

The actual construction of the brewery buildings was subcontracted to several firms. Peter Lind & Co. Ltd. was engaged to drive piles for the buildings' foundations, the steelwork was carried out by Sir William Arrol & Co., and the buildings themselves were the responsibility of Holland and Hannen & Cubitts Ltd.[47] The Guinness archive contains many images of the construction of the site, ranging from the grounds before any earth was moved through to the completed buildings. These were taken for various reasons at different stages. Often photographs were taken as simple charting of progress, while others were for engineering recording purposes—a visual record of where services were located. Many of the images were of high quality and portray not only the growing structures but the workers involved in the construction. These give clues to the number of people involved in the building and the types of mechanical support they enjoyed. In one image of the general building work, it is possible to see horse-drawn carts among much more modern equipment and machinery.

The archive also offers unexpected insights into contemporary building techniques. An example of this was the collection of photographs of the steel erection with a simple handwritten note: "Worst job I had was checking rivets on roofs of Hop Store and Brewhouse offices—no floors above ground—no hand rails or planks—just cold steel under my bottom and 100 feet of air! Checking a rivet needs two hands."[48] Presumably this was a foreman from the subcontractor engaged in the steel erection. The images make sense when read together with the written text; on their own, the photos are almost abstract in nature. It is here that Guinness stands out as a case study of corporate history at this time, for in addition to the wealth of visual materials there are many oral histories and written accounts of the building of the brewery, which appeared at various occasions in histories of the early years of the plant. George Gracie, a manager at Park Royal and later editor of *Guinness Time*, remembered the construction of the brewery in the first issue of the magazine:

> It was a thrilling experience to watch the gradual growth of this huge factory, from the start of work in November, 1933, to its completion in February, 1936. Once the site was cleared the task of pile driving began and owing to the nature of the ground it was necessary to use very large numbers of piles, some of which were 45 feet long. Then the mass of structural steel took shape as the framework to support the heavy brewing plant was erected. Most of the heavier machinery was installed before the walls were built, as in this constructional method the walls support no loads but serve only as a protection against the weather.[49]

The photographs also show just how amazing it was that the true purpose of the buildings was kept a secret for so long, for this was a site built alongside a busy arterial road, a Tube line, and a mainline railway. One of the intriguing features of the "cloak-and-dagger" process by which the buildings were constructed was the bizarre range of stories and myths that grew up about their eventual purpose. Owen Bulmer Howell, the solicitor acting for Guinness, related the way he had to field press speculation about the buildings:[50]

> A Sunday paper telephoned Mr. Howell's office one Saturday morning in about the June of 1934 and was told by his secretary that he was not in and, after much pressure, that he was probably watching cricket at Lord's. He was called out to the back door of the pavilion and asked whether it was true that explosives were to be made at Park Royal out of potatoes, Hitler having then begun to show his hand. He only replied: "If that were so you must surely realise that I could not tell you about it."[51]

Howell went on to say that the next day the Sunday paper led the front page with the story as their headline, which he says was "a story that fortunately persisted for quite a long time."[52] This military theme was echoed elsewhere in the stories that swirled around the mysterious buildings. Derek Wilson, in his history of Guinness, noted: "Local people believed that the hush-hush nature of the enterprise had something to do with the government's covert rearmament programme. It was even rumoured that the military were proposing to make poison gas at Park Royal."[53]

Others speculated that alcohol would be produced from potatoes or that the buildings at Park Royal were really a bicycle factory! Guinness maintained this secrecy until August 1934, when a formal announcement was made to the firm's annual general meeting. A week prior to this admission, T. B. Case met with Seán Lemass, the Irish Free State's Minister for Industry and Commerce. Case read a statement about the plans for Park Royal and sought to reassure the minister of Guinness's continuing presence in Ireland.[54] In the end the fears of a backlash from the Irish government proved unfounded, and, more generally, there was little negative reaction in Ireland—in part due to a fortuitous press strike at the time of the official announcement.

The building of the Guinness brewery did not go entirely smoothly, however. A report in the *Middlesex County Times* in March 1935 reported a strike among building workers. Under the headline "1,200 WORKMEN DISMISSED ON GUINNESS FACTORY BUILDING," the paper wrote of a dispute over the non-payment of a worker who seems to have failed to clock in for his shift. The paper quoted the London district secretary of the National Federation of Building Trade Operatives, Mr. J. Murray: "When the unofficial stoppage took place, the men refused to go back to work. The firm said they would not consider the claim until work was resumed." Interestingly, the rest of the piece rehearses the secrecy surrounding the Guinness brewery. The report, which made much of the "seven pale-brown brick buildings," concluded by saying:

> The work is being done in stages and present operations are on three of the main buildings—two storage buildings, and a third, in which silos—cylindrical bins, 80 or 90 feet high—will be housed. The foundations and girder work of these buildings have been completed, and the brickwork has reached varying stages of completion. The brickwork of these buildings can be seen from Hanger-Lane. Yesterday it gleamed in the sunshine, and in the distance the unfinished parts gave the impression of great building activity. Drawing nearer, one missed the sound of hammering and the bustle of men and machinery.[55]

When work resumed, the pace of construction was impressive, as Gracie's account of the creation of those same silos indicated:

> An interesting part of the building work was the erection of the Malt Store by the novel moving-form method. The concrete for the 230 storage silos was continuously poured into moulds which were moved steadily upwards at the rate of five feet per day, the whole job being completed in fourteen days. There were two hectic days during this process when dense fog threatened to interrupt the work which had to be kept going without a break.[56]

Another staff member interviewed for this same publication remembered, "The sense of isolation and mystery about the site; very few people locally knew what was to be made at the plant arising in their midst."[57] By the new year the brewery was almost complete and was ready to brew its first Guinness in England.

THE FIRST BREW

In Park Royal lore, much was made of the first brew of the new English brewery. Accounts of the building and initial brew were regularly featured in the pages of *Guinness Time*. Those who were involved in this story became almost mythical figures who had an authenticity within the brewery. It is striking just how well this ceremony was recorded and subsequently retold, and like the narrative leading up to this point there was a degree of secrecy surrounding these events. A sense of this narrative's foundation-like status can be heard in the account of Norman Wood, a brewery manager:

> The epochal day dawned on the 21st February, 1936, and at 8am the six young heroes and the twelve apostles were assembled on the kieve stage, when out of the gloom came a distinguished procession: Lord Iveagh, the Hon. A. E. Guinness, C. J. Newbold, W. S. Gossett and H. Deansley from Dublin. Lord Iveagh went aloft and pressed the button which started the rakes on No. 2 kieve, to signify the formal opening of the new Brewery.[58]

Wood went on to report that later a pressurized door flew open, covering most of the assembled group in sticky mash.

The company wanted to ensure that the beer produced in its English brewery was as close to the Dublin brew as possible. The early Park Royal product was sent to Dublin to be mixed with beer from St. James's Gate. Later the proportion of the Dublin brew in the blend was reduced until experienced brewers at both plants could not detect a difference between the "pure" Dublin and "pure" Park Royal brew. Indeed, so eager was the company to replicate its beer that it designed the process in London with much of the same technology as existed in Dublin. This was despite the fact that the head brewer in Dublin, when Park Royal was being planned, had argued strongly for brewing in stainless steel vats that could be sterilized, a technological innovation widely adopted on the Continent. Therefore, even as it opened, the new brewery was fifty years behind the times. Guinness was still eager to keep from its customers the fact that they were buying London-brewed stout, and much of the early distribution was kept secret, as John Beckett, a Guinness employee, described:

> Much no doubt will have been written about the secrecy of the early days occasioned by the anxiety to get Park Royal–brewed beer into trade without people being aware of its origin. An aspect of this was the actual delivery ex-Brewery and I recall cloak and dagger manoeuvres during Sunday nights on the racking shed floor and the road-loading bays, in order to get the early Park Royal brews into casks and away to the docks by stealth. Thos. Allen's drivers with their biggest lorries lined up to load butts and hogsheads[59] which (and we never knew the ins and outs at the dock end) could next day go into trade as if discharged from Dublin. Only when time had shown that the new product was indistinguishable from the genuine Liffey Water would it be feasible to supply our customer—rivals direct from Park Royal without raising a rumpus.[60]

Dublin was still to supply an important amount of stout into the British trade; only during the war did the proportion brewed in London reach 65 percent of the total UK consumption.[61]

While the senior staff members of the London brewery were sent from Dublin, as much labor as possible was recruited locally to Park Royal. The company made a distinction between "labourers" and "tradesmen"—essentially a distinction based on formal skills. For the laborers, Guinness followed the terms and conditions of other London brewers. Tradesmen were to enjoy similar trade union rates for the London district, but Guinness worked a shorter, forty-four-hour week. Some of the terms and conditions enjoyed in Dublin were replicated, but others were not. At a time of large-scale unemployment jobs were scarce and people wrote to the new brewery before it was even operational. Some of the new employees were sent over to Dublin to learn the company's systems and spoke of the awe in which the Guinness Company and especially the brewers were held. Some of the more specialist recruits were taken on from the contractors involved in constructing or fitting out the plant. Many of the accounts by the early Park Royal staff mention the lack of facilities of the early brewery and its grounds. Betty Mears, one of the earliest secretarial staff employed in the plant, remembered:

> All the secretaries, were housed in one office at first; there were no back-up services. We had to post our own letters, which, in the mud and the dark, could pose problems. I and one other lost the post in the mud and rain one evening. The Chief Accountant (O.M. Brown) wondered why he never got a reply to his letter; we never told him it had never been posted! Lunch was taken at the "Plumes" [a local pub] and we were issued with Wellington boots to go there because of the mud. In those early days there was great curiosity in the neighbourhood about the purpose of the buildings at Park Royal; it was generally assumed that they were going to be a munitions factory.[62]

Ion Commiskey, one of the Dublin draftees, related a similar story about the basic conditions of the first employees:

> My first day at Park Royal was spent washing out and lime-washing a sky cooler, with the help of Chubby Powell who later became Senior Brewhouse Shift Charger. It was freezing! Snow on the ground in mid January 1936 and we, open to the skies, at the very top of the Brewhouse. In fact all my early memories are of freezing conditions and mud; few stairs only ladders and hazardous planks for many gangways; great problems with the contractor's men and the blessed relief of lunch at the Plumes. So different from Dublin—we felt strangers in a strange land.[63]

Brewery life had not yet settled into anything approaching normalcy when the Second World War began in September 1939. The war had a huge impact on brewery life and workplace culture, with many male and female workers called up to different branches of the services, while demand for beer increased. Blackout procedures were put in place, underground shelters dug, and air raid precautions taken. The war was one of the dominant themes in Guinness company oral histories. Bob Nichol, a worker in the company's powerhouse, described wartime conditions:

> We had hardly settled down when we had to meet the challenges of War. Many of our experienced personnel were called up and could not be replaced, necessitating the swift training of raw recruits. All windows had to be boarded up, so we worked permanently in artificial light and when the Blitz started Power Station personnel had to remain in the course of an air raid shutting down to a minimum all steam valves, shutting off the gas supply and so on while everyone else was entering the shelters. We did in fact, have a shelter in the Station but it served little purpose as we had to stay at our posts feeling a little envious of those in the shelters. For this devotion to duty we were rewarded with an extra bottle of beer.[64]

As an industrial area to the west of the capital, the Park Royal area was subject to heavy bombing raids during the war. Two employees were killed in the ice house when a bomb landed and smashed through the roof. A number of remembrances mention this incident and the fact that it had occurred at lunchtime, when many of the staff were in the canteen just yards from where the bomb had exploded. Brewery employee John Webb recalled:

> When the Blitz started, we had trucks of dry sand available to cover any incendiary bombs that fell in the grounds. Some nights, we were very busy dealing with these bombs, and on one occasion, the enemy had started several fires in factories around the brewery, and they illuminated our premises, as a result of which the Germans must have thought we were a Power Station, because they showered us with incendiaries, most of which bounced on the concrete roofs of the Malt Store, Storehouse, Central Offices and Vat Store. They were quickly dealt with, using the dry sand, but I thought I should have a look and the Brewhouse—and there I saw several fires starting on the roof, which was of timber. With the help of one of the ARP volunteers, we managed to get the hose from the fire hydrant, through the spring door, and subdued the flames.[65]

Understandably, the war marked an important and unusual time in the life of the brewery and loomed large in the early history of Park Royal. There are numerous photographs of brewery life and labor in the archive taken of this time. Often they depict unusual events brought about by the hostilities, the uprooting of life and normal patterns of life. They show women working in jobs usually carried out by men, such as barrel washing and brewery vessel cleaning.

Priestley's work on *English Journey* quickly took him away from the modern, un-English, new factories of West London. Priestley was seeking out the authentic people of England on his travels and while he found and described them he also noted, to varying degrees, the poverty and degradation that many inhabited at this time. The interwar period was a pivotal moment in Britain, as it was for much of the world. The reportage of Priestley, Orwell, and others captured the decline of the old industrial areas and the type of work associated with this transition. At times what they were witnessing was the early deindustrialization of Britain, although they would not use the phrase. But their narratives also spoke of the emergence of troubling new and different forms of employment and organizations. The 1930s, in Britain at least, was an era when there was often a fear voiced of a new "mass" society. Intellectuals and others were attempting to understand what this mass society would mean, and work was one of the ways through which they framed their understandings. The decline in the traditional industries that had been thrown up in the nineteenth century was in stark contrast to the newly emerging ones of their own period. Novel things were being made for the "masses" by the "masses." New production-line technology was employed making new consumer durables and foodstuffs. This emerging workforce was more female in its composition, in stark contrast to the "heroic masculinity" of iron, shipbuilding, and coal industries. And the nature of the work that went on in these new spaces by turn amused, puzzled, and sometimes scared contemporary commentators. There was then a lament for the eclipse of the old and the sense of authenticity that was ascribed in the grimy industrial centers of the North, and the people who lived and worked there, a fear for the loss of character and identity bound up in national and regional sensibilities.

The interwar period was a time of upheaval and conflict, of dissonance and instability. There was disquiet about this new mass society and the prospect of social dislocation and disintegration manifest in industrial unrest and political extremism. But there was also concern about the creation of new "mass" workforces making uniform undifferentiated "mass" products for "mass" consumption. Here, too much unthinking integration was the troubling aspect of the emerging society; a mass workforce was open to manipulation by political demagoguery. One response to this atmosphere was a retreat into conservatism in the interwar period, the election of Conservative and National governments in the 1920s and 1930s and the rejection of the political extremes of the British Union of Fascists on the right or the Communist Party on the left. Electors were happier with a prime minister such as Stanley Baldwin, who spoke of an idyllic Englishness rather than radical change. This was an era marked by the expansion of the suburbs built not along European Modernist lines, but looking back to a mythical past through domesticated "Tudorbethan" styles.[66]

Many of these themes, tropes, and tensions can be seen at play in the story of Guinness's creation of its English brewery, and in turn that story helps to illuminate and make more intelligible the wider context of which it was a part. The decision to build a new brewery was effectively forced on a very conservatively minded firm that had been based in Ireland for 170 years and that still enjoyed some 8,830 years on its lease. It was the political upheaval and the economic uncertainty of the Irish Free State and the "economic war" between it and the United Kingdom that forced the hand of senior management. Once the decision to build a new facility in England was made, the search for its location shifted from the "old" industrial North to the "new" South, real estate ripe for Fordism.

Guinness planned and built a new factory on what was pretty much a green-field site, designing a set of buildings on ordered rational lines in stark contrast to their site in St. James's Gate, which had expanded in a far less ordered fashion. But for all this rational planning, the company installed at the heart of its brewing process technology that was fifty years behind the times because the officials wished to replicate the traditional product and processes with their mystical roots in Dublin.

This contrast between modernity and tradition was inscribed in the very architecture of the new buildings at Park Royal. West London was at the epicenter of Modernist industrial architecture, and yet Guinness built against the grain of this futuristic style. It chose to employ the premier architect of his day, one whose buildings were later to define their era, but who was in his own practice seeking to marry traditional and Modernist aesthetics. These were large industrial buildings with rational form and function and yet treated with that most traditional of material, brick, in a simple bond and minimal ornamentation. In its construction too we see the mixing of tradition and modernity with the use of steel framing, poured concrete, and industrial-scaled construction workforces simultaneously using horse traction alongside modern power equipment. In the midst of recession and depression, of social, political, and economic uncertainty, Guinness built a brewery that would "last a century or two."[67] This statement itself is at once both vague and confident and says much about corporate self-image and values at this time.

In terms of the workforce and the type of labor they would do at Park Royal, there was a pragmatic mixing of styles. Guinness made minor changes in the way it employed its staff in London, but none was a radical departure from Dublin practice. It aimed to replicate its reputation as a good employer in terms and conditions as well as wage rates. Though building on effectively a greenfield site, it did not actively seek to employ "green" labor as other employers did in newer industrial zones of the time. Instead it recruited key workers from within its own ranks at St. James's Gate and they in turn replicated many of the cultures and traditional practices from Dublin. For instance, Guinness would quickly establish an industrial cooperage at Park Royal to make its wooden barrels, with the new body of coopers adopting traditional customs and rituals that were two centuries or more old.

What, then, do the images of work from Guinness at Park Royal— photographic, textual, and oral—tell us about the wider nature of work during this period? What they show is something about the way that the modern is understood, assimilated, and even domesticated in one workplace. What these various images relate is the way groups and individuals drew on the past, their past, in responding to the changing nature of economy, society, and politics. They illustrate the pragmatic way in which people sought to normalize their environment, the creation of new routines, and workplace culture. The visual material presented by Guinness, and the narratives of personal recollections, give us an insight into how ordinary people felt about the work they did and the organization they worked for. What sticks in the mind is not fear of mass society, or of becoming a helpless automaton, but more pragmatic concerns, such as coping with the mud and negotiating the darkness of a building site. What fascinated them were the collective stories of the mystery surrounding Park Royal. These collective imaginings helped to create a powerful story about the foundation of the new brewery, images that would be built on in the future. Equally, when we study the photographs of this time and the building of the brewery, we are struck by a sense of modernity and tradition. And in the faces of those doing the work, we can recognize parents or grandparents attempting to make a living between the wars.

2

CREATING
INDUSTRIAL CITIZENS

In 1949, T. H. Marshall delivered a lecture in Cambridge that would become a seminal contribution to the understanding of the relationship between social class and citizenship. Later published as *Citizenship and Social Class*, this short analytical essay outlined the principal elements of citizenship—the possession of civic, political, and social rights. Hidden in the text was an important but largely neglected passage on what Marshall called "industrial citizenship," a civic identity derived from employment and the social and political relationships of the workplace. Marshall's essay is still widely read and influential in the fields of sociology, social policy, and political science and was a significant document of the postwar era as it recognized the elevation of the status of working people in society. *Citizenship and Social Class* is, then, a window into attempts to rethink the postwar settlement in Britain, to explore the role and meaning of class, and to think about how ordinary people might be supported to fulfill their potential in a modern postwar society. In its own quiet, understated, very English way, it was a revolutionary document of its time.[1]

Citizenship and Social Class was published in 1950, toward the end of the Attlee Labour government. This was poignant timing and perhaps marked the high-water mark of progressive politics, a period when social relationships and economic forces were being reshaped. The Labour Party had won the 1945 general election against expectations, defeating the Conservative Party led by wartime leader Winston Churchill. While Churchill retained personal popularity, his party did not. Historical consensus suggests that the popular mood in Britain seeped away from the Conservatives toward Labour throughout the war. Labour was part of the coalition government and held many of its senior posts. During the early 1940s, a succession of policies were introduced or planned for postwar Britain that were to become the foundations of the welfare state. Preeminent among the issues animating the electorate, certainly those identifiably working class, was that of unemployment and the need to ensure employment for all in the postwar recovery. Etched onto the memory of those old enough to remember the period was the post-Great War slump of the 1920s and recession of the 1930s. The economic consensus of that era dictated a classical political economy solution, a policy of cuts and retrenchment while the economy recovered and full employment would be restored by "natural" market mechanisms.

From the early war years, a new, more progressive and interventionist consensus began to emerge that eclipsed the failed ideas of the 1930s. Indeed, the 1930s take on the role of a critical foil against which subsequent generations were to fashion their own attitudes and policy; there was to be "no return to the 1930s."[2] This mood was captured by Jim Mortimer, an industrial worker employed in a factory not far from Park Royal:

> At the time I was working in a large engineering factory in the London suburban industrial belt of West Middlesex and I was an active trade unionist. In this factory and in other large engineering factories in West London and West Middlesex there was real enthusiasm for the election of a Labour government, pledged to a policy of social change. There was widespread consciousness of the kind of changes that were needed. The first requirement was that there should be full employment and no return to the mass unemployment, depression and hunger marches of the interwar period. This was felt more acutely in West Middlesex because so many of the workers had migrated there in earlier years from areas of high unemployment.[3]

The Second World War, in Britain at least, became known as the People's War, reflecting the mass mobilization of men and women in the services as well as in the workplace. This was an era of total war in which the productive power of the people was harnessed to defeat Germany and the other Axis powers. Part of what fed the hunger for change was the popular sense of betrayal ordinary people felt for the political class in the interwar period. While the electoral outcome of 1945 was seen as the victory for left-wing socialism, more radical left-wing sentiment had been evident during the war itself, as early as 1942, and if anything, this tide had receded during the remainder of the conflict.[4] Much has been written of the supposed radicalism of the Attlee government, but the reality was that Labour enacted a somewhat technocratic revision to the status quo.

Policy was aimed at the civil regulation of capitalism and the market, not its abolition. In this sense, the war years were a period when there was a genuine shift from cautious limited administration to a far more open welfare-focused spirit in government.[5] British society and its politics were divided not along the lines of capitalism and socialism but rather between different visions of how an economy should be managed. In his 1963 essay, playwright Michael Frayn made the distinction between what he called the "Herbivores" and "Carnivores." Both were groups of middle and upper classes who argued over the postwar spoils. The Herbivores were the gentle ruminators who, while not *of* the working class, were broadly sympathetic to less fortunate creatures. By contrast, the Carnivores believed that "if God had not wished them to prey on all smaller and weaker creatures without scruple he would not have made them as they are."[6] The Attlee government marked the high point of the Herbivores, but with their loss of office in 1951, the essential components of the consensus around the fundamental structures of the economy and the welfare state went largely unchallenged by either Conservative or Labour administrations until the 1970s. This broad consensus reflected the reality that reform was the result of nonpartisan policy development rather than partisan ideology both before and during the Second World War.[7]

Gradually, the austerity of the 1940s gave way to the growing affluence of the 1950s and what has subsequently become known as the long boom. Britain was still a major industrial power at this time. In 1951, the working population was 20.3 million people, with over 70 percent of them in what would be regarded as manual occupations.[8] Union density was high but uneven—55 percent for men, 25 percent for women; 49 percent for manual workers, 31 percent for nonmanual workers. Aggregate union membership slipped from 45 percent in 1948 with the creation of new jobs in less well-unionized sectors.[9] Industrial relations were dominated by a handful of large amalgamated unions, and while there was also a plethora of tiny craft and specialist unions, there were 735 unions in 1951, with only 183 of these affiliated with the Trades Union Congress.[10] This union profile reflected the state of British industry at the time, especially the labor intensity of many sectors where the use of skilled labor rather than large-scale capital investment was the norm. In some industries, such as shipbuilding, this allowed companies to compete in international markets by responding to demand fluctuation by recruiting or laying off their workers, both skilled and unskilled. The result was a singular system of industrial relations between employer and employees as well as intense rivalry between different unions, especially at times of economic downturn.[11]

The origins of this system can be found at the beginnings of industrialization in Britain in the late eighteenth century, and it is a system that reflected Britain's position as the first industrial nation, with few if any models to follow. Relative domestic industrial decline is often traced back to the late Victorian period, when Britain encountered increasing competition from France, Germany, and especially the United States. This industrial eclipse became increasingly apparent in the twentieth century, especially during the 1920s and 1930s. In the post–Second World War period this problematic industrial structure was hidden by the decimation of European industry coupled with strong and pent-up domestic demand. But whose fault was this situation? While many would recognize that Britain's problems were the result of being first in the field, others suggest that this was a function of poor, amateurish management rooted in a hidebound class system and ownership structure. There was a collective failure on the part of the business class to develop new management systems, to adopt new technology and industrial techniques, and to understand the nature of potential productivity gains. The result was that much of British industry remained small scale and fragmented and suffered from underinvestment.[12]

The other side of this narrative is that the decline of British industry was the fault of the workforce itself, portrayed as being lazy, inefficient, and above all subject to the whim of overbearing unions, in particular the growing militancy of shop stewards. In this vision, the problems of British industry were hidden by the immediate aftermath of the war and the subsequent boom. British productivity levels undoubtedly fell behind European and US competitors, interpreted as a reluctance on the part of domestic workers to work as hard or as long as their rivals—a trait supposedly indulged by a combination of strong unions and weak management.[13]

At roughly the midway point of the long boom, three British films were released that would help to mark and encapsulate, to remake and reimagine work in the era. In 1959 the Boulting brothers released their comedy *I'm All Right Jack*, set in a Midlands munitions factory; it was a satire of industrial relations in the 1950s, showing corrupt and incompetent management as well as slothful and indolent workers ready to withdraw their labor at the drop of a hat. The film's central character, former army soldier and university graduate Stanley Windrush, applies and is rejected for various posts in management before finding a place on the shop floor of his uncle's company. Stanley's uncle is eager to provoke a strike in order to manipulate trade. The film exposes lax management well but is best remembered for the character of the shop steward, Fred Kite (played by Peter Sellers), a communist-supporting militant bureaucrat who delivers his lines through a hail of political clichés. Windrush's haste to do his job well, and with enthusiasm, results in his breaking workplace norms and disturbing long-standing agreements, in the process generally exposing the chronic lack of productivity of the British shop floor.

In 1960, *Saturday Night and Sunday Morning* appeared, starring a moody performance by Albert Finney as Arthur Seaton, a hardworking factory operative in a Nottingham bike factory. The film opens with Seaton at his workbench counting off the pieces he has completed that day and reflecting on how much he hates his job. Seaton is one of the new wave of "angry young men" rejecting the deferential collectivism he sees in his fellow workers; Seaton's is a highly individualized worldview where progress and survival depend on the resources that he alone can draw on.

In 1961, top British comedian Tony Handcock starred in *The Rebel*. Less of a popular success than either *I'm All Right Jack* or *Saturday Night and Sunday Morning*, *The Rebel* showed Handcock trapped in a respectable middle-class office job, worn down by the all-too-predictable daily commute from the London suburbs into the City of London (the financial district). His accounting work is ordered and regimented and subject to time and motion study, but he longs to follow his true vocation as an artist. Perhaps the main theme that disturbs the central character most is precisely the order and predictability of his career. At various points in the film, Handcock is forced to confront the realization that his life will be entirely predictable, with little or no change envisaged, except for his annual pay raise and the prospect of a silver cigarette case when he retires.

Each of these very different films reflected contemporary concerns about employment and workers during the long boom. They portrayed work and workers in distinct ways, but their common themes include the order and predictability of labor, its stultifying hierarchies, its restrictive norms and values. Each of the central characters stands out from the crowd of his fellow workers; it is they who aim for something beyond what they are being offered or forced to conform to. These films speak to many of the themes of work in the long boom that animated academics trying to make sense of the postwar labor market, the workplace, and the workers who populated it. This was a cast that included bored workers, affluent workers, deferential workers, instrumental workers—and militants. In the late 1950s and early 1960s, there was real concern within the Labour party and the Left intelligentsia that the British working class had been "deradicalized" by a mixture of consumer durables and easy consumer credit.

Sociologists sought out so-called affluent workers to see if they were displaying outward signs of middle-class culture. Others lamented the decline of traditional working-class occupational communities that were on the point of being eclipsed by industrial change or the march of consumer culture. While Richard Hoggart fretted over the appearance of American-style coffee bars and the loss of the traditional working-class values of his Leeds upbringing, other sociologists visited communities soon to be subject to slum clearance, pit villages under threat, or industrial enclaves soon to be lost. Likewise, politicians thought about what was happening to work. They welcomed the growing affluence of the postwar period, some reminding voters that they had never had it so good, while Harold Wilson talked about the "white heat" of technological innovation and the need to eradicate restrictive practices on both sides of industry.[14]

Two years before Marshall addressed his audience in Cambridge, Edward Guinness, a newly appointed manager at the London brewery, was imagining his own form of Guinness Citizenship for the workers and staff at the Park Royal site. This version of industrial citizenship and the broader understanding of work and employment imagined and created at Guinness in this period provide a critical insight into broader ideas about the value and meaning of work in the three decades after the Second World War.

CREATING GUINNESS CITIZENS

The end of 1947 was not a hopeful time for many in austerity Britain, with rationing and shortages of many basic commodities made worse by one of the harshest winters on record. In a corner of West London, there were more positive signs of postwar recovery in the form of a statement of faith in the future. That year, the Guinness management decided to create a staff magazine for Park Royal, and this publication was sold to staff on a quarterly basis for the next twenty-eight years. The initial editorial made clear its purpose was to make a new start after "the social hibernation of the War and many of the old joys are returning." The editorial went on:

> Again most of us are now returned from the Services and are no longer just ships passing in the night. Gradually we are anchoring ourselves to this noble community, and any community that is worthwhile has a natural curiosity about the doings of its fellow members. Actual acquaintance is best achieved in the Social Club, but we need to expand that by a wider survey than can be there achieved. Thus it is with these objects in view that we have attempted to portray life at Park Royal.[15]

Produced from the start to a very high standard under the initial editorship of Edward Guinness and George Gracie, *Guinness Time* featured an illustrated color cover and copious photographs and other visual material. At the front of each issue was an editorial of some two pages that ranged in subject matter from details of brewery life and reflections on the passing seasons to wider consideration of politics and industrial relations. For the entirety of its run, *Guinness Time* featured a photo essay on aspects of work in the brewery, each piece reflecting on a specific trade or occupation and the staff in the department concerned while explaining how this particular aspect of labor fitted into the wider body of the brewery. There were also pieces on births, deaths, and marriages; reports on the various sports and social clubs; visits and events at the brewery; and articles about the brewing trade. An important feature of the magazine was the frequent historical accounts of various aspects of the Guinness Company, the Guinness family, and the brewery itself. The initial spur to produce a magazine was the wish to record sporting achievement by brewery staff, but it quickly went beyond this narrow remit. Edward Guinness recruited other members of the brewery staff, including the sports secretary John Beckett; Leslie Henry, the labor manager; and Martin Pick, the advertising manager. As Edward Guinness said, "We decided that ours would be a glossy, well produced quarterly magazine which would aim to reflect brewery life rather than have a message."[16]

The title, *Guinness Time*, was supposed to reflect that the magazine was to be produced on "Guinness time," during the working hours of the brewery, but as Edward Guinness explained:

> This was in fact unfair as we each had jobs to do and George Gracie and I used to work into the small hours in Bodiam or his house in Rossall Crescent, experimenting with layouts in which we had no expertise, writing, and editing articles we had persuaded colleagues to write. I remember captioning photographs was especially difficult as often one had failed to record all the names (at the start I was told that 99% of people like to have their photograph taken for a magazine but I never found the 1% who supposedly don't).[17]

The inaugural issue, which appeared just before Christmas 1947, featured a John Gilroy illustration of Alice in Wonderland, with the famous Guinness animals, such as the iconic toucan, at pantomime time and sold for sixpence per copy. As Edward Guinness remembered:

> I recall hanging anxiously around the lunch rooms and canteen as the first copies were sold, but the reaction was one of complete amazement and, as had been hoped, goodwill, as we were just recovering from the first ever strike in the history of Guinness three weeks previously (over alleged favouritism shown to non-Trade Unionists over the allocation of overtime).[18]

The run of the Park Royal magazine maps incredibly neatly onto the classic era of the long boom and acts as an important source of reflections on that era. By analyzing the nearly three-decade run of *Guinness Time*, it is possible to trace how brewery management reflected on the role of work, its nature, and their responsibilities as employers. This went beyond a general sense that Guinness should be, and wanted to be seen as, a "good" employer. Rather, Guinness managers felt they had a real responsibility to create a model workforce, not in a direct structuring sense but rather organically, by creating a nurturing environment in which employees could flourish. This can be read from the magazine in virtually every issue, potentially every page.

The magazine reflected on the brewery's division of labor and working life in a number of ways, most obviously in the work photo essays, but there were a wider range of issues covered around working life. Pensions, for instance, and the age of retirement were often discussed, as was long service. Younger people, both craft apprentices and what later came to be known as the Boys' and Girls' Scheme, were heavily featured, revealing insights into generational relations and concerns.

Guinness Time provides a window into how one management, at least, envisaged the possibilities for work and workers during the long boom. It was almost certainly a minority view, but numerous practices at Park Royal suggest how deeply notions of industrial citizenship could become embedded in both work and the contexts within which work takes place.

CRITIQUING IMAGE WORK

Industrial photography is really an invention of the late nineteenth century. To be sure, there were photographs of industry and workers before this time, but the deliberate and calculated use of photography was made possible and desirable by changes in technology and the reproductive processes.[19]

This availability of imagery is, then, both a function and a driver of the more general rationalization processes of the late nineteenth and early to mid-twentieth century. Nowhere is this more obvious than in the growth of company magazines. The rise of corporate staff magazines is a very important aspect of welfare capitalism in the United States, with the earliest example created by National Cash Register in 1887.[20] By 1915, large corporations such as Ford, US

Steel, International Harvester, Goodyear, and General Electric all had in-house magazines.[21] The impetus for expansion was the growth in the size of businesses during this period and the consequent erosion of the ties that had historically bound employer and employee in smaller shops and other workplaces. This nostalgia for the era of the small shop is described as "the Lament," a staple of business complaints about the growing distance between management and the shop floor. But this also represented regret at the lack, or loss, of the embeddedness of employers in the lives and community of their workers; it harked back nostalgically to an imagined "golden age" of employee relations, personal contact, and family values.[22]

"The Lament" was also the result of the growing distrust of management, especially of the biggest corporations, and their losing sight of the bigger picture of the role and function of business in society. Corporate communication was the key component in the attempt to stem and eventually turn this tide, and internal staff magazines were an essential part of this project. In 1921, a study of 334 employee magazines in the United States found that 91 percent had been founded between 1917 and 1920 and by 1925 there were more than 539 such publications.[23] By this time, employee magazines had become an important way of promoting employee loyalty, fostering cooperation between management and labor, and disrupting or challenging the power of trade unions. The Depression era of the early 1930s hit corporate publications hard, and many folded; however, there was a revival later in the decade, and by the first nine months of 1937, more than 400 company magazines were launched or revived. This trend marked a fightback against union power as well as a concern to combat what the business lobby saw as the New Deal attack on free enterprise and market capitalism more generally.[24] Photography was a crucial part of the makeup of these new forms of publication, rendering them more attractive and stimulating to their audiences.

But what of the content of the staff magazines themselves? How did they use photography, and how were images combined with written text? Clearly, with so many examples, it is difficult to generalize, and *Guinness Time* differs considerably compared to North American examples. A common trope in staff magazines is the projection of the company as a family; this was a shift from earlier examples that stressed the military-like discipline of big organizations. Moreover, John Mills, director of publication for the Bell Telephone Laboratories, emphasized how "the employees' house magazine has to sell, just as surely as does any salesman on the road."[25] Mills saw the employee magazine as the "great connecting unit running throughout all the organization . . . it inspires ambition, records advancements and promotions, and at its best, becomes the great binder which moulds the entire organization into one mass, all going in the same direction and for the same purpose."[26]

In addition to group photographs of corporate welfare activities, such as sporting events or company picnics, there were two varieties of images used in company magazines—the "domestic snapshot" and the "work portrait." Both of these were ideologically laden with meaning. The work portraits tended to show workers *idealized* and *individualized*, stressing the individual dignity of both work and worker while simultaneously excluding broader narratives of collective bonds and identities. Management actively used individual portraits of workers to create "a visual culture of dignified labour" and boost the idea of "artisanal republicanism" as an ideological bulwark against collective unionization.[27]

The domestic snapshot type of images, on the other hand, "articulated an ideology of corporate paternalism that safely knit the heroic worker into a hierarchical family system managed by corporate 'dads.' "[28] This theme of the absence, or rather controlled use, of images of actual work appears elsewhere. For example, while pictures of skilled workers served as cover illustrations for General Electric's company magazines, unskilled and assembly-line images were largely excluded; this allowed the nature and importance of the role to be obvious to the viewer of the photograph. However, inside, articles focused on visions of the factory as a community of workers who played sports and engaged in a range of other nonwork activities.[29] The paradox was that the element that united the workforce—the work they did—is not depicted. Rather, it was their leisure and social activity in, but also often external to, the workplace that was represented.

Editors quickly realized that the tone of their publications was important if it was to be successful; it could not talk down to workers or be as blatant or condescending as some early examples had been. A crucial part of this reworking of the staff magazine was to include as many images and stories from the shop floor or the workers' home lives as possible. There was a real attempt to drop as many names of workers as possible in every issue, each publication representing in its own way a "corporate family album."[30]

While company magazines were by their nature hierarchical and essentially top-down forms of communication, their tone was usually indirect; workers were not told directly what to think. They communicated "general values" rather than "direct orders."[31] Their simple role was to impart basic information about the workplace, but they had a secondary deeper and more complex role in shaping workplace identity and meanings. Through editorial material as well as visual prompts, business publications projected a new conceptualization of workers. They avoided direct attacks on unions or progressive political parties or even mentioning work explicitly at all. Indeed, Nye says of the portrayal of workers by General Electric that "these men and women are not working or producing; rather they are being produced."[32] Company magazines and the images used in them are ideological, but this ideology is complex and subtle. The messages sent, either overtly or covertly, were not uniform, nor were they consumed in a one-dimensional way. A large company such as General Electric uses a huge range of corporate photography and for many different purposes. Such image production also involved a great division of labor in the photographic and magazine sections—commissioner, editor, photographer, developer, cropper, and framer were just some of the hands through which images would pass.[33] The meaning, intent, and purpose of corporate images are open to negotiation and shifts with the passage of time. As for their audience, it is clear that workers were aware of corporate intent in both their image-making and in the content of staff magazines, and there are instances of workers refusing requests for photographs.[34]

The corporate image-making in company magazines was a social construction, largely but not exclusively by management. They structure the narratives that are told about the company and the workforce. In their use of photography and text, magazines mediate and construct a range of understandings about work and its meanings.

GUINNESS TIME, IMAGINING A BREWERY

From its beginnings in 1947, Guinness Time made extensive use of visual material—photography, sketches, and high-quality illustrations by John Gilroy. These images were scattered liberally through each issue but were most prominently used in the photo essays on brewery work. Over its three-decade run, each issue included a three- to four-page spread on a type of brewery trade or occupation. The photo essays featured photographs specially taken for the particular piece or archive photography alongside the text. This was a sophisticated combination in both style and form; the text was not merely a caption for the images, and equally the images were not simply decorative, there to break up and relieve the text. The editors instead set out to understand how a particular craft or element of labor fitted together, illustrating what a group of workers did and how that particular part contributed to the greater whole. It also set out to explain the technical competence of the trade and to represent workplace culture and tradition.

The photo essays covered virtually all the work at Park Royal, from skilled trades, to professional services, down to semiskilled and essentially unskilled labor. Some of the earliest pieces focused on the older trades in the brewery. In the second issue, the focus was on the coppersmiths. The article was written by one of their number, Mr. E. Blackborow, and was sandwiched between the regular column "Dublin Newsletter" (stories from St. James's Gate) and "Feminine Touch" ("a page for that most important cross-section of the Brewery—THE WOMEN"). The essay, titled "The Coppersmith," gave an account of the work of the craft in Park Royal, beginning not in 1936 and the opening of the brewery but with the origins of the trade in 2200 BCE. Blackborow drew on the Roman historian Pliny and St. Paul's Second Epistle to Timothy before turning to his own seven-year apprenticeship. By degrees his work ranged from tea boy and general gofer to learning his tools and becoming knowledgeable about metallurgy. He told of the culture of making "foreigners," unofficially made items like kettles that were smuggled out of the shop. Toward the end of the piece, he recounted completing his apprenticeship:

As the years of apprenticeship rolled by I grew more and more efficient, and at last the great day arrived when I was to become a coppersmith. At noon everyone assembled in the shop and I was "hammered out." All the 'smiths beat with hammers on anvils or anything else handy and my fellow apprentices pelted me with bags of red ochre, black lead, fireclay and whiting. I ran from the shop right into the arms of the boss who got his share of the missiles. This ceremony over I had once again to "pay my footing" [buying a round of drinks for the entire shop] to celebrate the occasion. I was now a fully-fledged coppersmith.[35]

The piece was illustrated with an engraving of a nineteenth-century coppersmith's shop, examples of the work of the trade, a photograph of a coppersmith at work, and a "school photograph" shot of the members of the Park Royal coppersmiths' shop. The text noted that the nine "smiths in the Brewery have between them 270 years in the Society of Coppersmiths." This relatively short piece touched on four millennia of history and went into the culture of the trade before finally giving the reader a sense of the science behind the craft.

Some of the photo essays were concerned with brewery processes and explained how and why work took the form it did. One such piece concerned the cooperage cleansing section responsible for checking, cleaning, and repairing wooden barrels after they were returned to the brewery from the trade. This piece was written by one of the editors, but it had the basic structure of the coppersmiths' article, taking the reader through the various stages of the barrel's progress on return to Park Royal: unloading and inspection, recording it in company records, smelling each cask to see if it was "off," sterilization, and finally refilling. Each element involved technical detail as well as portraits of the men and women involved. The parts of the process were illustrated with images and complemented by family portraits of groups of workers. The text was a skillful mix of technical detail and social observation, explaining the role of the workers in the wider story of the brewery and the outside world.

The first issue of *Guinness Time* had a photo essay entitled "The Cooper: The Craft and the Man." As its title suggests, this piece gave an overview of the production process and the history of the barrel—on this occasion, reaching back only to 500 BCE—before examining more contemporary aspects of the trade and its customs. Like the article on the smiths, "The Cooper" cited classical historians such as Herodotus. A good deal of the piece was devoted to the growth of the Coopers' Guild and to the system of apprenticeship, including a graphic account of the Truss-O ceremony at the end of the apprentice's time:

In England, for instance, when a man finished his apprenticeship and became a fully-fledged Cooper the occasion was observed with an initiation ceremony as befitted the admission of another skilled craftsman into the Guild. This initiation was designed to remain in the memory of the new Cooper for many a long day. First he had to make and then fire a cask. While it was still smoking he was placed in it; the truss hoops were driven tight and the victim, after being liberally sprinkled with shavings and well doused with water, was rolled down the street in his self-made chariot. He was then extricated and in front of the other members of the Guild was handed his indentures by the foreman of the shop.[36]

The article was illustrated with a fourteenth-century woodcut, a picture of Park Royal's first Truss-O ceremony, and a general view of the coopers' shop, alongside a more detailed picture of a craftsman at work. The piece was steeped in references to heritage and tradition, and it is interesting the way the brewery, laid out on thoroughly modern lines in the mid-1930s, was home to a revived craft ceremony dating back six centuries. Also noteworthy is that a staff magazine, effectively edited by management, would draw attention to craft tradition. The coopers' trade proved to be highly photogenic over the years in and beyond the pages of *Guinness Time*. The company archive was full of many aspects of the coopers' craft, including a series of black-and-white images of each element of making a barrel and a number of other Truss-O ceremonies, which occurred in the brewery until wooden barrels were superseded by metal casks during the 1950s. Guinness was clearly alive to the publicity value of this tradition; the advertising manager, Pick, arranged for one ceremony to be recorded by the *Illustrated London News*, and this scene was later used as the basis for a painting of the scene by Gilroy. This painting, in turn, formed the basis for postcards used in Guinness publicity in various ways. In the archive, there is a five-minute film of the ceremony that shows the whole procedure: from making the barrel and the apprentice climbing in to him emerging from his ordeal and later the presentation of indentures after he had cleaned up.

Over the years, the focus of the photo essays in *Guinness Time* included numerous other crafts and sections, reflecting both the changing organizational structure and its hierarchy. Ranging across blue- and white-collar staff, genders, and skill levels, the essays showed the work of the farmhands, the grounds staff, scientists in the laboratories, building workers, scaffolders, cleaning gangs, fitters, telephone operators, the advertising department, chauffeurs, cooks, pilots, and the wages staff. It seems there was a conscious effort to represent *all* the labor that went on in the brewery. The style of the pieces subtly changed over the years; some were written in the third person, others in the first. A good example of the latter is a 1963 account of the role of the Guinness Driver, which reads like an exercise in creative writing. While written in the first person, it is unlikely to have been written by a driver:

> Into the garage and park car. Still dark; five minutes to six. Overnight bag
>   out of the back; walk across the yard to Traffic Office window.
> "Morning, Jimmy."
> "Morning, Burt."
> "Here's your time-sheet; Thornton Heath then Birmingham."[37]

The piece continued with an inner dialogue about the job, the task in hand, the vehicles driven, and the other brewery staff. We see the driver's job in the round, what a typical shift looked like, including the need for overnight lodging at the time. The piece is illustrated with a variety of images taken in the brewery grounds and in the outside world. One of the pictures shows a group of drivers coming out of the all-important café stop. The dialogue finishes with an account of journey's end and the lodgings for the night:

> Yardley—into the lorry park—pull alongside Tanker 249, already parked. Turn Off engine, stretch, complete time-sheet, note mileage, 147 for the day, not bad with an early morning delivery in London. Collect overnight bag and overcoat—climb out of cab. Air chilly, going to be a frost again. Get sheet out of cab and cover windscreen—save a moment in the morning. Lock up cab. Cross park and pay fee. Could do with a wash; wonder what Marion's got for supper? Well, let's join the lads.[38]

An editorial character sketch of the brewery drivers completes the piece: "Thus does many a working day end for the Guinness driver, in places far from home. Often independent in character, working long hours alone, reliably he performs his important part in the process of providing our customers with their Guinness."[39]

There is a mixture of writing styles and genres, owing much to the documentary tradition of telling a story through a typical day or shift. It evokes this style in the manner in which it imagines a worker's inner dialogue about his work delivered in staccato, clipped sentences. Like the other essays of this form, it reinforces the sense of the interconnectedness of the brewery, both internally and externally. Most of the *Guinness Time* photo essays deal with labor internal to the brewery. To be sure, the outside world does feature occasionally but usually only where a worker has come from or where product eventually ends up.

That notion of interconnectedness was important in the photo essays and *Guinness Time* generally. The initial editorial had stressed the need to create social structures and linkages between people, creating community through understanding what others did in the brewery and the company more widely. A similar early editorial reflected on the meaning and value of work:

> In the passage quoted at the head of this page Aristotle gives his solution to this problem—to find happiness in one's work, whatever that work may be. To do this it is necessary to have an interest in that work and to understand how one's own job fits into the general scheme. *Guinness Time* hopes to help towards both these ends, for we do not believe in the Shavian pin-maker, who, while tending the machine that makes the heads, neither knows nor cares about the man who sharpens the points. We hold that men and women who spend half their waking lives working together must be interested in the results of their labours, and our pages are designed to foster this interest. We are proud of the organisation for

which we work, and of the product which we produce and our stories and pictures help to make them better known to ourselves, and to others.[40]

One way to read the work photo essays and, by extension, the entire run of *Guinness Time* is to see them as attempts to confront, and offer solutions to, the postwar problem of work. This reflection on work perhaps unintentionally echoes the French sociologist Émile Durkheim. Although the word *anomie* is not used in the magazine, this is what it hints at. In his book *Division of Labor in Society*, Durkheim is at pains to understand how modern workers in more narrowly defined roles accepted and embraced their place in a hierarchy. He tackles this head on, suggesting that this was to emerge organically out of the division of labor itself, predicated on a transparent, fair, and meritocratic allocation of tasks and positions, but that such an acceptance is itself rooted in an intelligibility of the overall division of labor. As he puts it:

> For, normally, the role of each special function does not require that the individual close himself in, but that he keep himself in constant relations with neighbouring functions, take conscience of their needs, of the changes which they undergo, etc. The division of labour presumes that the worker, far from being hemmed in by his task, does not lose sight of his collaborators, that he acts upon them, and reacts to them. He is, then, not a machine who repeats his movements without knowing their meaning, but he knows that they tend, in some way, towards an end that he conceives more or less distinctly. He feels that he is serving something.[41]

The role of *Guinness Time* in general but especially in the photo essays was to forge collective meaning by explaining to each member of staff how his or her job was interconnected with the others in the brewery. These stories build over time to reveal an organic community, one in which members relied on one another. In the combination of text and images, a sophisticated account of a modern industrial concern emerges. Technical and processional understandings are combined with social and cultural forms of everyday life. A humanized division of labor emerges across the pages of *Guinness Time*, where different parts of an interdependent but fragmented production process and the support functions have names and faces attached to them. The rationalized division of labor is reenchanted by reembedding economic actions into social and cultural structures. These articles were not trying to create uniformity across the workforce but actually stressed, indeed reveled, in difference. The images used to illustrate the photo essays were strikingly different from the American scholarly critique of corporate imagery that emphasized how workers were individualized and often removed from work settings altogether. While there was a great deal of coverage of sports and social activity, *Guinness Time* made a virtue of showing and writing about employees engaged in work. Even when workers were posed in school-type photos, they were rendered as workers, visually by their overalls, clothes, or tools and textually by captions recording their job title and name. In the case of the coopers and coppersmiths, there was no attempt to disguise the craft division of labor nor the fact that each of these crafts had its own long-established union.

IMAGINING PARK ROYAL

Images of the brewery and the work that went on inside it were created for many reasons and for numerous audiences, and these went beyond the photographic. In the 1950s, Guinness engaged a number of artists to record various aspects of Park Royal, and usually these involved the portrayal of labor in some form. The most famous artist associated with Guinness was Gilroy, celebrated for his long-standing relationship with its advertising campaigns.[42] Gilroy also painted a number of scenes of Park Royal in the early 1950s. These include general depictions of work such as "Unloading in the Malt Store" (ca 1951), depicting a loading bay with sacks of malt being manually discharged into a chute. The image shows thirteen Guinness workers involved in various activities and a brewery cat eying three pigeons attempting to eat some spilt malt. In another, Gilroy recorded two workers skimming yeast from the top of a tank. These paintings contrast with another Gilroy canvas of the same time, "Brewery Charger Inspecting a Copper." This picture is far more detailed and depicts a worker intently looking through a glass inspection porthole in a copper. These Gilroy paintings and others, including that of a cooper's end-of-apprenticeship ceremony, were displayed on the walls at Park Royal and were reproduced on company postcards as publicity material.

Guinness commissioned other artists to paint aspects of the company's trade both at Park Royal and Dublin and in the Guinness hop farms in Kent. The most notable was Terrance Cuneo, a prolific commercial artist specializing in military and industrial scenes.[43] Around the same time Gilroy was painting his canvasses, Cuneo was creating images of the raking sheds and a worker stirring an open mash tun. These pictures seem to be based on sketches and photographs of Park Royal. The Guinness directors were impressed with Cuneo's work and invited him to produce more paintings of St. James's Gate. Company archives record the negotiation over fee—the artist was paid 300 guineas for each canvas. Although both painters took a certain amount of artistic license in their commissions, both adopted a realistic style illustrating actual processes in a working brewery, warts and all. The canvases attempt to show not perfection but rather a working scene. The originals, copies, and reproductions of these paintings were hung around various offices and canteen areas in the brewery, and some were still displayed on office walls in 2005.[44]

In the Guinness archive, the pictures that stand out are those taken in the late 1940s and early 1950s by the commercial photographer A R Tanner. Tanner had worked for the photo magazine *Picture Post* before the Second World War and during the war as a member of the Army Photographic Unit. After 1945, he resumed his civilian career by working for corporations, including Guinness at Park Royal. Tanner took many shots of various types of manual labor in the brewery. The images were exquisitely framed and lit, transforming what were essentially routine production-line studies into beautifully crafted images of aestheticized labor. This image-making has its limits, however; although Tanner made the mundane beautiful, his lens and gaze were restricted to male labor. In the Guinness archive, I was unable to find any of these stunning images portraying females. This neglect is puzzling because women were certainly involved in some of the trades and sections he photographed.[45]

These images echo the work of industrial photographer Maurice Broomfield, a contemporary of Tanner, who coined the term "the New Look" in industrial photography. There are also stylistic similarities with German émigré photographer Walter Nurnberg. In a draft paper, "What, then, Is Industrial Photography?," Nurnberg distinguished between what he labeled "record photography"—buildings in long shot, machines, or industrial plant erection. This type of photography did not require creative ability; indeed, he described this genre as "arid reproductions." But "documentary photography of working processes and the imaginative portrayal of industry and its men" was inherently creative, as he described, to

> the portrayal of industrial life in general and to the dynamic story telling in general. With this type of photography the client is no longer interested to show merely an arid reproduction of floor space and machinery. Instead he looks for a vivid and visual expression of many of the skills which stand behind the making of his products. He expects his photographer to give him a coherent and eloquent story of working methods, indeed a forceful epitome of industrial endeavour.[46]

Nurnberg was the principal exponent of what was known as the New Objectivity, defined by its emphasis on sharp focus, contrasts of tone and form, visual rhythms, and a strong asymmetrical composition.[47] This approach had its roots in early Russian and Soviet film, added to along the way by interwar German influences, and the documentary film tradition in the United Kingdom. After 1945, Nurnberg turned away from advertising toward industrial photography, and his aim was "to fulfil not only his client's brief but also to express a heroic dignity in industrial labour."[48] At their best, Tanner's photographs for Guinness reflect many of these features of postwar photography. The images of Park Royal cannot be categorized as "record" photography in the narrow sense that Nurnberg suggested in his writing. Instead, they embrace many of the conventions of the more creative and innovative industrial photographers of the time. They also feature the same use of light, contrast, and asymmetricality of the New Objectivity style championed by Nurnberg and copied by others. Nurnberg said of his visual philosophy:

> Photography is the herald of Reality—a Reality to be found not only in the material aspect of life, but also in our spiritual experience. I, as a photographer, have thus to

do two things: to make others see what I see; and make those who understand my language share my emotional and intellectual attitude to life.[49]

Visually, in the postwar period, a number of industrial photographers and their clients, including Guinness, were trying to communicate a different disposition toward the industrial subject: they were invoking a visual industrial citizenship.

THE GUINNESS CITIZEN

The images and the texts written about the brewery's workforce conceptualized the Guinness Citizen. Both Marshall and Guinness were reimagining the status and possibilities for work and workers in the context of the postwar settlement. Each in his way mixed abstract philosophical ideas about the nature of labor with a more grounded account of employment practiced empirically.

The idea of industrial citizenship played a minor but important part in Marshall's *Citizenship and Social Class*. In the book, he addressed the question of modern work and the modern employee and the state's role in developing human potential in contemporary society. Essentially, Marshall recognized that the growing ranks of industrial workers needed to be cultivated into fully fledged citizens in the rapidly expanding welfare states. There was an imperative to create the context of an active, engaged, and moral citizenry. Work and the social structures that surround it could provide an important element of this new moral framework. Industrial citizenship, for Marshall, was a way of solving or at least ameliorating the fragmentary nature of capitalism, holding in check the corrosive effects of rationalization by reenchanting work culture. Such a form of reenchanted citizenship would allow a collective sense of society to emerge from the familiar, day-to-day setting of the workplace and work group.

This desire to solve the problems of modern industrial society through building social structure at work was immediately apparent in the postwar brewery at Park Royal. The stated aim of *Guinness Time* was to knit strangers together by explaining the different types of labor that went on in the brewery to anchor staff in their workplace. Although it used the phrase "Guinness Citizenship" sparingly, the magazine simultaneously reflected and created a sense of citizenship. This was evident in the magazine's coverage of working life, such as pensions, the age of retirement, and the issue of long service. However, some of the best examples can be found in its coverage of younger people, both craft apprentices and what later came to be known as the Boys' and Girls' Scheme, essentially a way of formally training young noncraft workers. In a 1949 article, "Theirs Is the Future," the magazine discussed the issue of youth employment, noting the problem of high school graduates: "Young people are at once faced with a great temptation to accept the first lucrative job which presents itself, without paying much attention to the prospects this job may hold out for their adult employment."[50]

This problem was compounded by National Service (compulsory military service for all young men, abolished in 1963) and its tendency to break up important structures and processes of socialization into working and adult life. Further, a particular group of youths were seen as especially at risk: those not engaged in craft apprenticeship.

> In a previous issue of *Guinness Time* we wrote of the Company's Long Service Award and of those who have received it. We now tell the other end of the story, how young people are recruited to the brewery and how they are trained and cared for here. It is our aim, not to provide mere blind-alley jobs for the newcomers, but by careful selection and suitable training to fit them into jobs to which they are best suited and to help them become useful members of the community. In doing this we hope they will become proud of their work and will become proud of their association with the Guinness Company.[51]

The photo essay that followed showed boys and girls at work in various parts of the brewery; the aim was to move them around the plant to give them an insight into a variety of tasks. In the case of the boys, it was to provide them with work experience before undertaking National Service. The piece finished by wishing the young recruits well and hoping that they too would one day enjoy long service awards.

This concern is echoed repeatedly in *Guinness Time*; in 1952, for instance, another article on the Boys' Scheme reflects on the possible fate of those working in nonskilled occupations:

> The problem, however, is not so easy to solve in the case of those non-tradesmen, and all too often the individual is employed in some capacity which can have no future for him in his adult life—the typical "dead-end" job. Our scheme is designed to overcome this problem. Its aim is to occupy the boy usefully during this period and to give him a thorough grounding in the work of the Brewery. It is also designed to bring him on physically and to simulate him in a sense of responsibility and self-reliance so that he will be best fitted to play his part, when an adult, in the industry and social life of the country.[52]

There are many instances of an innate conservatism in articles and especially the editorials. What was often stressed was the organic and the rooted, a Burkean conservatism; metaphors of stability were often deployed in the resistance to abrupt change or radicalism of various shades. What it returned to time and again was a concern for the modern worker and how the monotony and repetition of tasks could be removed or ameliorated. In one editorial reflecting on the success of Roger Bannister in breaking the four-minute mile, the editor ponders on the role of sport in work:[53]

> For sport is a wonderful medium for good international relations and equally is it important on the home front. If we were asked to comment on one aspect of

this, we would say that in an age of increasing mechanisation it does give a most valuable outlet to young workers who are so often beset with the monotony of industrial life. No more awful picture of the present day can be given than of the young worker watching different products of the industrial machine go past him all day and then watching motion or television pictures go past him all evening. Yet we know it happens.[54]

This observation highlighted that 80 percent of employees were members of the Guinness Club and noted the sporting activities within the brewery's environs; it also served as a call to arms for more staff involvement in activities outside of work. Interestingly, industrial monotony was bracketed with the leisure activities of affluence, especially television. The imagined passivity, both at work and leisure, of unengaged employees was a serious concern. By contrast, Guinness promoted an active engagement and vision of a particular type of creative citizenry, one inextricably linked to the workplace. The fear of passivity mirrored the views of contemporary politicians and social scientists over the negative aspects of growing affluence and what exactly the working classes would get up to when left to their own devices.[55]

The 1954 Christmas issue of *Guinness Time* paid close attention to the issue of retirement and the ageing demographic of society. Reflecting on longer working lives and the social problem of intergenerational tension caused by younger workers being blocked for promotion by older workers, it floated the issue of retired workers seeking employment elsewhere.[56] The phrase "Guinness Citizenship" was used in a 1953 article on the merging of the transport undertaking into Guinness. As the editor noted: "This change will extend to all transport workers at Park Royal what is probably best described as Guinness Citizenship, with all its advantages of Sick Pay, Service Pay and Pensions."[57]

This sense of citizenship can be seen in a later piece on the Boys' Scheme: "Guinness is a family firm and likes to foster a sense of belonging throughout the Brewery":

> The Boys' Scheme was not devised just to train a boy for work in the Brewery. It was framed to give him an opportunity to develop his character and to express himself in worthwhile and pleasurable pursuits. The training allows him to be placed in a job within the limits of his own abilities and above all, it helps him to meet the many demands and responsibilities of a rich and full adult life.[58]

Later still, the purpose of the scheme was explained as being to "train boys in Brewery work and also as good citizens."[59]

It is clear from both the contemporary and retrospective accounts of the training scheme that Guinness had a vision to develop staff and that, through work, all sorts of other qualities would emerge and be nurtured in the brewery. Guinness drew a distinction between four main aspects of a young person's life at Park Royal: on-the-job training, character training, physical fitness, and further education. The Boys' Scheme was based on a system of on-the-job training where the youths would begin their working lives as uniformed messengers, allowing them to understand the geography of the brewery and developing an appreciation of its social structure. This was followed in the second year by exposure to different departments, both production and support. The character training aspect of the scheme was aimed at developing notions of leadership among the boys, encouraging them through competing groups within the brewery and taking part on the Duke of Edinburgh's Award Scheme. Each feature of the training scheme had a strong moral purpose and conviction, best illustrated by the focus on physical fitness:

> Indeed one found that the leisure time of the boy was compounded too often by a futile and sometimes dangerous boredom and the inclination, with opportunities these days unknown to his father, of always being a spectator. To meet this we engaged a sports coach who for one afternoon a week has each boy under his charge, training him principally in team games and I am convinced that a boy's loyalty to his company can be much enhanced by being a regular member of one of the teams. Further, although team spirit appears to be a phrase temporarily out of fashion, it can none the less encourage constructive group activities with highly beneficial social consequences.[60]

These aspects, together with further education, described a particular vision of the power of work to shape both the individual worker and a wider collective body in the brewery. This piece illustrates how a vision of an industrial citizenship was an amalgam of two potentially contradictory impulses. First was a desire to create individuals of character who were independently minded, committed to the company, and capable of leadership. Second, however, there was a real sense that this independence was a quality to be fostered by benign intervention and a positive and enriching environment, one that was inextricably social and collective.

There are clear parallels between the issues Guinness management sought to address and those of Durkheim, Marshall, and a host of nineteenth- and early twentieth-century writers on work and welfare: Essentially, how does society provide adequate, even generous welfare while not deterring work? This debate over the relationship between work and welfare evokes T. H. Green's notion of developing people's "best selves," a moral ethic rooted in both the individual and collective worker.[61] Here, a collective moral sense of the need to be a good worker and therefore a good citizen was implied. This was an ethic that had to be nurtured rather than imposed.

Durkheim's major intellectual contribution to this same debate was to ask, "How can we find a system of moral restraint which is relevant to modern conditions?"[62] The answer lay, at least in part, in the workplace professional or occupational groups whose norms and values would act as the basis for moral regulation of the individual *and* the group. Crucially, such groups provided a space between the immediacy of the family and the remoteness of the state: "Professional ethics find their right place between the family morals already mentioned and civic morals."[63] The increased division of labor had created a more marked diversity of professional ethics, each occupational grouping possessing distinct positions from another. As Durkheim put it: "We might say in this connection that there are as many forms of morals as there are different callings, and since, in theory, each individual carries on only one calling, the result is that these different forms of morals apply to entirely different groups of individuals."[64] It was in the economic sphere that social stability was fostered, compensating for the decline of religious observance in what would otherwise be a moral vacuum for society generally and for the individual. Professional ethics filled this vacuum with a set of norms and values regulating individual ego and desire by appealing to a wider intelligible collective sense, close enough to have concrete expression in workplace norms while distant enough to provide critical space between the individual and corporate group.

Just like Marshall, Durkheim, and others, Guinness management at Park Royal wrestled with this problem of work. From a variety of material, we get a clear sense that senior members of management on site and in the company had a broader vision for both work and the workforce. They were imagining both in an expansive and positive form. They recognized that the task of building character could not be left to itself or the individual; rather, there should be an informed intervention on their part to enable the individual and collective "better self" to emerge in the postwar workplace.

IMAGINING WORK AT PARK ROYAL IN THE LONG BOOM

How, then, does what Guinness management was doing at Park Royal fit with or vary from the insights offered by other, mostly North American accounts? We can certainly recognize the different genres of photography developed in the portrayal of the postwar brewery: the portrayal of heroic workers, the elements of their home and family life, and sports and social activity. However, in both written and visual texts, management set out to show workers engaged in labor, in contrast to the General Electric workers, who were framed either as heroic individualized workers or at play. *Guinness Time* editors made an active choice to show what people did in the brewery. They sought to portray the division of labor on the site rather than hide it, wanting to explain how seemingly small or trivial tasks fitted into a wider whole. They tried to anchor workers into the plant and the wider organization. Workers were shown as individuals at times, but more frequently they were portrayed alongside others, emphasizing their shared collectivity.

A widespread dissatisfaction developed with the growing distance between management and shop floor as firms grew more complex in the late nineteenth and early twentieth centuries; the result was that corporations sought new ways to engage their employees. Corporate magazines were an attempt to bridge this gap, to reintegrate and re-create a sense of family in the corporate body. There are, undoubtedly, strong parallels in this line of analysis for the Guinness material. The firm had always prided itself on its strong identity as a family firm, deeply paternalistic with a reputation for welfare; there was perhaps less cause here than for a full-bodied "Lament." Park Royal was barely a decade old when the war ended. The workplace norms, cultures, and patterns of everyday life had had little chance to settle before the war. Peacetime represented an opportunity to start anew, offering the staff in London the chance to do something distinct from Dublin traditions. If there is a lament in *Guinness Time*, it takes a different form: it is a desire a return to normal, for rootedness, for everyday certainty. To be sure, part of the background in management thinking across a range of labor policies at Park Royal was the threat posed by militant trade unionism and the specter of communism. Unlike the North American examples of corporate imagery, or indeed wider corporate welfare, Guinness took a more relaxed view of its staff's politics.

The pages of *Guinness Time* did not attempt to disguise work, nor more broadly did the magazine try to stymie collective bargaining. On the contrary, the Park Royal site actively encouraged blue-collar staff to join relevant trade unions. This was unusual in the brewing sector at the time and even raised eyebrows among managers and directors in Dublin. This move can be interpreted in a number of ways. On the one hand, it was a cynical attempt to head off more militant confrontation and political organization in the immediate postwar period. Conflict between capital and labor would therefore be contained by industrial relations bureaucracy, with disputes dissipated horizontally rather than vertically. Alternatively, we could read what happened at Park Royal in a slightly different way, one where there is a recognition that labor policy needs to change. This emerges from a complex set of reasons and stimuli. It was a reflection of changing attitudes in industrial management as a result of the war: a generation of men and women had gone through a life-changing experience that had shaken up preexisting values, norms, and expectations on both sides of the capital/labor divide. Labor had, during the Second World War, held a seat at the table. With the election of a Labour government in 1945, there was a real sense that this was labor's time, the era of the common man and woman. We can witness this ideological shift in the upper reaches of government and the wider public sector. This spirit also animated Marshall in *Citizenship and Social Class*, in which there is a clear recognition of the full flowering of working-class citizenship as part of a modern social democracy.

In the case of Guinness at Park Royal, this sense of new potential is translated into trade union recognition, and, through the pages of *Guinness Time*, into a broader, deeper, and more profound reflection on the role and meaning of work in the postwar era. Welfare and industrial relations concessions are not cynical maneuvers, a ploy or pretense; rather, they are genuine attempts to develop men and women in a workplace. "Guinness Citizenship" could be read as simply a refreshed and updated paternalism, and that could be a legitimate interpretation. However, within the texts, what was being offered was recognition of the need to help individuals to grow so that they could become independent, thoughtful, and even critical citizens within and beyond the workplace. This more generous reading of management motives has parallels with Marshall's vision and also that of Durkheim. Both these theorists could and have been interpreted as being conservative thinkers; however, each, in his own right, can be read in far more radical ways. Both emphasized the importance of work groups in imposing collective norms and values on individuals but argued that this moral order is essential for creating citizens who recognize their individuality in a collective, an essentially societal setting. Norms and values are not fixed but rather are the emergent property of the collective; they have moral authority over the individual precisely because they are collectively derived.

In his introduction to a book of Broomfield's images, Jon Levy writes:

> Embodied in these pages are the realisation of many dreams. The stunning photographs attest to the ingenuity of the medium, the hard work of individuals and the lofty ambitions of a generation to build and shape a productive future for society. Inherent in the subject matter is a sense of the optimism of an era and, perhaps most importantly, pride. Workers, workplace, work; this is not a romantic setting for a photographic body of work yet the secret ingredient that makes it taste so sweet is of course the photographer's eye.[65]

Levy's observation echoes many of the themes of this chapter, both in the industrial photography of the period and a far wider spirit of the time. The documentary style of postwar industrial photography attempted to idealize the mundane, the ordinary, and the everyday. It sought, if not heroic workers, then at least to dignify the work and lives of the common people. It was part of a wider spirit of generosity for, and recognition of, the labor of working-class people. It showed confident working-class subjects engaged seriously in doing things. These images invite, even instruct, the audience to pay careful attention to the work itself and the worker. Through the lens of Broomfield, Tanner, and countless other industrial photographers, what is revealed is a new way of seeing work; we are invited to take a new look.

This optimism of the period was expressed in other media and ideas of the time. It is a positive reading of the potential of humanity. It was labeled by Frayn as the outlook of the Herbivores: "Gentle ruminants, who look out from the lush pastures which are their natural station in life with eyes full of sorrow for less fortunate creatures, guiltily conscious of their advantages, though not usually ceasing to eat the grass."[66] Against these Herbivores Frayn opposes the Carnivores, who have a completely different outlook on society and the role of the individual in it. Frayn and others saw the postwar settlement as the work of the Herbivores, and after 1951, when they lost power, this essential vision of society was accepted by a large part of the political caste. The essential idealism of that settlement could not have remained intact; it was eroded from the very beginning by the realities of austerity Britain and the pragmatic need simply to survive.

What happened at Park Royal in the same period represented in microcosm this wider story of work. The management and labor policies of the brewery were a mixture of traditional paternalism coupled with the idealistic and pragmatic realization that things had changed. The text and images of the Guinness brewery at Park Royal serve as a witness to the struggle over the role and meaning of work in the era of the long boom. Guinness grappled with the issues of staff returning from the services and their reintegration into brewery society. Later, management attempted to think seriously about workplace citizenship and the role and meaning of work to try to inculcate an active Guinness Citizenship in its staff. This vision itself was challenged and eroded by the pragmatic considerations of the mundane day-to-day working life of the brewery—abstract notions of human potential became bogged down in the detail of pay differentials. What remains impressive was the breadth and depth of a humanistic vision for work and workers that emerged at Park Royal in the three decades after 1945.

3

THE GARDEN IN
THE MACHINE

In 1953, Ealing Studios released *The Titfield Thunderbolt*, a light-hearted comedy about the attempts of the fictional rural community of Titfield to save its railway branch line from closure. Predating the infamous "Beeching closures" of the 1960s,[1] the film tells the story of a group of amateur enthusiasts who seek to run the line themselves after the closure, on economic grounds, by the state-owned British Railways. *The Titfield Thunderbolt* in many ways is an archetypal Ealing film, with its storyline of a small tight-knit village battling against the large-scale, impersonal forces of the bureaucratic state. The narrative arc of the studio's films is often portrayed as stability, disturbance, fight back, return to order. At one point in the film, the leading characters—the vicar, the local squire, and a local landowner—plead with the authorities to be allowed to run the railway themselves after British Railways pulls out. During the public inquiry into the closure, it appears that the group has lost its chance. This elicits an outburst from the local squire:

> Don't you realize you are condemning our village to death? Open it up to buses and lorries and what's it going to be like in five years' time? Our lanes will be concrete roads, our houses will have numbers instead of names, there will be traffic lights and zebra crossings . . . [the railway] means everything to our village.[2]

Titfield fits into the wider Ealing genre; where once the studio had been progressive, even modernizing, in its portrayal of national character, this film represents part of a decaying arc where more progressive ideals are tamped down underneath a growing sentimental conservative anti-Modernism. While the film certainly pokes fun at the quaintness of rural English life—as Ealing often had before—Titfield is a rural community under siege from the forces of modernism, modernity, organized labor, planning, and state bureaucracy.[3] This is an old England surrounded and threatened by the postwar consensus. In many ways, Titfield can tell us a great deal about the tensions in postwar Britain over modernization versus tradition, progress versus heritage, rural versus urban.

One of the best academic examples of this sense of threat can be found in W. G. Hoskins's *The Making of the English Landscape*, first published in 1955.

The majority of the book illustrates how the English landscape changed over time at the hand of human inhabitants; what unfolds is a natural, organic pace of development that subtly improves and adds character to the rural aspect. Even the upheavals wrought by the Industrial Revolution in their own distinct way complement the landscape. In the final chapter, "The Landscape Today," Hoskins's narrative takes on a darker hue: "Since that time, and especially since the year 1914, every single change in the English landscape has either uglified it or destroyed its meaning, or both."[4] Hoskins rails against the encroachment of the countryside by large-scale mechanized farming, opencast mineral extraction, and industrial ribbon development:

> What else has happened in the immemorial landscape of the English countryside? Airfields have flayed it bare wherever there are level, well-drained stretches of land, above all in eastern England. Poor devastated Lincolnshire and Suffolk! And those long gentle lines of the dip-slope of the Cotswolds, those misty uplands of the sheep grey oolite, how they have lent themselves to the villainous requirements of the new age! Over them, drones, day after day, the obscene shape of the atom-bomber, laying a trail like a filthy slug upon Constable's and Gainsborough's sky. England of the Nissen hut, the "pre-fab," and the electric fence, of the high barbed wire around some unmentionable devilment; England of the arterial by-pass, tree-less and stinking diesel oil, murderous with lorries; England of the bombing-range wherever there was once silence, as on Otmoor or the marshlands of Lincolnshire; England of the battle-training areas on the Breckland heaths, and tanks crashing through empty ruined Wiltshire villages; England of high explosive falling upon the prehistoric monuments of Dartmoor. Barbaric England of the scientists, the military men, and the politicians: let us turn away and contemplate the past before all is lost to the vandals.[5]

Hoskins's dystopian vision is one that stresses change while at the same moment calling "time" on the idea of progress, for the gradual improvement of the English landscape until the early years of the twentieth century gives way to unnatural despoilment and debasement. This modernizing moment is one that goes against nature's grain, one that is incapable of being organically folded into the contours of the soil. Hoskins was not alone in this negative reading of postwar progress and its impact on the English landscape.[6]

There is a distinct shift in attitudes toward the countryside and modernity after World War II. In the period before the war, modern technology and new design were often understood as improving the English landscape through the adoption of new techniques of husbandry and technology. Planning was an essential part of preserving and enhancing natural landscapes and the built heritage of England. The Festival of Britain in 1951 was the highpoint of this modernizing vision that "offered a national vision aligning the modern and traditional, city and country, reconstruction and citizenship, history and future."[7] Poignantly, however, Matless adds that although this was perhaps the fullest expression of landscape and citizenship, it was also the point where it began to degrade from internal and external attacks: "Traditional landscape, local heritage and anti-modernity line up against visions of a planned and ordered country."[8] Matless examines the impact and legacy of Hoskins's interpretation of twentieth-century modernization on the English landscape, showing how he adopted a powerful voice of authority, creating a series of positive/negative dichotomies through which to read the contemporary landscape:

> Hoskins signals the emergence in recognizable contemporary form of a series of powerful cultural oppositions; urban against rural, national and international against local, individual against state, shallow theory against deep particularity, planning against landscape, modernity against tradition. Hoskins also crucially sets past against present.[9]

The result is to effectively stop history dead in its tracks. The past now is something to be escaped to rather than something to be drawn on in understanding the present. It creates a "formulation of despair" that provided a powerful context for postwar preservation and heritage movements.

It is important that this reaction against modernity should not be seen as just a rural phenomenon: the urban, too, in postwar Britain was subject to increasing attention from those who sought to preserve what was being lost of the Victorian and Georgian built environment.[10] It was, however, the countryside that really exercised the nostalgic imagination. As sociologist Howard Newby notes:

> Ever since England became a predominantly urban country, rural England has been regarded as the principal repository of quintessential English values. Culturally English society has never adapted itself to urban living, has never adopted an urban way of life. *Real* England has never been represented by the town, but by the village, and the English countryside has been converted into a vast arcadian rural idyll in the mind of the average Englishman.[11]

Newby sought to understand the relationship between rural settlement and social forms, especially those around work in the countryside. He was interested in how ideologically agricultural work was shaped by a nostalgic view of the countryside, the idea that work and economic bonds were rooted in structures of tradition and mutual respect. There was a sense that such work enjoyed a social stability, rootedness, and order absent from modern industrial labor carried out in urban settings:

> Embedded deep in English culture there is now a strong belief that work on the land has some intrinsic value which renders it more morally beneficial and that to dwell in an English village is to be more attuned to traditional realities.[12]

At times, rural landscape and the type of work that went on there have been elided; character and quality merge in a vision of authentic, rooted workers.

These types of vision are in turn compared unfavorably to the forms of work and workers who dwell in urban settings, the character and rootedness of the former juxtaposed with the narrow instrumentality and shallowness of the modern urban worker.[13]

It would be wrong, however, to characterize postwar society and polity as exclusively antimodern or vehemently against change. The 1945 Labour government was certainly a modernizing one, wedded to improving people's lives through a mixture of planning, reform, new technology, and development. The Festival of Britain, in its own quaint and very British way, was a celebration of the future as well as the past. The reforming zeal of the wartime administrators and technocrats was still evident throughout the period under consideration. This modernizing desire can be detected in both urban and rural settings, beautifully illustrated in Edward Mills's account of the modern industrial architecture and design.[14] In *The Modern Factory* (1951), Mills promotes orderly and effective factory planning, landscaping, and the use of light and new technologies: "In spite of town planning legislation many hundreds of acres of beautiful countryside have been overwhelmed by ill-considered, badly planned and un-neighbourly industrial buildings." But, he continues, "industrial development is an economic essential in the life of Britain to-day, but there is no reason why this essential part of British post-war recovery which provides work, food, necessities and luxuries for the world, should at the same time disfigure the land to which it brings so much."[15] There is, then, no contradiction here between planning, industrial development, and the landscape. There is a real sense that they could and should have a mutually beneficial relationship.

The Guinness brewery at Park Royal, and the work that went on there, represents a "privileged occasion" for understanding work in the twentieth century. Guinness adapted itself to the postwar settlement in labor policy terms. Reflected in the pages of *Guinness Time* and in the images it produced, the company attempted to create Guinness Citizens. The company was trying to mold, however imperfectly, a stable work community. In doing so, the organization made sense of the tension between modernity and tradition, the urban and the rural, at Park Royal. These tensions are inscribed and embedded in the landscape and very fabric of the brewery. Guinness developed its very own, very English modern version of vernacular "pastoral capitalism." As this story unfolds, new notions of the pastoral, the rural, and the country estate surface and resurface time and again. A continual narrative is woven around the Park Royal brewery whereby its extensive grounds and environs are imagined as a village—but this is a village that is not simply popular and sentimental, a static throwback to another age, but rather one that is imaginative and complex, one that stressed movement, development, and improvement. What happened at Park Royal in the long boom sheds new light on the changing nature of work in this period and the values that inform it.

AN ESTATE IN FACTORYLAND

Three miles away from Ealing Studios, an amateur cinematographer at the Guinness brewery made scores of films between 1948 and 1952, which, in their own way, again speak for England.[16] These short silent cine films, some in beautiful rich color, show life at Park Royal over those five long-distant postwar years. One film stands out from the rest, the one depicting the Truss-O ceremony, because it is the only one directly concerned with the portrayal of work—even though it recorded the rite of passage rather than the labor itself. The remaining films document a huge variety of leisure activities for brewery staff and their families, from dinner-dances to lawn bowling matches, amateur dramatics to sports days and children's parties. In all these glimpses into a long-disappeared life, the brewery and its landscaped grounds provide a benign and dignified backdrop. That so much celluloid, an expensive and still rationed commodity in the late 1940s, was devoted to leisure, pleasure, and play at a place of work is noteworthy. This idea of leisure and pleasure at work was not merely a positive alternative to "work" but rather was the alternative side of the same coin, reflecting an enlarged and generous vision of labor and economic life. It provides a very different vision of work and how it formed part of a wider set of social relationships and values. This was a landscape carefully cultivated over the thirty-year period beginning in 1945, a physical, social, and cultural one.

One of the films from the late 1940s has the intriguing title, "A Ride on a Jet-propelled Bicycle." In this sped-up film, viewers spend two minutes careering around the brewery grounds at breakneck velocity. Some of the distinctive brewery buildings are apparent, but what strikes the viewer most is the extent and nature of the grounds themselves: the bushes, trees, shrubs, flowers, and immaculately cared-for lawns. This is an interesting juxtaposition of the semirural ordered landscape viewed from a vehicle labeled as "jet-propelled." Jet propulsion was perhaps the most exciting cutting-edge technology of the day. It had been invented in Britain and was just about to see service on the de Havilland Comet Jetliner, and it was more widely symbolic of a new Elizabethan era in the postwar period. This contrast of modernity bursting into the landscape is recorded elsewhere in images of Park Royal, such as this 1948 *Guinness Time* editorial:

> At Park Royal we play cricket in a beautiful setting and in a few seasons in which the Club has been functioning we can claim a fair measure of success. In spite of the fact that the background is distinctly modern and trains on the Piccadilly Line emerge noisily from behind the kitchen garden, there is sufficient space and leafiness in the trees to give a rural aspect. It requires only the merest flight of fancy to find the blacksmith, butcher and possibly even the curate from among the coopers, engineers, accountants and others who comprise the eleven, and our picture is almost complete.[17]

In both these images, then, there is a work of artifice occurring. The film invites viewers to experience the fantasy of "jet propulsion" around the actual brewery grounds; the editorial evokes an idyllic village green in a rural setting while an electric Tube train bursts onto the scene.

These imaginings are similar to Nathaniel Hawthorne's reflection as he sat down in the woods near Concord, Massachusetts, in 1844 to record "such little events as may happen." After a long period of tranquility, he recorded:

> But, hark! There is the whistle of the locomotive—the long strike, harsh, above all other harshness, for the space of a mile cannot mollify it into harmony. It tells a story of busy men, citizens, from the hot street, who have come to spend a day in a country village, men of business; in short of all unquietness; and no wonder that it gives such a startling shriek, since it brings the noisy world into the midst of our slumberous peace. As our thoughts repose again, after this interruption, we find ourselves gazing up at the leaves, and comparing their different aspect, the beautiful diversity of green.[18]

In *The Machine in the Garden*, Leo Marx reflects on the enduring theme of pastoral tranquility disturbed by modernity in the form of the machine in American literature. Indeed, this theme of disturbance, or lost innocence, first finds its expression in the ancient Greek poets Theocritus and Virgil and their evocation of symbolic landscapes that blended myth and reality. The premise of much of this genre is the depiction of Arcadia under threat. In the case of the ancient Greek poets, this rural pastoral simplicity is endangered by urban culture and settlement rather than modern technology. These evocations then enjoy a static, antihistoric quality: Arcadia exists outside the mainstream of history. As Marx argues:

> The sudden appearance of the machine in the garden is an arresting, endlessly evocative image. It causes the instantaneous clash of opposed states of mind: a strong urge to believe in the rural myth along with an awareness of industrialization as a counterforce to the myth.[19]

What the images offer is a complex reading of the relationship between the rural and the pastoral on the one hand and modernity in various guises on the other.

The Park Royal site was by no means a blank slate before Guinness purchased the land and built the brewery in the 1930s: it had been settled for thousands of years before then. The area of Hanger Lane, just yards from the brewery's southwest perimeter, was named after Hanger Hill, a derivation of the Anglo-Saxon word *hangra*, meaning a wooded slope. The first record of the land is in the *Domesday Book*; the owners were listed as the Canons of St. Paul, who had been presented with the land at Twyford in 930 CE by King Athelstan. This manor was later leased to lay owners in the early twelfth century. In 1361, the lease was assumed by a London fishmonger, who paid the Dean of St. Paul's a red rose at Midsummer as rent. In 1540, the land was purchased by grocer John Lyon, who later became Lord Mayor of London. The property was held in the Lyon family but was allowed to deteriorate before it was purchased in 1800 by the Douglas-Willan family. Later in the nineteenth century, the family sold some of their holding to the Royal Agricultural Society, which intended to use the land as its permanent showground.[20] A 1963 article in *Guinness Time* recalled the era of the showground, mapping what had existed in 1903 and orienting the reader by explaining what Guinness had built on top of it. Park Royal—as the site became known as a result of the Royal Agricultural Showground having been built there—was at the time a largely rural area, although the Great Western had built a railway line alongside it. As the editor noted in 1963, "The bowling green and part of the playing fields was allotted to veterinary Inspection. In 1903 this area must have somewhat resembled an Irish horse fair as it was also used for sales by auction and space was set aside for prospective buyers to 'try out' the horses."[21]

The editor made no attempt to hide the way the brewery's construction had overlain that previous aspect: the horse ring and surrounding poplars were replaced by the racking sheds and the main garage, and the Royal Pavilion and official buildings gave way to the Guinness power station. There was even mention of the asymmetrical oak trees that stood outside the brewery's central office block. These had been planted originally by the Prince of Wales (later King George V) and King Edward VII. The article notes: "The smaller one owes its somewhat irregular appearance to the fact that it was severely damaged by a bomb blast in 1917."[22] This is a good example of the ways in which the company recorded progress and change. It made no attempt to hide history or to minimize the impact of the brewery's construction. Nor was there an attempt to disguise modernity—the bomb blast was almost certainly the result of early German zeppelin raids carried out over England during the First World War. What this account of the pre-Guinness history of the site shows is the complex understanding of the process of historical change. In its explanation of why the Royal Showground failed, the piece notes that this was due to essentially economic forces: by the turn of the twentieth century, the largely urban audience of London was seemingly uninterested in rural agricultural displays, and the Park Royal shows attracted the lowest audiences ever.

DOWN ON THE FARM

Farming and agricultural topics in the pages of *Guinness Time* were some of the many elements that lent a rural aspect to Park Royal over the years of the long boom. Guinness had adopted the name Associated Agricultural Processes Limited to facilitate the purchase of land and the construction of the buildings at the site in the 1930s, and this theme continued after that phase was completed. From the beginning of the Second World War, Guinness created a farm on the Park Royal estate in response to the "Dig for Victory" campaign. During wartime, this served as a vital source of vegetables and meat for staff, and after the war, the farm continued to serve an important function as part of the brewery's food service, with produce grown on site used in the extensive catering operation. In the first issue of *Guinness Time*, three pages were devoted to an article entitled "On the Farm" about the wartime origins of the firm's farm:

> So we at Park Royal, who had been brewing for three years when the war broke out, decided that the many acres of land not needed at present for the brewing processes should be made full use of in the production of food. Some of the land was given over to employees for allotments, and to this day, and in particular now, these plots are flourishing. Mind you, the heavy Middlesex clay land is hard to work, but the yield of vegetables is good if the land is treated intelligently.[23]

The piece was illustrated with photographs of cows, hens, pigs, and the twenty-five estate workers. Much was made of the ten thousand eggs deemed surplus to the brewery's needs sent to the packing station and the one hundred pigs per year dispatched to market. The article also records the herd of Guernsey cows given to the brewery by Guinness Chairman Lord Iveagh from his Surrey estate. This was not hobby farming. The scale of the operation—attested to by the size of the labor force—can be seen in the fact that the farm supplied enough produce to provide the eight hundred main meals served daily and milk throughout the year. The article explained the interesting symbiotic relationship between the farm and the brewery. The sheep, for instance, foraged for spilt grain after unloading, but this had its darker side: "The sheep became excellent scavengers, but once or twice met a sad fate, when for example, one or two of them wandered behind the Power Station to sample the acid liquid in the Coppersmiths' Scouring Shed."[24]

News from the farm regularly appeared in *Guinness Time* over the years and at various points, it was the subject of a work photo essay. In the summer 1951 issue, an essay covered both the farm and the wider gardens of the brewery:

> With the coming of spring, our thoughts turn to outdoor pursuits and we may reflect thankfully that, in its surroundings at least, the Guinness Brewery is not as (most) other Breweries are. Now, as we come to work and go home in the light, we can watch the growing of flowers by the Bowling Green and the ever-changing form and colour of the trees on the Estate.[25]

The author then invited readers to ponder what the estate cows were thinking about their surroundings: "For those of a more reflective disposition there is the pleasant prospect of sharing that particular form of deep content enjoyed by Pyrford Patreena, Flossie and their pedigree Guernsey companions as they roam in the deep summer grass."[26]

This piece, like the other photo essays, reminded readers how integral the labor of the estate workers was to the wider brewery as a whole. What could be thought of as a marginal, even peripheral, role is reimagined as central and vital. Although the majority of the text takes the form of captions, these reinforce this sense of importance. Readers see, for instance, coppicing on one of the three thousand trees on the estate and are informed that the kitchen gardens supply six thousand lettuces, one and a half tons of runner beans, seven tons of cabbages, and large quantities of other vegetables and flowers for the brewery, in addition to two hundred gallons of milk per week.

Agricultural issues more generally loomed large in many editions of *Guinness Time* over the years. Regular pieces appeared on the Kentish hop farm owned by Guinness, and there were also features on experimental techniques for improving grain and hop yields. Images of agriculture and rural labor were often featured in the staff magazine, as were pieces on hop picking and pickers. The photographic archive has hundreds of images devoted to the hop farms, from planting to harvest and packing. These photographs were supplemented by paintings done over the years by a variety of artists that captured various aspects of hop picking. Collectively, these images, both pictorial and textual, stressed rurality and nature, emphasizing an organic connection among the brewery, its product, and the land. This image of agricultural husbandry was echoed in other rural aspects of the brewery.

LANDSCAPING

References to landscape and landscaping abound in internal and external descriptions of the Park Royal site. One writer uses the term "garden city brewery" to describe Park Royal,[27] and internal Guinness publications made direct and indirect reference to the brewery being in a pastoral setting, as "an estate in factoryland," or its otherwise rural aspect. The decision to create and improve the landscape around the brewery was neither accidental nor inevitable: it was the conscious decision of directors and other company staff and was the subject of disagreement at the board level. As the managing director, Hugh Beaver, later explained:

> There was a great deal of debate as to the amount of land we should buy. On the whole it was thought well to buy ample land which in those days of depression was not dear; but every now and again there used to be murmurs . . . Those who were in favour of ample space all around us got nick-named the Parkites, and the others the anti-Parkites. Once when the battle was going against the Parkites, I produced a complete layout plan for houses, flats, shopping centre and some light industry all over the present cricket field and over the cows' field next to Bodiam and Udiam and along Coronation Road to the bridge.[28]

This more intensely urban plan seems to have done the trick, and the "Parkites" emerged from the struggle victorious. Beaver's piece, part of a reflection marking the twenty-first year of Park Royal's existence, was illustrated with a panoramic view of the brewery grounds taken from the vathouse roof in 1951. The photograph is captioned, "The final vindication of the 'Parkites' cause."[29] The firm was very proud of its landscaping at Park Royal. In 1950 it created a display about its efforts to be shown at the Royal Agricultural Society's annual show. *Guinness Time* ran a photo essay—"Trees for Beauty and Utility"—on the project, showing a number of "before and after" comparison shots of the grounds. As the piece notes:

> The stand showed, by means of plans and photographs, the transformation of the Park Royal site from dreary waste scarred by the builders' operations of 1935 to the green lawns, neat hedges and beautiful trees of to-day. These pictures showed especially the effectiveness of the "screen" and "blackout" planting of such quick growing species as Poplar and White Willow.[30]

A later article went into more depth about the tree and shrub planting in the brewery grounds. Much was made of the "arboricultural advisor," A. D. C. Le Sueur, who had been involved in the estate since the brewery's initial construction phase. The piece noted, "We thank him for this green and pleasant oasis which is not normally associated with a brewery or other place of work on a factory estate."[31] Also mentioned was the brewery's "Tree Man," George Lancaster, who had planted trees for the building contractor in the 1930s before joining the Guinness staff. The article highlighted the difficult soil conditions and the various arboreal problems faced by the estate staff, as well as the huge amount of planting the company had engaged in since the mid-1930s, including 1,380 trees of sixty varieties and 410 ornamental shrubs.[32] This included 500 Lombard poplars planted for screening purposes and four hundred yards of *Berberis stenophylla* hedging planted alongside the brewery on St. James's Way. Improving the landscape was a regular topic in brewery literature. Beneath a picture of the gardens in front of the brewery buildings in 1957, an editorial, "Summer Landscape at Park Royal," observed:

> Much has been written of the need to preserve our countryside from the ravages of industrial development. But it is not a question of preservation alone; landscapes can be made by men. The harmony of the brewery buildings in their garden setting reminds us of the debt we owe to our gardeners for their particular achievements.[33]

This is an important theme in the accounts of the brewery and what Guinness management was trying to create at Park Royal. While there are many instances of rural fantasy, of pastoral hyperbole, this was almost always tempered by an understanding of the human agency involved in the creation and maintenance of the landscape. In one of the earliest editions of *Guinness Time*, Le Sueur wrote a short piece on his planting philosophy at Park Royal. During his first survey of the grounds, he wrote, he recalled the "gaunt skeleton of steel that was eventually to become the Brewery." Describing what he found as "a rather dreary expanse of land, covered with brambles and weeds interspersed with piles of builders' material and earth," it was, he concluded, "the landscape planter's nightmare!"[34] Le Sueur's approach emphasized rational, ordered, and scientific planning to maximize the impact of vegetation and the general improvement of brewery vistas:

> In any case the effect produced by a modern factory rising out of trees which must always overtop is not particularly good, so that planting ought to be done over as wide an area as possible rather than as a concentration of trees around the central building. In the case of the brewery there was fortunately plenty of space, so that planting could be gradually worked up to the buildings from a considerable distance.[35]

The piece is interesting as a philosophical account of landscape aesthetics but is also a highly technical discourse on planting techniques and the effect of wind, shade, and moisture on tree growth. As with many *Guinness Time* articles, the piece had high expectations of its audience, a number of whom were avid gardeners themselves.[36]

The issue of human agency in shaping the landscape was particularly apparent in a discussion about the company's role in the building of the Hanger Lane underpass just beyond the brewery gates. Beaver had been attempting to screen the brewery from adjacent properties and realized that the spoil from the road excavation, while a problem for the contractor, would provide an elegant landscaping solution for Guinness. The subsequent landscaping project, dubbed by some "Beaver's folly" or the "Guinness Hills,"[37] was positively recorded in a *Sunday Times* article in April 1962. Robert Harling begins the piece, "The Art of Creative Dumping," with an account of traffic congestion:

> The view on the right is well known to any motorist anywhere; the bleak and desolate semi-industrial townscape of our major motorways. Mr Kelly's drawing, however, is of a particular stretch of one motorway as it used to be. This was the Park Royal Junction of the A40 and the North Circular Road, which has recently been subject to a great deal of replanning and rebuilding. Part of the development was an underpass which smooths out what used to be one of London's traffic snarls.[38]

Harling goes on to reflect on the otherwise high cost of transporting the waste spoil out of the area but then continues:

> In this instance, Guinness allowed the soil to be dumped on land which they owned on the side of the A40 which faces London Transport's Park Royal Station . . . Somebody at Guinness had the bright idea of asking the eminent landscape architect, Geoffrey Jellicoe, to shape the dumps into gently curving hillocks.[39]

The article was accompanied by two line drawings of the site after the landscaping was completed. Both portray a recognizably urban environment but one softened by trees, hedges, and rolling hillocks. The underpass excavation works had begun over four years prior to the *Sunday Times* article. Jellicoe was a renowned landscape designer and theorist who was influenced by Jungian psychology, abstract modern art, and sculpture, and through his designs, he explored the role of the subconscious in landscape design.[40]

Jellicoe was proud of his achievement at Park Royal, and in his book *Studies in Landscape Design*, he notes of this commission: "The company were anxious to ensure that the view of the considerably widened road from the brewery, and conversely the view of the brewery from the road, should not only be impaired, but if possible enhanced."[41] He explained how, with the soil excavated from the underpass,

> it has been possible not only to model the land, but to create a hill some thirty feet high as part of design composition. With the shape of the land established, it was now necessary to design the groups of trees. These have been so placed as to conceal unsightly features, to cause concentration on the brewery scenery, and to give an interesting changing panorama of light and shade to the motorist moving in either direction.[42]

A photograph of the construction was reproduced as a *Guinness Time* frontispiece in the autumn of that year. Where images of spring flowers, blossoms, or trees in full leaf were often reproduced, readers were confronted by an altogether different vision of the brewery's grounds. Under the title "The Changing Scene at Park Royal," the caption read: "This year Autumn has seen more change than usual in the landscape at Park Royal. Work on the Western Avenue Under-pass has meant the destruction of our screen of Lombardy poplars which has revealed a fresh, and rather severe, view of the Brewery."[43]

The image is an intensely urban one, with four lanes of traffic in the foreground and construction work going on behind that. Concrete shuttering, mechanical excavators, and pile drivers compete for the reader's attention with the brewery buildings brooding in the near distance. The editorial, "North West Passage," picked up the theme of the roadworks. After reflecting on exotic travel, the author referred to road repairs of old before writing:

> It is, therefore, refreshing for us to witness almost on our doorstep an example of highway engineering different in essence and in scale from what we have had before. This is clearly road-making instead of road mending: the belated realisation in England of a new conception for our roads. And as might be expected the new road makers bear little resemblance to the old in their methods of work. Great machines and cranes scoop and reshape the earth and high boarding surrounds the scene of operations.[44]

The author lamented the loss of the brewery's trees: "The Lombardy poplars which preserved the Brewery as a visible but unobtrusive part of the landscape have been cut down and now the five great blocks seem strangely stark and dominant."[45] But the piece finishes with a strong affirmation of faith in progress:

Those of us who work at Park Royal will almost certainly suffer many irritations and delays in the months that remain before the project is completed. But the motor car that has destroyed distance and brought far off counties within easy reach has also in recent years too often made the neighbouring parish seem infinitely remote, and there can be few who are not willing to suffer short term inconveniences so that a proper solution can be found for this wasteful and vexing problem.[46]

Landscape was obviously important to the firm's management and board, but this desire to shape and beautify was not a backward-looking attempt to create Arcadia anew in North West London. The regret at the loss of the screen of trees was tempered by a pragmatic acceptance of progress in the shape of the car and its attendant infrastructure. It also afforded the opportunity to engage in further improvements to the estate by recycling the spoil from the works. Guinness went out of its way to harness the skills and insight of one of the premier award-winning landscapers of the day, a designer whose ideas meshed with the role of the workplace the firm was promoting.[47]

This pragmatic relationship between the natural and the human-made environment is illustrated elsewhere throughout the long boom at Park Royal. An early example of this was in the piece "Birds and Park Royal," a two-page spread illustrated with line drawings of a variety of avian visitors to the brewery:

Here, at Park Royal, our normal preoccupation with man and his works could easily leave us insensitive to the sights and sounds of Summer were it not for the number of birds upon our lawns and their chatter in our hedges. It seems a far cry from the roar of motors and the clatter of machinery to the singing of a thrush, and yet, it is only a matter of yards—from the office windows to the Berberis, from the Vathouse to the bowling green.[48]

Insight into nesting patterns and behavior was obvious in the short piece, which recorded in loving detail how different species had adapted themselves to the brewery's presence, finding ecological niches among the factory setting despite the "invasion of industry." Sparrows lived in the engineers' department and the powerhouse, kestrels nested in the vathouse and malt store building, and the author noted that a night clerk had been startled by a resident owl. The article concluded by expressing thanks "for our small bit of country in this great city."[49]

Guinness was not the first, nor would it be the last, organization to landscape its factory site. By the time the Park Royal brewery opened in 1936, there were examples stretching back two centuries or more where industrialists had attempted, with varying degrees of success, to blend modernity with the rural.[50] Organizations often used images of their factories and their surrounding grounds to promote their corporate values or the wholesomeness of their products. They were also directed at internal and external audiences to reinforce messages of corporate paternalism and beneficence.[51]

Factory owners have also long sought to use the physical isolation of a factory and its grounds to concentrate and control their workforces.[52] A twentieth-century twist on this geographic isolation is what some have called "pastoral capitalism": US corporate resettlement from the inner cities to the suburbs or countryside. There were three distinct waves in this process: the corporate campus, the corporate estate, and the office park. The move to the suburbs represented a desire to flee urban labor unions and served as a recruitment strategy aimed at maintaining a predominately "white" office and clerical staff. The belief was that building workplaces in pleasant green surroundings would make it easier to both recruit and retain staff. In this sense, the corporate evacuation of the American downtown neatly maps onto and is a stimulus for the postwar "white flight" to the suburbs. However, the corporate campus model had another role. Buildings set in attractive landscapes can tap into utopian social visions of the American imagination. They create powerful models linking corporate values to progressive trends.[53]

These types of corporate spaces should not be read as simply a crude control mechanism or ideologically loaded terrains. While landscapes tell us something about control, they also reflect wider, more complex ideas about industry and its relationship to society—shared notions of rurality and nature, for instance the enjoyment of the pastoral and the appreciation of vistas, cut across structures of class and power. The factory landscapes are rationalized spaces, but they also offer spaces of reenchantment and imagination.[54]

CULTIVATING THE SOCIAL LANDSCAPE

If Park Royal was a garden, it was designed as a social space as well as one for wildlife, trees, and flowers. From its beginnings, the brewery had promoted a wide range of social and sporting activity; events for the 1948 London Olympic Games were held at Park Royal, and Roger Bannister trained for his attempt to smash the four-minute mile on its running track.[55] Some of this activity was actively created and supported by the company; other clubs and groups emerged by the initiative of the workers. In the Guinness archives' films, many of the shorts record the various activities of the brewery's year, from golf, rugby, football, cricket, and hockey, through numerous sports days and amateur dramatic plays, to other groups such as the photographic club. *Guinness Time* devoted a great deal of attention to nonwork activities and was eager to stress the importance they had for creating individual character and wider social bonds. An early *Guinness Time* editorial made the link between active leisure and finding interest in one's work:

> Nor should this interest fade with the end of each working day. Once again using wiser words than my own, this time William Morris. "The true secret of happiness lies in taking a genuine interest in all the details of daily life." So, when the

tun-brush is laid aside, the ledger closed and the typewriter covered, let us take some part in those other activities of the Guinness community which then begin. The Guinness Club provides variety wide enough to satisfy everyone.[56]

The piece goes on to talk about the way these leisure activities cut across work-based groupings and social status, emphasizing the role of sports to build character among brewery staff and in particular among the youth, either formal craft apprentices or members of the Boys' and Girls' Scheme. And it viewed sports and wider social activity as vital to the creation of well-rounded men and women. Features on the Boys' and Girls' Scheme trainees devoted more attention to the leisure side of their lives than to the work aspects.

Rudimentary facilities were created during the war for various leisure activities, and these had grown over the years. Things radically changed in 1959 with plans to build a new clubhouse at the company's expense, marking its bicentenary. The building featured a main hall, a refreshment room, a bar area, and a gymnasium. The main hall, designed for dancing, amateur dramatics, and banquets, had room for 350 people seated or dancing, or up to 200 for dining; the floor was sprung maple. Each of these areas was supported by its own ancillary rooms, such as changing areas and kitchens. The building would in time support a huge variety of activities, including a range of sporting activities, two theater groups, darts clubs, a cinema, and a television room. A *Guinness Time* piece was accompanied by both plans and an artist's impression of what the completed buildings would look like.[57]

The construction of the new clubhouse featured prominently in the staff magazine. In the final issue of 1959, a photograph in the frontispiece showed Lord Iveagh laying its foundation stone. Underneath the stone the company decided to bury a time capsule with various documents and ephemera representing the work and social life at the brewery. The *Guinness Time* editorial writer was in a reflective mood:

> Therefore, when the Chairman placed beneath the foundation stone of the new Clubhouse a casket containing copies of the Guinness House Journals, *The Times* and the *Guinness Book of Records*, any sadness at the contemplation of the disaster or decay which would reveal these documents to our distant descendants was tempered by the thought of the benefit and real pleasure we were bestowing upon them.[58]

The writer then turned to imagining the landscape in which the time capsule might be discovered:

> Some future archaeologist would rejoice indeed to find in *Guinness Time* a plan of the ruin with each room labelled for its mysterious purpose: historians will perhaps find in *The Guinness Harp* and the emblem on the casket, evidence of a hitherto unsuspected colonisation of Britain by the Irish, and politicians will ponder the strange workings of democracy and the tantalising conundrum posed by *The Times* on Election Day. . . . What ever value our descendants may place on the

documents we have bequeathed to them, with the total obliteration of our civilisa-
tion a technical possibility it seems a wise precaution to leave in a safe place some
record of our lives at Park Royal.[59]

This poignant piece imagines the brewery landscape in a dramatically different
way from that which precedes it. While it is difficult to imagine future archaeol-
ogists making a priority of decoding what occurred at Park Royal in the context
of a nuclear winter, the piece speaks again to a real sense of the importance of
the historical record and to the idea that what happened at Park Royal was in
some way special. It was, in other words, worth recording.[60]

Perhaps the most frequently documented of brewery occasions on the Park
Royal cine films were the sports days and fairs. These involved various sporting
events—competitive running over various distances, relays, egg-and-spoon runs,
sack races, and tug of wars between brewery teams—and rides, attractions, and
entertainment. One year a sea cadets' display was the central piece of the day,
the next year a Scottish country dancing troupe. The films, many of them in
color, show these were well attended both by staff and their families. An editorial from 1948 describes a typical scene: "Printed frocks and the many-coloured
shirts of small boys vied with the gay hues of the flags and bunting to present as
pleasant a spectacle as one could wish to see." After describing the many attractions available, the writer notes:

> Four o'clock brought that satisfying time, the interval, satisfying in that now one
> can either join in the siege of the tea-tent, listen to the Band, or saunter round
> the various stalls without the feeling that one may be missing some vital part of
> the programme. At one stall it was possible, for a small charge, to satisfy a long-
> frustrated emotion—the desire to throw things at all the china in the house. . . .
> Elsewhere there were Darts, Bowling and many other attractions which comprise
> the fun of the Fair.[61]

This piece was replete with rural images and allusions. In many ways, articles like
this created a sustained and deliberate image of the brewery and the land surrounding it as a village. Indeed, Guinness built a number of houses just outside
the brewery perimeter in Moyne Place, colloquially known as "The Village."[62]
Over the years these images, and the rural pastoral tropes they employed, build
to form an "imagined village" largely at peace with itself. To push this reading
further, it is possible to identify the basic elements of this rural idyll—the
landscapes of the brewery, including the farm and kitchen garden. There were
the different occupational groups and the division of labor found in rural communities. In many ways, the brewery during the long boom was a self-sufficient,
self-sustaining community, with its own farm, power station, canteens, maintenance workers, grounds workers, painters, and decorators, not to mention all the
craft trades. Also present were the various rites of passage of a village: *Guinness
Time* recorded births, marriages, and deaths. *Guinness Time* can be imagined as a

parish magazine for the brewery, with its own brand of "small c" conservatism. Like all villages, Park Royal had its divisions and hierarchies—witnessed in the cleavages within and between parts of the workforce and between the blue- and white-collar workers. This social hierarchy is further evidenced in the distinction and career trajectories of Oxbridge and "Red Brick" graduates recruited to the firm, with Lord Iveagh as the village squire.

This conservatism took many forms over the years. In 1953, for instance, an editorial drew heavily on an organic metaphor in its reflection on brewery life and wider politics. What started as a piece seemingly concerned with gardening suddenly shifted tone:

> At the same time the keen gardener can be the most sane and resourceful of men and it is interesting to reflect on how many of the truly great men and women have spent much of their time in their gardens; for gardening will teach the same lesson as history, that changes which are to have a lasting value cannot be achieved without forethought and hard work and there is no short cut to attaining a worthwhile ideal. Gardening gives a man roots, in more ways than one and we wonder on occasions, when reading some of the utterances of our more radical politicians and public men, if their views would be not have greater balance had they learnt some lessons which Nature can impart to any who are willing to learn and who can put to one side the slogans and artificial prejudices which so often pass for "progressive" thought.[63]

The column was followed by a piece and accompanying photograph of the Earl and Countess of Iveagh marking their golden wedding anniversary and their "fifty years' joint service to their fellow men and women."[64] Earl Iveagh and his extended family were often the subject of articles and images in the staff magazine, and this radical/conservative tension was replicated on numerous occasions. In 1955, for example, *Guinness Time* had as its frontispiece the John Gilroy painting of the Earl and Countess in their coronation robes. This was accompanied by possibly the angriest editorial in the entire run of the journal, "Honour without Ceremony." It marked the planned ceremony in which Queen Elizabeth was to confer the Most Noble Order of the Garter on Lord Iveagh and Prime Minister Winston Churchill, which had been canceled due to the national railway strike. The piece made clear the lack of respect that these events showed to the Guinness chairman and the wartime leader, but the majority of the text was devoted to a critique of industrial militancy:

> Frequently we hear nowadays that as a method of settling a dispute the strike is out of date and certainly it is encouraging that the more responsible bodies who govern our industrial life are deeply concerned at the present position and have deplored the wanton recklessness which has characterised so many recent disturbances. There are signs that the seed of good and amicable negotiation on the basis of give and take will flourish wherever it is given a proper chance. Such methods however are not sufficiently exciting for some appetites and it is the

wholly disproportionate power of these which is one of the greatest dangers to our national survival.[65]

The piece was almost certainly written by Edward Guinness, at the time Park Royal's personnel manager and still editor of *Guinness Time*. He mentioned his "boyhood spent in the North of England" and lamented "those tragic years of misery and frustration when unemployment and short term working dogged the lives of those who endured it."[66] He continued:

A black cloud descended on town after town and home after home as more and more factories became idle and the queues at the Labour Exchange grew. Full employment, as we know it today, would have seemed a Utopia only to be attained in dreams. How much would men of that time have envied our position today. And yet memories are tragically short, for each break in our industrial life means a deterioration in our national livelihood and our vital export trade, which, unless it is arrested, can only lead to a return to those conditions which men have sworn should never be allowed to return.[67]

This piece was itself a time capsule buried deep within the long boom. It revealed a progressive yet innate conservatism, a relatively privileged manager from outside the main Guinness brewing family whose formative years had witnessed industrial depression and hardship. This account had been filtered through the experience of the Second World War and later through industrial relations at Park Royal. It also reflected a fear for the fragile nature of the postwar settlement. Ten years into the long boom, economic stability felt far from permanently secure; as the editorial noted, "prosperity is not something which is a human birthright and which willy-nilly can be maintained." The passage drew parallels between the individual and the nation, and without using the word "citizenship," it made clear that this understanding was in dialogue with the established model of industrial citizenship:

If we fail at this time, the verdict of history will be that we were incapable of accepting prosperity and full employment without abusing them. If we fail, we will have squandered a wonderful position which has been built up from the chaos of a quarter century ago and we will have denied the efforts of many great and honoured men whose lives were devoted, even sacrificed, to the common cause.[68]

This was a statement about industrial citizenship and the dangers, as the writer saw it, of a lack of moral regulation, both at the collective and the individual level, that would undermine the ability of society to provide a humane welfare state. The piece was an urgent appeal from within the long boom era for recognition of what was at stake, and it spoke directly to the idea of moral hazard that exercised T. H. Marshall and a host of nineteenth-century thinkers on work, welfare, and citizenship. "Honour without Ceremony" was bookended by another Iveagh portrait and an article on the Order of the Garter, which had its roots in feudalism and over a thousand years of English history. Whether done consciously or not, this historical juxtaposition both reflects and reinforces powerfully an organic conservatism that emphasized slow, considered change rather than radical, sudden upheaval. With its appeal to history and pragmatic rootedness in prewar experience, the reader can gain a glimpse of thinking about the postwar settlement by one sympathetic to reform and gradual improvement.

INDUSTRIAL CITIZENSHIP IN THE LANDSCAPE OF THE LONG BOOM

How, then, do we make sense of what was going on in the era of the long boom at Park Royal, and what lessons does it have for a wider understanding of industrial and social tensions at the time? One reading of the Guinness archive material, especially the texts of various kinds from *Guinness Time*, would be a highly conservative corporate interpretation of the countryside and its fate, with its emphasis on the rural, the landscape, and the organic. Park Royal was depicted through text and pictures as a rural landscape, a pastoral space. The brewery was described as a farm, a kitchen garden, at times even as a semiwilderness home to wildlife. At other moments, the site was described as carefully manicured, subject to planning and scientific landscaping, where trees have "utility and beauty"—planting masks, diverts, shelters, or indeed emphasizes and frames. Finally, Park Royal can be imagined as a rural town where the brewery workers were characters in a traditional village setting set adrift in time. *Guinness Time*, in this reading, takes on the appearance of an Ealing film; its pages offer an amusing, backward-looking fantasy projecting a cozy, nostalgic, one-dimensional view of its own times.

Such a reading, while easy, would also be lazy. While tradition and landscape were strong features of these images, a progressive modernity keeps bursting through in a variety of ways. We are never left long with the impression of rurality without being reminded that the brewery is "an estate in *factoryland*" or a "garden *city* brewery." As a late article in *Guinness Time* reminded readers: "In the summer when the grass is green and the trees and shrubs are in full leaf, it is easy to overlook the fact that Guinness is part of a factory estate in a highly industrial area. And long may it be so."[69]

While the various planting schemes may have sought to shield or hide other buildings and the increasingly busy arterial road, there was never a sense of a wish to escape to the past or deny progress. In simple terms, the brewery "would not try to seem anything else than a large and efficient factory."[70] Guinness, in truth, could not have done anything else but to acknowledge its "new" English brewery. It was built to a rational planned model and was the most modern and largest brewery in the United Kingdom. It was situated amid a large, industrially developed part of West London. Modernity, often positive, sometimes less so, kept popping up in the various images created around Park Royal—the Piccadilly Line train emerging from behind the bushes, the roar of Western

Avenue on the brewery's doorstep. Development and modernity are seen as progressive and valuable. There was a real faith in the future, although the past was valued. History was seen as something to learn from and to be built on; Modernism did not need to represent a clean break from the past.

In a variety of ways, Guinness managers were attempting to reenchant work and to emphasize and draw out more creative and romantic notions of labor, evidenced in notions of Guinness Citizenship. Here the reenchantment took the form of reuniting understandings of work processes with the parallel development of well-rounded individuals who can provide leadership while creating community. This was most forcefully realized in the Boys' and Girls' Schemes, which emphasized four interrelated elements of training: on-the-job training, character training, physical fitness, and further education.

Another aspect of this reenchantment was the creation of an attractive and stimulating physical environment, one capable of allowing quiet contemplation, intense physical activity, or more cerebral pursuits. This reenchantment can be seen in the combination of these factors rather than the fragmented elements of it. Park Royal, in the thirty years from the end of the war, represented an explicit attempt to create, or re-create, community in the workplace, with the recognition that the disruption of the Second World War had prevented the brewery's staff from really becoming embedded in Park Royal. This move was also an attempt to distance work and community from the social dislocation of the interwar years. If this was paternalism, then it was a revised formulation of it. The recognition of trade unions, creation of a Works Committee, and consultation are one element of this, but the organization was deliberately creating capacity in its workforce to think and act independently for the collective good. They were trying to mold industrial citizens, imagining an enchanted modern workforce. The pages of *Guinness Time* both reflected these ideas and were designed to reinforce them.

In 1975, at the end of the run of *Guinness Time*, the autumn issue featured a photo essay on the pilots who flew the company's executive jet around Europe and Africa. It emphasized the modernity of the aircraft; the company had owned three different ones since the first one was purchased in 1963. The piece stressed the international linkages the company had across the globe as it serviced its existing markets and sought new ones. At the back of the magazine, a two-page spread, "Pastures new . . .," reported the departure of the final members of the Guinness Guernsey herd from the brewery grounds. The cows were returning to Lord Iveagh's country estate, and for the first time in thirty-five years, the brewery would not be producing its own milk. In their place, forty beef cattle were installed, but the piece has an unusually melancholic feel to it. The new cattle would be grazing the next summer on the field bordering Western Avenue containing the hill created from the underpass. The article reminded readers of other aspects of the grounds, recalling the "Dig for Victory" campaign of the war years, the creation of the kitchen garden, and the livestock kept, including, for a time, peacocks. "It would appear," the writer noted, "that we have now reached the final stage in the development of the estate." While proud of that spring's daffodils, the author concluded:

> But, nevertheless, we shall miss the cows. Twice a day they were taken across Twyford Abbey Road to be milked at the farm in the grounds of Twyford Abbey. But no more. However, the beef herd are now grazing the meadows and Guinness can be proud that they can still provide a farm in the middle of industrial buildings in North-West London.[71]

The two stories from the final *Guinness Time* speak to wider issues in the United Kingdom and the world beyond. Perhaps it is no coincidence that the staff magazine should come to an end so abruptly in the mid-1970s: the period from 1973 to 1975 is often seen as the ending of the long boom or the Glorious Thirty. By this time, a magazine that was created to allow workers and staff to get to know one another was being undermined by the growth of Guinness itself, from a firm brewing one product in 1945 to a larger corporation diversifying into a dizzying variety of products and markets. The focus on Park Royal was no longer adequate or tenable for the organization and its wider workforce. Internally, too, social and economic changes were afoot. When the first editions of *Guinness Time* rolled off the press, work was a priority in people's lives; far fewer leisure and sporting opportunities outside meant that nonwork time was spent at home or in one of the many activities in and around the brewery. By 1975, low-cost foreign holidays, rising standards of living, almost universal access to television, and increasing car ownership allowed workers to exercise real choice over how they enjoyed their leisure time. Perhaps, too, they were less tolerant of the account of work and industrial citizenship offered by the magazine.

If 1975 marks a turning point, an end of an era, it also marks the point where inequality in Britain was at its narrowest. Wage differentials were small, and the gap between blue- and white-collar workers was closing. British families were more likely to mix socially and at the school gate. They lived in closer proximity than before or after, and they shared substantial parts of a national common culture.[72] In 1973 Britain had sloughed off most of its imperial possessions and had joined what was then the European Economic Community. While still a major manufacturing nation, it was steadily losing ground in terms of productivity and innovation. The oil price shocks of the early part of the 1970s were to emphasize Britain's connectedness to a world economy, and the pressures introduced by these shocks created considerable inflation and industrial unrest. All of these factors are part of the story of the breakdown of the long postwar consensus, a consensus that had witnessed the victory of the Herbivores over the Carnivores. Perhaps it is apt that in 1975, Park Royal's gentle ruminators were themselves replaced by a beef herd destined for the plates of Carnivores. If the previous Glorious Thirty had been the time of the Herbivores, able to make an argument for a wider enriched sense of industrial citizenship, then we can surely read it in microcosm through the story of Park Royal. The next thirty would come to be seen as the time of the Carnivores.

This photograph of the construction of the Guinness Office Block Park Royal was likely taken as a record shot by the construction contractor in 1935. *Guinness Archive, Diageo Ireland*

Park Royal Brewery Block "A" under construction in March 1935. These buildings were built in secret, their purpose disguised from all but a few company employees until after the opening. Guinness wanted to avoid sanctions from the Irish government if it had discovered that the company was planning to build its "English brewery." The slope in the ground aided gravity in the brewing process. *Guinness Archive, Diageo Ireland*

The twenty-one-foot coppers (seen during their construction in 1935) were used at Park Royal Brewery until the 1980s. These vats, which were essentially kettles, boiled the grain liquid with hops to create beer. Park Royal was for many years the largest and most modern brewery in the United Kingdom. *Guinness Archive, Diageo Ireland*

A foreman took this photograph of the fourth to seventh floors of Block C (Storehouse), capturing his view from under the roof in 1935. His job was to inspect the rivets on the beams: "Worst job I had was checking rivets on roofs of Hop Store and Brewhouse offices—no floors above ground—no hand rails or planks—just cold steel under my bottom and 100 feet of air! Checking a rivet needs two hands." This was a handwritten note found in the Diageo archive in Scotland. *Guinness Archive. Diageo Ireland*

The brewery buildings of Park Royal, photographed here in 1960, were carefully landscaped over the years with shrubs, trees, and gardens. *Guinness Archive, Diageo Ireland*

"Lady Cask Smellers" sniff used barrels on their return to the brewery to see if they had suffered from a chemical reaction, which was best detected by the odors released from the wood. Guinness made extensive use of female labor in production at Park Royal during the Second World War. Photograph ca 1940s. *Guinness Archive, Diageo Ireland*

Two workers weld a seam in a vat at Park Royal in the late 1940s. The style of this and other photographs is clearly influenced by European photorealism and was part of the "New Look" in postwar industrial photography. *Photograph by A. R. Tanner, Guinness Archive, Diageo Ireland*

Production workers wash out an emptied vat after a brew at Park Royal. The photo was taken through the vessel's hatch, which the workers had to climb through in order to clean up after a brew. The foam is spent yeast. This job was a routine part of the production work after every brew. *Guinness Archive, Diageo Ireland*

Workers fill casks from the "Iron Cow" at Park Royal in the late 1940s. The Iron Cow held the finished beer from which individual barrels would be filled. This is one of a large number of images taken by A R Tanner showing most aspects of the brewing process. The filled barrels would be sent to bottlers for dispatch to public houses. *Guinness Archive, Diageo Ireland*

Guinness workers purchase the first edition of *Guinness Time* at Park Royal in 1948. The editor, Edward Guinness, recalled that he was "hanging anxiously around the lunch rooms and canteen as the first copies were sold." In the background, workers line up to collect their wage packets. *Guinness Archive, Diageo Ireland*

Guinness workers read the first edition of *Guinness Time* at Park Royal during lunch in one of the brewery's canteens. All of the Park Royal canteens featured waitress service for staff at all levels. *Guinness Archive, Diageo Ireland*

A painting by John Gilroy depicts the "Truss-O" ceremony at Park Royal. The apprentice is about to be put in the barrel, where all sorts of things will be thrown over him before he is rolled around the workshop. The victim's smiling parents stand to the right of the barrel. *Guinness Archive, Diageo Ireland*

An apprentice cooper celebrates at the end of his "Truss-O" ceremony, which was the rite of passage from apprentice to fully qualified cooper, at Park Royal, about 1947. At this point, the newly qualified journeyman would be presented with the indenture papers marking his new status. This was an ancient ceremony resurrected by Park Royal's coopers beginning in the 1930s, when the brewery opened. The apprentice is the first person to the right of the barrel in shirt, tie, and suit, having cleaned up from the ceremony before the photograph was taken. The consumption of beer was an integral part of such occasions. *Guinness Archive, Diageo Ireland*

Three coopers work at Park Royal in 1949. The rough wooden hoops are being hammered into place on the barrel and were temporarily holding the individual staves together before the iron rings are in turn forced into place. Wooden barrels were held together by the shape and pressure of the parts acting on each other rather than by glue or nails. The company took many photographs of various stages of the coopers' work; this one was part of the Tanner series. *Guinness Archive, Diageo Ireland*

A worker visually inspects a copper to check that all is well with the brewing process. Workers used sight, sound, smell, and taste in the production processes. This is a 1952 painting of Park Royal by John Gilroy. *Guinness Archive, Diageo Ireland*

A worker inspects one of the mash tuns where hot water and germinated grain, called a "mash," were mixed as part of the brewing process. This stage in the brewing process converted the naturally occurring starches from the grain into a sugar liquid called a "wort." The painting is by the renowned British industrial artist Terrance Cuneo, done at Park Royal in 1951. Cuneo was active during the postwar period, working for a large number of corporate clients. *Guinness Archive, Diageo Ireland*

A Terrance Cuneo painting of the racking shed at Park Royal shows the filling of the barrels, about 1950. *Guinness Archive, Diageo Ireland*

Barrels returning to the brewery were always sterilized by steam A R Tanner took this shot of routine production work in the late 1940s. *Guinness Archive, Diageo Ireland*

A R Tanner photographed the washing of returned casks at Park Royal in the late 1940s. These images illustrate how Tanner made extensive use of light and shadow in his photography, drawing on prewar theories developed by photographers in continental Europe. *Guinness Archive, Diageo Ireland*

4

REMEMBERING
THE WORK OF THE
LONG BOOM

In 1963, the British Productivity Council sponsored a forty-four-minute black-and-white film, *People, Productivity and Change*. The film's commentator and interviewer was sociologist Tom Lupton. Viewers meet him first as the camera pans through his office door at what was to become Aston University and eavesdrops on an important debate about social change. The film itself is a wonderful time capsule of social and economic life in the early 1960s. One thing stands out through the haze of tobacco smoke that the film's participants produce: the centrality of history in shaping the classed experience of work. For many of those explaining their reaction to plans for productivity, their thinking was powerfully framed by events of the 1920s and 1930s rather than the concerns of the "swinging sixties." Suspicion of employers' motives and the memory of real poverty more than three decades before animate these mid-twentieth-century conversations.

Like other films about work, *People, Productivity and Change* draws out some of the important themes and contradictions of the era of the long boom. Often, in popular memory, the thirty years after the Second World War are portrayed as homogenized, a period of unalloyed prosperity and growing affluence. While this homogeneity was undoubtedly true, for many there remained real poverty.[1] Sociologists of the era were often drawn to new types of workers, labeling them "affluent workers" in the vanguard of changing social attitudes, assumptions, and cultures. Elsewhere, industrial sociologists were fascinated by the persistence of class-based occupational communities and cultures, debating at length why workers continued to cling to trade and craft identities, exposed through seemingly byzantine demarcation disputes.[2] As Lupton's film made clear, postwar affluence was experienced not always as a smooth increase in living standards but rather as gains and losses.

Retrospectively, many of these nuances in the postwar workplace and society have been ironed out and rendered into something else. Sociologists looking back at this earlier time from the comfort of the late 1990s observed something different. French social theorist André Gorz wrote:

> Even in the heyday of wage-based society, [modern work] was never a source of "social cohesion" or integration, whatever we might have come to believe from its retrospective idealization. The "social bond" it established between individuals was abstract and weak, though it did, admittedly, insert people into the process of social labour, into social relations of production, as functionally specialized cogs in an immense machine.[3]

Sociologist Zygmunt Bauman suggested that "factories turned out many and varied commodities, but all of them, in addition, produced the compliant and conforming subjects of the modern state."[4] What Gorz, Bauman, and their colleagues saw was a workforce enjoying prosperity but somehow devoid of agency—robots, or cogs, playing out meaningless lives on the line. Here workplace culture is reduced to mechanical interaction between those who happen to be laboring in the same place. This totalizing account seeks to seal off the era from further discussion, suggesting that those finding value in the work of the era are, like the workers described, suffering from false consciousness and are indulging in a romantic nostalgia for the industrial past.

Recent social historians have begun to think more critically about this era and the issue of affluence and growing real income levels and how highly contingent the working-class experience of affluence was. Many in the postwar era slipped in and out of poverty or felt vulnerable to potential changes in the economy and their local community. As social historian Selina Todd put it, "Working-class lives were lived 'on the borderlands.' "[5] For others in certain industries in more prosperous areas of the booming economy, underpinned by the welfare state, there could be a great sense of security and optimism. On one level, this affluence was an achievement, not a problem; it represented the democratizing of capitalism, the widespread provision of goods and services for almost all. However, the combined effects of inflation and low productivity created growing levels of frustration and anger, resulting in industrial relations conflict. The accepted explanation offered by those who studied so-called affluent workers was that high earnings had revealed a moral weakness, the simple pursuit of high pay and regular raises rather than a deeper attachment to a particular form of work.[6] These increasingly instrumentally oriented workers were unrestrained by a more traditional working-class culture and morality. It would be wrong to see affluence as simply creating a narrow, selfish class of workers. Working-class people in this period enjoyed rising living standards, high demand for their labor, and greater job security than ever before. They had agency in their workplaces and homes and exercised it.

It is clear, then, that the period from the end of the Second World War until the mid-1970s was varied and complex. The working-class experience of this era was highly contingent on a number of variables; arguably the most important of these was access to good, stable, and well-rewarded employment.[7]

During the era of the long boom at Park Royal, management portrayed work in the pages of *Guinness Time* as a benign set of relationships. In the photographs and accounts of brewery life, and more concretely in a set of labor policies, Guinness management offered a pragmatic accommodation with postwar labor. But what was the experience of work at Park Royal during the long boom? How did workers inhabit the spaces so carefully laid out for them? What did they make of the notion of industrial citizenship being offered by Guinness? At Park Royal, a group of workers created, enjoyed, and reproduced a rich autonomous work culture far removed from the sterile atmosphere imagined by later social theorists. They were employed by a large, profitable firm that actively encouraged union membership. They enjoyed good pay, terms, and conditions in the buoyant London labor market, underpinned by a progressive welfare state. This gave workers, both individually and collectively, a tremendous sense of security and confidence, both about their present and future. Park Royal's workers did become industrial citizens—although not quite as either T. H. Marshall or Edward Guinness would have imagined.

MEMORY WORK

The stories that follow come from those who worked at Park Royal from 1960 until its closure in 2005. Not all of those recorded here were employed all the way through; indeed, some worked in the brewery for short periods. A number remained on the shop floor throughout their careers; some climbed the promotional ladder, while others were recruited to the ranks of the junior managers.

Many of the recordings were carried out in 2004 and early 2005. The announcement that the brewery was to close had been made public earlier in 2004, and production finally ended in the summer of 2005. These recordings were made against a backdrop of "managed uncertainty," with many of the workers unsure what the future held for them. Some knew they would take early retirement, others wanted to continue working even though they were financially secure, and a final group had to find a new source of income after the plant closed. What all of the interviews capture is a sense of uncertainty, change, and flux. Often it is difficult to disentangle ideas and accounts of the past with the "now" of 2004, the certainty of the past juxtaposed with the uncertainty of the present. Often, the workers remember the previous four decades fondly, especially the period up to the 1980s. Interviewees intertwine their own positive personal narratives around that of the brewery. They describe the way they become deeply, and willingly, embedded in the life of the brewery; at times, it is difficult to distinguish the person from his or her work. Revealed here is the richness of working life and the emergent culture of the time.

But what of the charge of nostalgia? Are the workers interviewed here, and myself in recording them, complicit in a "retrospective idealization" of the past and the "heyday" of industrial work? Were we jointly engaging in bouts of "smokestack nostalgia," a romanticized, rose-tinted remembering and recording? It is a staple of oral history approaches to consider the status of memory and the validity of interviews. While critics emphasize that memory is inherently selective and fallible, there is a long-standing defense of oral history that makes a virtue out of these very flaws.[8] In their introduction to *The Myths We Live By*, historians Raphael Samuel and Paul Thompson draw attention to this weakness, noting that "memory is inherently revisionist, an exercise in selective amnesia. What is forgotten may be as important as what is remembered."[9] This position is difficult for some academics; we trade on notions of truth, replicability, and falsification, with myth residing in the province of the arts. However, oral historians have continued to make a compelling case for the power of understanding collective and individual beliefs that do not neatly fold into dichotomies of "true" and "false." The choice is not necessary: "Oral history offers a double validity in understanding a past in which, as still today, myth was embedded in real experience: both growing from it, and helping to shape its perception."[10] Samuel and Thompson's ideas draw heavily on Alessandro Portelli and his assertion that the validity of a story is less important than its structure; as he says: "The oral sources used in this essay are not always fully reliable in point of fact. Rather than being a weakness, this is however, their strength: errors, invention and myths lead us through and beyond facts to their meanings."[11]

For many oral historians, then, form and meaning rather than simply content is important since history is made both at the time of the event and in the subsequent retelling of that event. Put another way, these are images that have been rendered of events and that continue to be worked on in the present. This does not mean that there are no discernible patterns and tropes within memories of the past. Samuel and Thompson note two categories of remembering. The first is the narrative arc marking progress from darkness to light, stages in a life or career invested with meaning and significance, as signposts. The second style of narrative is shaped by symbolic notions of the past. As Samuel and Thompson wrote:

> In one version of autobiography it is "the good old days": a state of primal innocence corresponding in some sort to the Lost Eden of the Old Testament or the Golden Age of the poets, an enchanted space as remote as the "once upon a time" of the fables. The past here functions as a kind of reverse image of the present, a time when "everyone was neighbours," and life was more secure.[12]

This type of narrative tends to be overlain, or mediated, by a sense of loss. In both tropes there is a tremendous sense of morality, expressed as either "look how far we have come" or, in the latter example, "look what we lost/had."

Both of these visions of the past and present are open to the charge of nostalgia. Like other oral historians, I am eager to challenge this interpretation by examining in more detail what we mean by "nostalgia." Over the past three decades or more, there has been a growing and sustained interest in nostalgia above and beyond the simplistic sense in which it is often used. Fred Davis's *Yearning for Yesterday* is central to understanding the complexity of nostalgia. Davis suggested a taxonomy for studying this elusive emotion, identifying three orders of nostalgia: *first-order* or *simple nostalgia*, *second-order* or *reflective nostalgia*, and *third-order* or *interpretive nostalgia*. Simple nostalgia is what most people refer to when they use the phrase; here a reflection is dismissed, in a pejorative sense, as false or highly selective memory; the past is imagined as unproblematically better and more real. Reflective nostalgia, by contrast, refers to the notion that those expressing or experiencing nostalgia examine more critically what they are thinking and doing: "Why am I thinking like this?" Finally, interpretive nostalgia extends this critique and self-reflection to ask deeper and broader questions, such as, "Why am I feeling this now?" and "Was the past really that much better?" The essential point is that almost all nostalgic reflection questions memory in a critical way; there are few instances where the remembrance of a past is completely devoid of any form of balance or critique.[13]

One of the core shared tenets of writers on nostalgia is that it tells us more about the present than it does about the past. While the past is the raw material for reflection, it is the present conditions that one finds oneself in that stimulates the emotion. A number of writers have suggested that nostalgia is the basis for a progressive and, indeed, radical critique of the present in the comparison between then and now. This could be a passive critique or take on a more active stance, but crucially nostalgia is not simply conservative and backward-looking.[14]

In the interviews that follow, we have to be cognizant that the reflections on the past were being collected at a moment of turbulence. The past for these workers represented an intelligible "known" against which they were comparing and contrasting the unstable present and the unknown future. The interviews capture the period in the brewery's history from roughly the early 1960s through to the late 1970s, exploring themes such as early socialization, the work itself, workplace culture and humor, authority and management. Apparent here is the sense of continuity as well as change across these twenty years. While aspects of the work and the organization of the brewery shift, much remains the same. Most notable across all the interviews is the expression of a collective workplace culture, an industrial atmosphere, or an industrial structure of feeling, which reflects many of the aspects of industrial citizenship—though not always as Edward Guinness envisaged them.

GUINNESS AT WORK

Beginning a new job, especially one that would come to dominate a life, understandably makes a lasting impact. Henry Dawson started work in the print trade, but after he was laid off in 1969, a friend told him about vacancies in the brewery:

> Went to the interview and Edward Guinness himself interviewed me 'cause he was in there at the time. And he said to me at the interview, "You can have the job, but I don't think you'll be staying. But we need people now and you're used to shift work. . . . You'll soon pick up the work itself, so, yeah, we'll employ you." He said, "Can you start on Wednesday? Or Thursday?" And I said, "Yeah, course I can." And he said, "Thursday night on nights," and that's—that's when I started, St. Patrick's Day.[15]

Workers who had begun their careers in the 1960s mentioned how many vacancies there were in the contemporary London labor market. Many did not believe that they would stay for long; Guinness workers often remarked that, initially at least, they assumed the brewery would be just a temporary stopgap. As Graham Bayford explained about his expectations of his working life:

> Not a clue really, didn't have a clue what I wanted to be, wanted to do; it was just a case of going into one job, if I liked it. Come to Guinness's, didn't think I'd be here longer than a couple of years, but all of a sudden it grabs you.[16]

When men look back at their younger lives and selves, it is sometimes hard to disentangle their current concerns—the imminent closure of the brewery and the insecurity they felt—alongside the far greater sense of stability they enjoyed at the start of their careers. This was a wider feature of the labor market in London and elsewhere in the 1960s through into the 1970s. One worker said:

> And there was plenty of work about—we were talking about that this morning. When I left school, there was never a problem: it was where you *were* going to work, not *if* you were going to get work. I'm working with a young lad today and he's twenty-eight now, and he's had to take this job for six months just to get some money. Whereas I left school, there was loads of work about, plenty of manufacturing, plenty of building work all the time. So come here, had, like, I suppose you could say, a job for life.[17]

What emerged across the interviews was a real sense of an industrial milieu during the 1960s and 1970s in which Guinness represented one attractive employment opportunity among many others. This reflects the wider stability and confidence engendered by being in the midst of the long boom era. The narratives emphasized tremendous freedom and ability to choose from a wide range of possibilities.

Often the initial impressions of the company were formed on the first day, even before workers entered the brewery proper. The workplace environment can make an impression on all the senses—smell, taste, vision, touch, and sound—and workers often related their memories through a combination of these. Dave Bathurst remembered through his sense of smell:

> In those days . . . I mean, that's the first thing when the day I came for interview, you sort of walked across from Park Royal Station: "What's that smell?" And then you could smell all day long would be malt, the smell of mashing of malt, but particularly what you'd smell is this, is that smell which would be hopped wort, quite bitter, and probably for a year or two would have gone by before I stopped noticing it. Gosh, that was strong, almost in a sort of medicinal way. Neither unpleasant or pleasant, it was just, "Oh, that's a bitter smell." But you could smell it because that vapour would be blowing out from the wort coolers.[18]

Henry Dawson went on to describe his first day at work, comparing the experience of Guinness with his previous smaller employer. His and other accounts conveyed a sense of awe at what workers discovered at their new place of work:

> When I went into Guinness's—totally different world. I mean the first time I went up to the canteen and everything was silver service. Whoa! I wasn't expecting that. People coming round with big silver tureens of soup and potatoes and vegetables and waitresses laying them on the table in front of you! For an ordinary working man, that was a bit strange. You expected the staff to have that, but not the men on the shop floor. But yeah, that was what it was like. But overall I think it was quite overpowering the first—not my interview but my induction because I went all the way round the brewery in one day, and you were trying to remember things. And the brewery was quite vast, and there was so many nooks and crannies and little places that you could get to. But, once I got onto the shift—actually got onto the shift and started working with the shift I was gonna be with, it was a lot easier. Because you quickly formed working relationships because you all relied on each other.[19]

Terry Aldridge, who started at Guinness in 1975, had previously worked in the automotive sector. He started at the brewery after a friend alerted him to a vacancy for a process operator, a job Aldridge described as "the lowest of the low." He was attracted both to the pay and the firm's reputation. Relating his first impressions of working at the site, he said:

> So it came to me as a bit of a shock when I first walked through the—the gate—doors into the Brew House. I'm looking at a sort of an engine room in a ship. Was absolutely flabbergasted, couldn't believe it, never been in a brewery before.[20]

Aldridge also articulated his shock on first entering this strange new environment:

> But I know that when the doors opened up there was this massive structure, I mean
> it was up to about—I dunno—eighty, ninety feet high. They were very high build-
> ings. And there was mains, like all pipes, but they're not pipes, they're mains,
> y'know—There was all these mains, there was all these vessels, and there's steam,
> noise of machinery. I just stood there and I thought, "What the hell is this?"—
> absolutely no idea. I was quite flabbergasted, to be honest with you, 'cause I'd never
> been in a brewery before.[21]

Another worker, Mike Thomas, spoke in similar terms about his first impressions of the plant at the time:

> It was just a mass of cylinders and pipes and things, and quite . . . well, a bit fright-
> ening in a way, too. You had to get to know all this stuff, where it all went and how
> it all worked. And, of course, it was all very mechanical. There was no pushing
> buttons and computer operated or anything like that. It was all valves.[22]

Both Aldridge and Thomas were describing their awe of an industrial sublime, at
once impressed and a little scared by their new environment.

One of the striking features of the interview I carried out with Thomas was
the subtle way in which he expressed his discomfort at the male-dominated atmosphere in the brewery at this time:

> Yeah, I turned up, I think I turned up on a six-to-two, we used to do twelve-hour
> shifts so but—on a six-to-two in the morning. Been issued with Wellingtons, an
> overall. Put those on. As I say, it felt very strange to me, 'cause it was full of men
> and I felt quite intimidated really, especially in the locker room. But they were all
> very friendly and quite nice and we always had to go over to the foreman's office,
> through the brewery and we were allocated jobs then: "You're doing this, you're
> doing that," whatever. And because I'd only just joined for the first—I think it
> was probably a week—I would shadow somebody else. And that was quite nice.
> Whatever jobs they gave the fellow I was shadowing, I went along with him. It was
> very different, I'd never seen anything like it—I'd never been in a brewery.[23]

Ray Snook started at Park Royal in 1960 as an apprentice coppersmith serving
a five-year apprenticeship:

> We actually worked in copper, and all the brewery pipework in those days was all
> in copper pipework, and it was all tin and everything was made out of flat sheet,
> whereas now it is stainless steel. I had a very good apprenticeship here, excellent
> apprenticeship, very, very good craftsmen in the workshops.

Snook was obviously proud of the skills he had gained earlier in his life, skills
that had been rendered redundant by changing technology. He was, though,
still able to draw on a residual identity as a skilled craftsman, even though he no
longer had cause to practice that craft in his current position. In 1965, Snook was

forced to leave Guinness after he qualified so that he gained outside experience, a common practice in craft trades at the time. He rejoined the brewery after nine years. Snook's interview was a good illustration of the way past and present intermingle in the narrative of work:

> It was fun, it was; to be honest, I still enjoy coming to work here, I do, but, I mean, I have seen the changes here. The management have changed big time; they're not the good old Guinness family firm that they were—you're a number now. Chief engineer in the old days would walk around and he would know your name, boss now wouldn't even know your name.[24]

Later in the interview Snook spoke of the family atmosphere of the brewery, which again mixed past and present:

> It was very good, as I say, it was family orientated, there was a lot of family. They always say, "How on earth do you get in here?" You know, in those days, if you had a relative who worked for Guinness, like everyone wanted to work for Guinness in those days; no one ever left. No, it was an excellent firm, but as I say, people had— they knew you then, you're just a number now.[25]

Snook here struggles to find the right phrase that will do justice to the sense of being embedded, comfortable in a working environment. "Family" is a close approximation but does not quite sum up what he wants to say. Snook stresses being known, a sense of being acknowledged by fellow workers and respected by management.

Mick Costa was going to stay in school, but his mother saw an advertisement in the local press for vacancies on the brewery's Boys' Scheme, and he started in 1970. Costa spoke of how the company's reputation was reinforced by relatives in Ireland as well as local knowledge. Guinness, as he put it, was a "highly respected place to work":

> I started off in the Guinness Boys' Scheme, which ran from whatever age you started at, but the early stage was sort of fifteen and a half. I was going to stay on at school, so I didn't start until sixteen and a half. Again, very much character building basically. Outward Bound, Duke of Edinburgh's Award Scheme, up the mountains every other weekend. So your time really wasn't your own, but it was a good period to be in. And, as I said before, very, very sport orientated. Came out the Boys' Scheme at eighteen and then for certainly the next twelve years, you would find yourself having certainly at least a day off a month in the summer to play cricket. Football, being more of a weekend game, sort of didn't happen, really, but exchange tours with Dublin for all sporting events. Darts, snooker, anything you could think of. Very, very, very sociable company to work for.[26]

Importantly, Costa hinted at a discomfort at the level of expectation the firm had over both his work and social life, suggesting that his time was not his own, while simultaneously seeing the experience as a positive and rewarding one.

This was echoed in an interview with another recruit to the Boys' Scheme, Mick Costello:

> The Boys' Scheme itself revolved around job experience throughout the company. So, for approximately three to four months, you worked in various departments. You were also given opportunities to join the Duke of Edinburgh's Award Scheme— but it wasn't really a choice; you were sort of told that you had to go. In the Boys' Scheme, your time was really not your own. Most were at day-release college once a week, evenings once a week, football training two nights a week. As character building, the Guinness Boys' Scheme, I very much doubt you could fault it.[27]

As in other interviews recorded at this time, in the next breath Costello compared his initial experience with later trends: "And then, of course, belts were tightened and like a lot of high-profile companies who had big sporting facilities, they're diminishing very, very quickly now."[28] Here, past and present were inextricably linked, the understanding of one era embedded in another. Costello was interviewed with his colleague Dave Bathurst, who had joined the company as an underbrewer in 1970 from university:

> Came for an interview—I mean, I think the thing that struck me was that they, at that time, even before I joined the company, was this image. They actually invited me up for two days of testing, which I thought was extraordinary. In that sense, at that time, they were probably way ahead of the game in terms of recruitment practices, testing, and you did a whole load of things, including then, you know, it was, I was only going to be a fairly humble, quite low-grade trainee shift manager equivalent underbrewer—and yet you had dinner that, one of those evenings, the middle evening, with members of the Board.[29]

This idea of image that cropped up at several points in Bathurst's narrative speaks to an external presentation as well as an internal culture:

> Certainly there was this image when you came in, and before you came, of, "You're joining a family. Here are all the things you need to know about sports facilities, club, all the things that you can have," and certainly people outside who had been exposed to industry, even then, said, "Yeah, Guinness is a really, really good company to work for." I mean, even then, it, it was a big name, well known.[30]

Bathurst recounted his initial impressions of Park Royal:

> When I first came here, there were about 1,500 people on site. I have to say, I was very impressed. Even to me, Guinness was seen as a good company, a good employer, everything they did, even interviewing and things, and the benefits and all the other things they offered. It was quite funny because I remember going back home and, at that time, in 1970, my starting salary was just under a thousand quid a year—and I thought that was absolutely wonderful.[31]

David Hughes was recruited into a more senior role from university, but his memory was similarly positive:

> Well, I joined the laboratory, so I didn't join the brewing department first off; I moved into the brewing department about nine months later. But my first impressions were . . . a big company, big reputation. I enjoyed being in the brewing industry; I thought that was quite good fun. They had loads of sports facilities onsite. There were clubs. There was a big social scene going on. There were 1,500 people onsite. There were loads of, you know, young guys and young girls, and everybody started pairing up and, I mean, most of my friends married Guinness girls. You know, there was a big secretarial scheme, which my wife was on. Three or four of my best friends married secretaries or women who were working in the brewery. So yeah, it was great, you know. I got immersed in this.[32]

His choice of the word "immersed" is interesting, as it gets at the way work possessed a more all-encompassing quality; it speaks to attachment or being deeply embedded. To push this further, we can see how life is lived through work here in a way that becomes more difficult later. At points in his interview Hughes was critical of the company and the way it was run, even in the early 1970s. This was leavened by a more-than-residual affection for the plant and the people he worked with and managed.

Time and again, workers talked about joining a "family" or experiencing a "family atmosphere." This phrase has a number of potential implications. First, there were a number of families employed in the brewery across generations. There were also members of the Guinness family themselves, who populated the management and the company's board, although their presence was diminishing by the 1970s. Workers on site may well have been aware of the Guinness family through direct contact or in the pages of *Guinness Time*. There was, however, a broader and wider sense of family being recounted here, contributing to this notion of the industrial atmosphere of the workplace. What workers are describing is entering a preexisting social community based in and around work, one that helped to humanize economic life.

LIFE ON THE LINE

For production workers, life was hard: many of the routine brewery tasks involved heavy manual labor, such as cleaning the brewery plant. Until the new investment of the 1980s, the machinery used at Park Royal was much the same as it had been when the site was opened in 1936, and it was highly labor-intensive. Much of the work of the process staff involved a constant cycle of starting off brews, monitoring, and then cleaning. Thomas described the beginning of the typical routine:

One of the major jobs, I suppose, was at the beginning of the brew. You'd always have a charger, who would be in charge of getting the water temperature right, 'cause in a brew house—right at the top of the house were the water tanks, and they used to heat those up, and then the water would be allowed to come out of those tanks and be mixed, 'cause it was red hot—really hot water—and it'd be mixed with cold water to get the right temperature. And then they'd be sent to all of the various tuns and coppers—anyway, cylinders where we used to have all the grain put in. One person would be standing at each of these, and I think there was about six of these big vessels, and he would shout, "Turn in!" And that would be your time to turn the wheel and start the grain coming in. But the grain would be mixed with this water, and it would go into the vessel. Fill up the vessel. Finish that, and then we would have got what they call sparging arms over the top, which are just like hosepipes, really, but arms with holes in. And they would spin round and drop water, hot water, onto the top of the grain to percolate through the grain, and then the liquor would come out the other end. So that was one of the jobs, and that would take quite a while to do that. By the time—that was always a nighttime job, as far as I remember. You do that job at night, and by the time you finished that, it was time to go and have a cup of tea and then breakfast.[33]

All of my interviews with workers included detailed descriptions of the process of industrial brewing. Their oral descriptions were accompanied by extensive hand gestures enacting long-disappeared tasks, traces of a former way of life.

The next stage in the process, after heating the grain with water to create a liquor, was adding hops:

That used to get pumped up to what we call the coppers, and . . . the coppers were just great big coppers. Like a kettle, but massive things. And it used to get mixed with the hops there. So another job we had to do was when they—when these are being filled up, we had to go right to the top of the house and undo these—they used to call them pockets; they were great big sacks and they used to have the hops in them. They must have been seven foot tall, I suppose? Very tall. So you'd open those up and you would have to carry them. They were heavy, yeah. So what I would do is, I would just push one over, really. Let it go down onto the floor so it was like a big sausage, and then split the end open and then gradually empty it out down the top; it was quite a physical job, really, to do that.[34]

The work of brewing often involved manipulating the raw materials needed to produce beer, coupled with operating the many flow valves in the brewery's complex web of piping. The cleaning that followed each stage of the brew was the hardest labor, involving heavy lifting in a hot, steamy atmosphere. As Aldridge explained:

I suppose the only hard work for a process operator was at nights, when you had to get inside these vessels called hop backs,[35] and they had these series of bronze plates inside and there was about, I dunno, two hundred of them to lift up in very hot conditions. Stripped to the waist, lifting these plates up, dragging the plates up against the wall, and you stack them all up and you get your hosepipe out and you have to wash all these sludge down the waste, what is the end products. So, yeah, it was probably the hardest; you used to come out of there knackered.[36]

Fellow production worker Thomas described the process of cleaning the coppers:

The coppers actually had—they were like a kettle with steam rings in the bottom, so that would be full of steam and that'd heat it up and boil it. Well, he was sup-posed to shut off the steam to these rings so that we could get in, and it was always two people again. We'd get in, take a hosepipe in there, and then hose all these spent grain out and hops out. Sometimes they were a bit of a devil, sometimes, these chargers, because they had to get these heated up again, ready for next shift. They wouldn't always turn off the steam, they'd just keep it cranked open, and I went in there once with Len, this big strong man, and we got in there and we started hosing them. Well, once you hit one of these tubes with the steam in it, steam suddenly comes out. Well, your—well, no, actually he was in there. I was outside. You always—you could only have one person get in there, one to watch. So he was in there hosing down and he hit this and suddenly the steam comes up. Well, he—it's awful, it's like being hit with a wall of steam. And it's the only time that I've ever thought that "He's not gonna get out," y'know? [Laughs] And if you were to collapse in there you'd get badly burned 'cause you'd fall on one of these rings. So you always need two people there, one to stand outside and watch to make sure everything was all right and one to do the job. So that was a very hot, uncomfortable job if it wasn't done properly, if they didn't shut the steam off properly.[37]

Thomas went on to describe other manual aspects to the cleaning process:

And the other physical, really physical, job there at that time, I remember, was at the bottom of that vessel, and it must have been from wall-to-wall there round. It was a very big vessel. The bottom was made up of plates, triangular—sort of trian-gular plates that fitted all together like a Meccano set. And so once you cleaned the tops, you had to lift all these and stand them up on the side and clean underneath, and then put them back; that was a really heavy job. They must have been half a hundredweight each, I think, these plates; they're big copper plates or bronze. So that was a really hard, physical job. But again, it was easy to do if you knew what you were doing, and that was usually done with two people as well.[38]

Production-line workers made it clear that often the work itself had little in-trinsic value and indeed was quite boring. One process worker described his first jobs in the brewery after he joined Guinness from the building trade:

I didn't particularly like the job. I preferred the job I was doing before [plumber]. It was a very boring job. It was production line, and you stood in one position doing something, where the job I'd done before was very . . . like, you had to think about it. The very first job was in the Draughts Out Department, where I said I'd been for twenty-five years, and that was when draught Guinness was first coming out, so we had to hand-fill the kegs, basically; wash them and hand-fill them.[39]

Although the topic of boredom often cropped up in conversation about the work, interviewees talked at length about how they sought to overcome industrial tedium. One described how taking breaks helped him to cope:

All I can say is everybody was looking for a break as soon as they could get it; they just wanted to get away from the job. So it bred a culture, I would have said, of what was perceived as laziness and looking how the job is now and how it was then, I can understand why people did it because I used to do it myself: I'd go for a break. That used to be boring as well, but it was often doing one operation all the time. And people that have never done that don't know. The managers used to say, "They're always on a break" and all that, but if you are a manager, you're sitting at a desk and you want a cup of coffee, you can just go and get one or walk away and have a chat with somebody. Then you come back, you've relieved the boredom, if it was boring what you're doing—probably isn't. But when you're doing the same maneuver all the time, that's the only way you can get out of it.[40]

He expressed a kind of moral economy: he and his colleagues needed these breaks so they could cope with the boredom they encountered on the line. Those little pauses in production made the job sustainable; they broke up the working day.

One of the key features of Park Royal was that it was a fully integrated site, both vertically and horizontally. This had been one of the recurring themes in the pages of *Guinness Time*, and perhaps naturally this was a topic that all the workers interviewed mentioned. This integration was often addressed in discussions of what had occurred at the site since the 1980s. Bathurst described the feel of the place in the early 1970s:

There were a lot more people then. Each department ran as a separate unit. So you had raw materials, brewing, fermentation, the vat house, kegging, as it was then—all of them operated as standalone units with large numbers of people. So, yes, a much busier site, and everything was done in house then, it didn't matter what it was—transport, site services, building, painting. Anything that had to be done, which in some ways was why the numbers then would have been so high, was done in house. Anything and everything. There was someone on site who you could ring or ask who would be responsible for doing things.[41]

This quality of the brewery as an integrated site in the 1960s and 1970s was a feature of lots of narratives, often emphasizing the sheer scale of the workforce then compared to that at the time of the interview:

When I came here in '70 there was nearly two thousand people on this site, all of whom were geared to producing Guinness. There would be another three or four hundred offsite doing sales, but there would be a couple of thousand people all geared to this site producing Guinness. But when you bear in mind, then, that everything, but everything, associated with the company was in house—gardens, estate, building maintenance, distribution, the maintenance of those distribution vehicles. You know, they would take lorry engines out down the bottom there. Scaffolding was in house. There wasn't a thing you could mention that was not in house.[42]

This integrated past was in stark comparison to the organizational structures that had emerged from the 1980s. The narratives display an almost reverential awe for how things used to be done, for the reach and ambition of integration of the organization in the postwar period. In their accounts the workers mull over the process of change and offer a defensive account of the past, an emphasis on understanding work organization then in its own terms. As Costello said:

It was very, very sociable—very sociable. I guess you could say, looking back now, and being quite harsh, that from this perspective, the whole shift, the whole site was vastly overmanned. You know, you had . . . there was nineteen people on a shift in the brew house and three shifts a day. The fitters had mates; electricians had mates. There were coppersmiths who had mates because most of the brewery's vessels were made of copper, so that was a trade then in itself.[43]

But then he went on to talk about change and explain the historical context:

I mean, everything's stainless steel now, so you don't need coppersmiths anymore. And now on the trade side, maintenance is basically multiskilled and mechanics can do electrical work and vice versa to a certain extent. So because of the overmanning, if you like . . . but in those days, okay, I've said overmanning, but there were great big valves to open, you know, enormous wheels to turn, whereas now they're all automatic.[44]

When asked about the charge of overmanning and potential inefficiencies a few minutes later, Costello emphasized the context:

Well, no, I say quite, because you, you've got a different perspective of things these days. You know, it's just a matter of, it was all part and parcel of the whole thing in those days, you know. You weren't conscious about how many people there were there: they were there, and that was it. But now, because of all the streamlining's been carried out, I mean, you can, it's for that reason that you look back and say, "I can't believe we had that many people!" But it was a lot more manual than it is now.[45]

There is, then, a complex, multilayered narrative within the interviews and the memories that the narrators draw on. There is a critical account of the present and a critical evaluation of the past. The workers defend the past; they concede that things were not perfect but argue that they made sense and were rational within their own time. This attitude defends the workers' individual and collective history and protects the memory of the firm. They need to be fair to the past, to judge it on its own terms and in its own time.

INDUSTRIAL RELATIONS, DEMARCATION, AND THE UNION

By recognizing unions since the early postwar period, Guinness was ahead of its time in the brewing industry, where outright hostility to unionization was the norm well into the 1950s and 1960s. Guinness was very unusual in effectively enforcing membership on its blue-collar workers. This process of trade unionization was rooted in the experience of the Second World War. Ben Newbold, then the managing director, believed that "unorganised labour under the stresses of post-war conditions would be very undisciplined."[46] Both the Dublin site and, initially, the Park Royal site had traditionally been opposed to unionization, but in the early postwar period Newbold's successor, Hugh Beaver, signed an agreement recognizing unions on the Park Royal site for the purposes of staff representation and negotiation over pay and conditions. The agreement included a provision that new entrants were to be encouraged to join a union, with the brewery being 100 percent unionized (rather than the formal description of the "closed shop"). Skilled workers were represented by one of six craft unions, while semiskilled and unskilled workers were represented by the Transport and General Workers' Union (TGWU).

In the semiofficial histories of Park Royal, industrial relations takes on a benign countenance, with a broadly good-natured management alongside a passive, committed workforce. In his account of the first strike at Park Royal, resulting from a dispute over overtime allocation, Edward Guinness reflected on the increased militancy of the late 1940s:

> Those were heady days for Trade Unionism and in the general "togetherness" of the workers during the War the mood was militant in seeking to strengthen bargaining power and achieve recognition from very reluctant employers by enrolling as many members as possible. The advent of the Labour Government in the immediate postwar period and the strength of the Communist Party on the fringe (copies of the *Daily Worker* were constantly to be found on the benches of Sun Works and the Laboratories) augmented the unrest created by the difficulties of fitting back into industry those demobilised from the Services.[47]

The account of the strike is one of well-meaning officials who had little or no idea of how to take or organize industrial action. Edward Guinness recounts that the strike committee unwittingly, albeit briefly, accepted aid from local Communist Party activists. The strike, described as "half-hearted," ended after four days.[48]

Rather counterintuitively, perhaps, the strike encouraged Beaver to strengthen the firm's commitment to trade union recognition. After the strike, he felt that sporadic unrest would persist until Park Royal was 100 percent unionized. This narrative of union tolerance is interesting as it highlights a tension in the brewery's self-narrative as a happy, self-contained space. Guinness was undoubtedly a good employer in terms of wages and conditions. At Park Royal, and especially in Dublin, the company had a long track record of corporate welfare.[49]

Management interpreted industrial tension as disruption caused by outsiders, rabble-rousers, or militants within. Edward Guinness wrote of the strike: "There were a number of militants in the Forwarding area at that time."[50] Clearly, the decision to recognize the various unions in the plant, indeed to actively encourage them, must be seen within this context of competing pressure and circumstance. Trade union consciousness had been heightened during the Second World War, and ideas from the Left of the political spectrum had gained considerable traction. There was a clear appreciation that Communist Party activists were at work in London, especially in the new factories that had sprung up in West London in the interwar period. Union recognition was therefore a pragmatic acceptance of political, industrial, and social reality during this period, one that can be seen as a continuity of a type of already established welfare capitalism that Guinness had practiced. It was an attempt to institutionalize potential sources of dissent or conflict in a process production facility vulnerable to unofficial walkouts.[51]

By the mid- to late 1960s, the period when most of the interviewees began working at Guinness, industrial relations at Park Royal had settled into a formal, established pattern. There were four strikes on site before 1969.[52] In addition to the two sections of the TGWU (transport and production), there were six craft unions representing various trades, with a total of forty shop stewards representing the entire blue-collar workforce.[53]

This division between unions may well have split the workforce, but it also had the effect of ratcheting up pay levels in negotiations as a result of "leapfrogging." Management at Park Royal was concerned with these divisions for both pragmatic and more idealistic reasons. In the late 1960s until the early 1970s, much of the United Kingdom, especially London, was experiencing a very tight labor market, with effectively full employment. Labor turnover during 1969 was very low at 0.3 percent per month for men at the brewery, representing a 3.6 percent annual turnover. To put these figures in perspective, labor turnover in the brewing sector nationally was around 3.3 percent monthly, or nearly 40 percent a year.[54] Unemployment in the region was 1.4 percent—effectively zero—and the number of unfilled vacancies rose to 202, 200 by 1973.[55] Clearly, this was a comfortable moment for labor to push its case, but the low turnover of blue-collar staff in the brewery indicates that Guinness seems to have been genuinely perceived as a good place to work, if a little too paternalistic at times.

Some of these issues and tensions were apparent in my interviews with staff as they recalled that era. There was a great of deal respect for the union and what it achieved for workers, but there was at times a residual unease at some of the features of the process. Aldridge relates his induction into the union in 1975:

> I was explained that there was the Transport and General Workers' Union to join. How'd you feel about it? Well, doesn't matter where you feel about it or not, you're gonna join anyway. Eh? So, yes, I joined the union. The one thing I found a bit disturbing with it, though, was there was a chap, there was a chap there called Larry Grogan. I suppose he was the chief of the Transport and General Workers' Union. He worked there, they come round with a ballot box. Okay? Walk into the locker room and it's sitting there. They come up to me and say, "Right, Terry, there's a bit of paper here." Gives you a bit of paper, and you got all these people's names down there and a box to put your X in. I don't know any of them. How would I?[56]

Aldridge continued with the story:

> I don't know who they are. "Oh," he says, "just—just put—just put Grogan. Put a cross in there." Well, I'm naive, ain't I? I'm not gonna challenge it. I don't know who the other guys are, so I just put a cross in it. Y'know, that's how it was. I think the plus side, I suppose, with unions was that if there were any gripes or any issues, the unions were pretty strong, like pay rises and stuff like this, y'know?[57]

There was a divide between the shop floor workers and their representatives. As one union steward explained, "You find that most of the blokes are just as suspicious of shop stewards as they are of the management."[58]

This is another nice illustration of nuance within the oral histories. There is a reflexive quality to Aldridge's account: he is uneasy with established structures of power while recognizing the union and its place within the brewery. Another production worker, Henry Dawson, reflected on this same union steward:

> Larry Grogan, who was head of the union, was quite a stern Irishman but very fair. And he knew—he had this knack of knowing just how far to go with the company and knowing when he was not gonna get any more. And I think because of the way he conducted himself, the Company respected him that way and all. So they knew how far to push him. So it was an amicable agreement.[59]

Many of the workers I talked to took a similar stance toward the union, and like Dawson, described negotiations or disagreements as "theater" or "pantomime." Also common was a sense of the collective presence of the union for the workers. Aldridge, for example, contrasted Guinness with his previous employer:

It's a funny thing, really: in all the time I ever worked for the brewery, I never thought that I should ask for a pay rise. If I was in garage, Lancia's or whatever, you might think, "Hang about, come on, let's go up the office and see if we can get a pay rise."[60]

Bathurst tried carefully to represent the power of the union at the beginning of his career: "I suppose some departments were—perhaps militant is the wrong word, but let's say more, perhaps, unionized or from a union procedure point of view, stronger than others, but that never became a problem."[61]

Alan Mudie started work at Park Royal as a shift brewer in 1973 straight from university; he too related the power of the union at the time:

At shop steward level, shop stewards were very militant, and swearing and thumping desks and storming out of meetings was not uncommon in those days. It actually made it quite interesting; it was quite an exciting time to come round and join an industry.[62]

Hughes worked as an underbrewer at Park Royal from the early 1970s and gave a fascinating account of his relationship with the union stewards:

I was never really very good at managing people, unfortunately, until after I left Guinness, because we got no training in man-management really, properly, and it was one of the things that I regret, that I didn't get better trained there. Guinness didn't do it. They trained the shop stewards to deal with the managers, but they never trained the managers to deal with the lads. It wasn't until I joined my next company that I actually got some really good-quality man-management training. In the brewery, you didn't really need to manage people too badly, because everybody knew what they were doing. They had been there for so many years. We were doing the same thing repetitively. You didn't have to manage people too badly. There was very little stuff going on that needed, you know, reprimanding.[63]

Hughes went on to explore the role and nature of the brewery stewards:

They kept the discipline at work. You know, the unions were quite strong. Yeah, they seemed to get their way most of the time. I mean, the brewery was quite profitable, so they didn't have to fight them tooth and nail. But there were shop stewards onsite, and the stewards were quite powerful. As a manager, I felt fairly emaciated. I felt that I didn't really get a good shout from Personnel. Personnel took [made] most of the decisions about what was going to be allowed.[64]

The unions at Park Royal were firmly embedded into brewery life and had been for a number of decades. All of the workers I interviewed were very conscious of the union and its presence in shaping working life at the plant—one aspect of taken-for-granted employment structures at the time.

AUTHORITY AT WORK

Hughes's reflections afford a good opportunity to consider authority structures in Park Royal during the period up to 1980. There was clearly a developed hierarchy in the brewery in terms of its management structures, levels of supervision, trade unions, and the workplace rule of law, as well as within each of its departments. In the latter case it is possible to detect structures of grade or job hierarchy, seniority, and age, all of which help to create an intelligible set of relationships and social order. There was a strong moral order to this structure of hierarchy. Barry Hubbard talked in terms of a moral order existing in the brewery at the beginning of his career; once again, in remembering the past, the present was a critical foil against which ideas and memories are played. Asked about his desire for promotion, he answered:

> No, not early on, no. I mean, that was the thing with Guinness as well. They used to pay very well, you know, so you didn't even sort of think about what you were going to do because you were earning quite good money anyway. You weren't striving to get up there. And in them days, it worked on a pecking order. It didn't work as it works now. You didn't get sort of a young bloke coming in and going straight into a management position; you progressed. Which is what I did, you know. I did it the old way, but now it's not the way. Now it's—they bring people in from outside, or at least people at the bottom sometimes really jump up, and it's not done on a pecking order. In some ways, it's right, and in some ways, it's wrong, because they gave you a bit of a reward for loyalty. Obviously, they didn't promote people that couldn't do the job; you know they had to be able to do it. But you could almost dictate who was going to get the job before it happened. Or you got, someone got a nod, you know: "You can put in for that job." But it doesn't happen now. And if they haven't got the right person within now, they bring them in from outside, which never happened before. There was always progression up from below.[65]

Seniority systems have their drawbacks, of course, not least the fact that they disadvantage women, but they were a common basis for promotion within British industry in the postwar period. What Hubbard was reflecting on here was the way legitimacy is sedimented within the organizational structures at the brewery and how these features of the workplace were seen to be fair and in turn accepted.

Each department had a developed pecking order, as Thomas revealed:

> We had process men. These are the bottom of the pile; that was me. Then you had SPMs, special process men, which were a little bit higher. Then you had chargers, and then foremen, and the overall foreman. So that was the structure. So people like us, the SPM, the ordinary process men, we used to work fourteen days on a trot. As I say, we got on with it, we didn't mind it, and there was always a foreman

in charge of you, but very rarely showed his face. Y'know, as long as everything was going all right, he didn't bother you.[66]

In interview after interview, workers stressed the absence on a day-to-day basis of senior management and how they were largely left to perform tasks in the brewery. The exception to this rule was when something went seriously wrong. Aldridge gave an example:

> One of the most common—I probably think one of the most common things in the brew house, all connected with the process of beer, was what we call a "smiler." Have you ever heard of a smiler? Well, y'know, if you did something wrong—say, you did something wrong and you did a misfigure on the computer or something—and then you gone into the boss and you're standing there going— you just put that smiling reflex—you kinda think psychologically it's gonna make things better by smiling, perhaps.
>
> So the guy's gonna say, "What're you smiling at?"
>
> "I've gone over the dip." Now if you go over the dip, you muck all their figures up.[67] You haven't lost beer, but you've buggered up their figures 'cause they've gotta now go back—shut the job down, shut all the pumps down, goes back to the office and they gotta refigure it all. Because you put too much in on that particular fill. And I've had a couple of smilers![68]

Aldridge stressed the importance of owning up to mistakes, not attempting to cover up an accident. Hughes gave a similar account from the position of a newly qualified underbrewer on his first night shift in charge:

> There was a very formative thing that happened to me. I was on shift, on night shift I think, or late shift, one of the two, and we had what was called a "works smiler." I think it was called "smiler" because when this happened, you basically mixed up the brews—you'd put too much of one thing in or another, diluted it too much. or you'd got it horribly wrong in terms of mixing. The guy who was doing it would come down to the brewery office smiling, you know, trying to put a brave face on it, so it was called a "smiler." So, anyway, this happened on a shift. I was phoned up by the supervisor to say that we'd had a smiler, it was quite a bad one, and I'm sitting down there, and it was my first night shift, I think, and I'm aware that, you know, you're up in front of the head brewer next morning to explain it, and you're going to get a bollocking, di-di-di-di-di-di. So I'm thinking, "Oh, bloody hell!" and I'm starting to get myself angry and starting to work myself into a bit of a lather, because I'm twenty-two and I'm not that confident with man-management. I've never had any man-management training. Guinness didn't train you in man-management because they had this belief that you had it innate from time on the sports field and, you know, dealing with, you know, the gardener! So I'm won-dering how to deal with this guy, what am I going to say to him? So I'm starting to work myself up into a bit of a lather.[69]

He then related the meeting with the man responsible for the smiler:

> The guy responsible comes into the office about quarter of an hour, twenty minutes later, and he's about forty-five, married man, been in the brewery a long time, really nice chap, tough as nails. He's short, built like a little blockhouse, you know, Dan Dare type, thick arms, strong hands from turning valves for years, crying. I haven't seen a grown man cry. He came in the brewery office, and I just thought, you twit, you absolute idiot, Hughes—what on earth are you thinking about?! This guy feels it more than you do. This guy's in tears, not because he's going to get a bollocking from David Hughes—he couldn't care less about David Hughes—pride in the job! He's let himself down, he's let the shift down, he's probably had a bit of an ear-bashing from the supervisor. The supervisor is probably saying, "Oh, that young shift manager, he's going to give you a bollocking now—he'll be tearing strips off you!" But he's not bothered about that. He's let everybody down. The guy was bawling his eyes out. I couldn't believe it. I couldn't . . . I don't know what I said to him. My brain was just a jumble at that stage, and I thought to myself, you're an idiot. You've got to rethink how you manage people.[70]

This long passage reveals many of the aspects of the moral economy of work at Park Royal and elsewhere in industry more generally. Positions of authority are underpinned and overlaid by personal relations, attitudes of respect for age and experience. Hughes had talked before this passage of his insecurity of being put in charge of workers who had two decades or more of experience in the brewery; indeed, these same workers, now subordinate to him, were the very people he had worked alongside when he was training. The moral economy of the workplace is, therefore, not simply something in which workers are embedded but a set of norms, values, and customs they create collectively over time, and that come to be shared by management as well.

WORKPLACE CULTURE

Former Guinness workers frequently referred to the strong and vibrant workplace culture in the plant. These are memories filtered in various ways with earlier experience framed by more contemporary concerns. The interview with Graham Bayford epitomized the issue of workplace culture. He talked about his early life at the brewery:

> Very hands-on manual labor, team spirit, having a crack, having a good time at Guinness, yeah. It's not been a bad time at Guinness even with the reduction in labor. They do look after, they *did* look after, their employees. From working in other places and then coming to Guinness's and working, it wasn't like work; it was like coming in for a laugh and having a game. In the early days, it was a case of, "I'll just come in and have a laugh" rather than thinking, "Oh, well, I could do that job and get more money."[71]

This sense of fun and joy at work, at least in the past, was common in interviews with craft workers, production staff, and supervisors and management. Snook contextualized his earlier working life with the present:

> I still enjoy coming to work here, you know? I can't understand people when they say, "Oh, I've got to get up for work today." I've never had that; I've had a really good time. I do think it's changed, as I say, with the managers; the managers are not so—uh, what's the word? They are not as family orientated, as this place *was* a family place, and you tell them some of the stories and that now and they just don't believe you. And I don't mean stories in a nasty way, it was about parties when people retired, or the apprentices coming out of their time, we had excellent parties and the guys would get the workshop all set up and by the following morning it would all be back as it was and you wouldn't even know a party was there.[72]

Snook's account is complex as it layers time as well as value, simultaneously valuing the past while critically evaluating more recent times. There is also a strong morality here, as he emphasized that the pleasures of the past were not derived at the expense of getting the job done: production was maintained *and* the workers enjoyed themselves. There is a real sense here that the work and the social aspects of life at the brewery folded in on themselves. Humor at the site was a common theme in the interviews.

Speaking ten years after the closure of the brewery, Henry Dawson related how his wife had recently caught him smiling. " 'I know what you're thinking about,' she said. 'You're thinking about Guinness, aren't you?' " He went on:

> I think it's the best thirty-seven years' work I've ever had. It was like a holiday. I can honestly say that. It was like going on holiday every day, y'know, because you never knew what was gonna happen, but you always knew it was gonna be fun. And if anyone out there has got a job like I had, I'd like to know where it is, because that was one hell of a job, y'know? It really was.[73]

One aspect of this humor, for the production workers at least, were the water fights that went on in the brewery, especially during the process of cleaning after a brew. When I interviewed Aldridge, most of our time together seemed to consist of our laughter as he recounted getting wet or retaliating:

> I think when you—this is a little bit like when you go to school, isn't it. You're a new lad, you're in a new class, and you don't know anybody, and if you show weakness you get picked on. And I was probably one of them, because I was not used to that environment. I wasn't used to all this steam and noise and water and that. I just wasn't used to it. And of course, for quite a while, I was getting wet. Buckets of water were coming down, hosepipes. I got wet so much I had no clothes left, y'know. I'd go into the admin office and say, "Look!" I'd be standing there, and he'd say—I think it was Monty, the Irish chap, he's long gone now—and he was

doing something. And I was standing there soaking wet and he said, [Irish accent] "You been playing with water?" And I said, "Well, no, I haven't. Somebody's wet me!" and he said, [Irish accent] "Get yourself a bucket, go up the top of the house, and wet him." That was it. If you were gonna get wet, wet them. That's how you survived. I mean, sometimes it used to go on and on and on. You used to get wet all the time, y'know. That did get to me a bit.[74]

This, like many other observations, shows the considered complexity of these workers' attempt to balance contradictory thoughts and feelings. Aldridge, like others, was careful to frame his account of play at work as something that did not interfere with the work itself, or that it was in some ways functional to the smooth running of the brewery:

They were—they was . . . I mean, obviously a lot of camaraderie, there was mucking about. And anywhere there's hosepipes, y'know, you see some really good hose-pipe fights. On nights when you've wrapped everything up, and then out come the hosepipes! I mean, it was like, good God, it was like gardens of Tivoli! [Laughs] Water all over the place! I mean, some of the things were a bit idiotic, the sort of things they did to water. [Laughing] Oh God, my—I'm still trying to think. You used to have these detergent suits, and it was a full suit that zipped up with pop-pers, right? And hood over the top, because you're dealing with detergent. Big, black gloves on, and you go and deal whatever. Well, I remember I got wet so much, I had no clothes left. I thought, "I'll show you, you buggers." Put the suit on, walked up on to the mash floors. Walking around and obviously they grabbed me. On the floor, they stuck the hosepipe up me leg, [laughing] they turned the water on—now, we're talking about hosepipe, the big hose, not a garden hosepipe, big pipe. And that goes up your trousers [laughing]. And then you blow up, water coming out all orifices—and they'd run off and leave me there, soaking. And it's bloody cold 'cause I only had pants on.[75]

Reflecting on this anecdote, he tried to explain what these types of events had meant to him. As he continued to laugh, he said, "It just worked. I dunno, per-haps it might make [laughs]—funny sort of way, perhaps it made you feel hap-pier to go into work."[76]

One of the major themes that workers spoke of as part of brewery life and culture was the consumption of the daily beer allowance given by the company. Hughes discussed the drinking culture in the early 1970s:

Most of them [production workers] smoked on shift. You know, you went in the locker room at six in the morning, and there would be a cup of tea brewed, and you'd sit down, you'd have a couple of fags [cigarettes] or a bottle of Guinness, and then you'd start your shift, and an hour and a quarter later, you'd come back and have another fag, another bottle of Guinness and—not the healthiest of lifestyles [laughing]! And then after the shift was over, you'd go down the clubhouse and you'd have another few and a bit more of a bevy, but that's the way it was in those days. Manual workers did drink a lot of beer because they burnt a lot of calories.[77]

A production worker remembered his first impressions of the drinking culture at the brewery: "What I first saw in the 1960s, when I first walked in that workshop at seven that morning, seeing blokes drinking a bottle of Guinness instead of a cup of tea."[78] One of his colleagues reflected on the ever-present alcohol at the plant: "So the beer was always in the shop, and then at lunchtime, the real rule was you had two quarts to drink anyway during the day and one with your lunch, and there was a beer bar in the canteen as well."[79]

Hughes has written several books on Guinness; he wrote about such consumption as a twenty-one-year-old graduate shift supervisor in the early 1970s:

> Before every shift began we assembled in the foreman's locker room for the customary smoke and a beer. Can you imagine the shock to the palate for one so tender, of drinking a bottle of Guinness by the neck before 6am? Tea was made about seventy-five minutes into the shift from a huge pot. Such was my first introduction to bottled Extra Stout.[80]

He explained the context of work-based drinking at the time at Guinness and more widely in industry:

> Brewing was still a physical job in the '70s, with much running up and down the stairs in the seven-story brew house and across the bridges to the connecting houses of raw materials. . . . Many miles would be covered during a shift and most of us being keen sportsmen declined the lifts and ran the stairs. Beer was consumed throughout the shift to sustain body and soul. On nights, several stouts consumed at the end of shift helped one to sleep.[81]

The culture of a workplace encompasses many different elements and changes over time. At Guinness, various elements contributed to this particular industrial atmosphere: the job roles and identities of brewery workers; the different craft and work traditions workers were socialized into; the individual personalities and histories people brought to the company; the humor and horseplay; the hierarchy and workplace rule of law all helped to shape workplace culture. It was through this environment that workers articulated knowledge of their surroundings and of others. This was a culture that clearly had a moral order; it made work intelligible and helped to humanize what could often be mundane, for some boring, repetitive work.

INDUSTRIAL CITIZENS?

The pragmatic acceptance and active recognition of trade unions, the creation of schemes for noncraft apprentices, and a panoply of welfare measures and staff benefits aimed to create Guinness citizens. This vision for workers at Park

Royal was advanced and recorded in *Guinness Time*, which was itself an embodiment of a particular form of postwar UK industrial welfare capitalism. While the magazine was undoubtedly largely written by management, its intent was more liberal than this perspective might imply. There was a genuine attempt to reconfigure workplace relationships in the era by encouraging an active, engaged, and involved workforce. Part of this vision was that workers should be afforded considerable autonomy.

But how did the beneficiaries of this benign, expansive management regime embrace this vision of workplace citizenship? As a sociologist interested in questions of identity and meaning at work, I have almost never encountered workers who volunteer thoughts on abstract concepts such as "occupational identity." Workers do not think like this; it is not part of their grammar. However, when relating their life stories, especially those who were employed in the long boom, workers offer accounts saturated with these themes. They express the process and practice of *being* and *becoming* embedded in work, *their* workplace, and in *their* work culture. These are processes that workers generally, not just those at Guinness, find difficult to articulate precisely because they experienced this quality as an ongoing process rather than a moment of revelation or discrete event. What interviews recover is both the form and content of the experience of being embedded in work. But what does this idea of embedding mean, and what does it reveal about the workplace?

The notions of embedding and embeddedness can help us think through the ways workers inhabit, individually and collectively, workplaces and industries, especially as they did during the long boom era.[82] The concept speaks to attachment to a particular form of work. This can encompass a firm, and Guinness would be a good example, but it goes beyond that to allow us to describe a broader sense of ownership and confidence in work present in the period. It reflects an industrial atmosphere often reported in interviews with workers from the era.[83]

Industrial atmosphere captures a similar sense of the quality of working life in the long boom. It was a self-confidence born of a time of relative stability, affluence, and security. These features, both interior and exterior to particular workplaces, allowed workers to attach themselves to the jobs they did, to demand things of work, but also to feel responsibility and ownership for their work. This was a confidence that came from knowing that they were not going to be arbitrarily dismissed or subject to unfair sanction. People were comfortable in their skins; they could be relaxed in their working and social interaction with their peers as well as management. The dominant culture that emerges after the war embodied the more expansive sense of human capacity and possibility; there was a general sense of being ambitious to achieve one's human potential. The Guinness narratives illustrate how those dominant ideas of the progressive, expansive Herbivores were translated into a workplace vernacular by the workers themselves; they are an articulation of an industrial structure of feeling or a culture of industrialism.[84]

Raymond Williams made the distinction between three forms of structure of feeling—*dominant, residual,* and *emergent.* The interviews from Guinness workers at Park Royal reflect both a dominant structure of feeling and the process by which that structure of feeling is made residual. They reveal this through a series of layoffs at the brewery and ultimately its closure. Industrial loss serves as a fundamental break with established patterns and meanings. It creates the space for reflection, concern, and questioning. It is what sociologists call a "breaching experiment."[85]

At the level of deindustrialization, this economic loss tells us about the values and meaning associated with work more generally in society. These interviews at Guinness show a similar pattern of revelation after disruption. Although most of the workers I interviewed were speaking before they lost their jobs, they had learned that this was to happen. At the moment I was interviewing them, they were being forced to reevaluate a whole series of ideas and memories, individual and collective, about work. What they were recalling, through the lens of impending redundancy, was this more settled time. It would be easy to disregard these as simply nostalgic reminiscences, but the workers are evaluative, critical, and at times analytical in their reflection. They are aware of the charge of nostalgia but are attempting to express value in that past, their past. They are giving an account of the past while simultaneously considering what they gained from it. They are living momentarily in their history and reimagining or repopulating it. This is a landscape of the imagination, one of value and loss. There is defensiveness here because in their stories they related previous ways of being at work that to modern eyes might appear inefficient, indulgent, or wasteful. In the critical telling of the past, the workers are imagining themselves back in the past and defending their work in the context of the time—socially, culturally, technologically, and politically. They want the listener to at least acknowledge that historical context. There is also a profound sense of value within the patterns of social interaction that the work organizations of the long boom afforded. Part of what made work enjoyable, or even at times bearable, was the way social relationships overlaid and underpinned the mechanical act of labor.

What, then, of citizenship at work at Park Royal? There was an identifiable tangible industrial citizenship present at Park Royal, and it was part of a more general industrial atmosphere across many workplaces at that time. It was undoubtedly shaped by individual organizations such as Guinness, and the role of trade unions and industrial relations and workplace rule of law was another significant factor. But while these are important structures that shape, constrain, and enable, there was also space for an autonomous workplace culture to emerge and to be transmitted, transformed, and changed. This industrial structure of feeling structured action but simultaneously represented the lived experience of work. We can think of it as a set of norms and values into which people are socialized and which they live by, but these are not static values, even though they appear to be so. Marshall stressed the need for moral regulation to emerge from the work group itself rather than being imposed externally. This identification of the need for autonomy is more directly articulated by Durkheim, who laid emphasis on this set of workplace morals:

> A system of morals is always the affair of a group and can operate only if this protects them by its authority. It is made up of rules which govern individuals, which compel them to act in such and such a way, and which impose limits to their inclinations and forbids them to go beyond. Now there is only one moral power—moral, and hence common to all—which stands above the individual and which can legitimately make laws for him, and that is collective power. To the extent the individual is left to his own devices and freed from all social constraint, he is unfettered too by all moral constraint.[86]

In other words, true autonomy, freedom, and individuality are predicated on collective moral constraint. What the Guinness interviews reveal, especially those carried out in 2004–2005, as the factory was about to close, was precisely this sense of collective understanding of social relations of work. This was a form of Guinness Citizenship to be sure, but not necessarily the form envisaged by Edward Guinness or others in the firm's management.

The voices recorded here allow us access to another privileged occasion in industrial life—the experience of working-class stability in a benignly managed workplace. These are workers who experienced work in the long boom era and tell how they thought and felt about it, both at the time and much later in their lives. Their narration of this period is not uncritical, but they recount real value in the social relations of the time and the industrial atmosphere that shaped them and that they in turn helped to shape. This is in stark contrast to the sociological accounts of sterile, desiccated working lives reported by theorists such as André Gorz and Zygmunt Bauman. The power of oral history lies in its ability to capture the lived experience of those who inhabited this time and space and in the process "rescue" those who experienced the long boom "from the enormous condescension of posterity."[87] Our job is to try to make sense of these reflections both in the context of the times they describe and in our own. The era of the long boom is a contested space for both the Left and the Right. With the passage of time and the detachment it affords, history is rewritten, reevaluated, reimagined, and overlaid by a variety of concerns.

5

CHANGE AT WORK

One of the defining images of 1970s Britain was a poster about work—or, rather, the lack of it. In 1979, the Conservative Party's advertising agency, Saatchi & Saatchi, created its iconic image of a welfare line snaking beneath the banner "Unemployment Office" under a simple tagline in uppercase, boldface, black letters: "LABOUR ISN'T WORKING." The poster purported to show vast swaths of the unemployed waiting to receive state benefits, reminding the audience that under the Labour administration of James Callaghan, unemployment stood at an unprecedentedly high rate of just under a million people.[1] Although the poster itself had limited exposure during the lead-up to the 1979 election, it has taken on a half-life detached from its original context: it somehow acts as short-hand for Britain in the 1970s, or arguably the whole of the period of the postwar consensus, which was by this time being openly questioned across the political spectrum. It seems to distill the essence of a wasted decade of stagnation, labor unrest, and inflation, acting as a background to other stock images of the era of mass union meetings in factory parking lots and groups of disgruntled strikers warming themselves aside glowing braziers of hot coals on cold picketlines.[2]

During the 1980s, images of industrial militancy still dominated the visual record of the time, but they were joined by others illustrating a newer British economic order: those of workers in the financial sector speaking into what now seem like unwieldy mobile phones or barking across noisy trading floors over the tops of equally oversized desktop screens. This new economy seemed to trade in invisible commodities rather than in the manufacture of tangible things. Likewise, its workforce was younger, still male-dominated but dressed in suits rather than overalls or uniforms. If the blue-collar workers of earlier images had been bound by hierarchy, restrictive practices, and demarcation disputes about allocation of tasks, these new city workers ushered in an era of deregulation, entrepreneurship, and risk taking.[3]

Both sets of images are stereotypes, of course; the vast majority of British workers did not go on strike in the 1970s, although many were members of a trade union. Not all those employed in the financial sector were amoral traders, although the decade was marked by one financial scandal after another brought on by corporate excess. Both images do, however, mark a reimagination of the postwar world and its values. Tory prime minister Margaret Thatcher's greatest legacy was the way she oversaw a rewriting of the 1970s before, during, and after her time in power (1979 to 1990). She and others constructed the industrial unrest of late 1978 and early 1979 as the Winter of Discontent, a moment of crisis from which Britain was saved.[4] Moreover, Thatcher sought to rewrite not only the 1970s but the whole of the era of the postwar consensus, reimagining it economically, politically, socially, and culturally. In this reading, Britain's status as a "failed state" in the 1970s has its roots not just earlier in that decade but in the choices and decisions made after the Second World War, with its emphasis on social engineering, nationalization, and the managed economy. The new conservative orthodoxy portrayed the long boom era as breeding slothful management and lazy workers; compromise and accommodation had laid the seeds for economic failure. This rewriting provided the intellectual underpinning for wholesale changes to the way the state was organized and work was managed. In many ways, this is a reimagining that still has great resonance today. With the passage of time, the decade of the 1970s has become subject to greater historical scrutiny, but at the same time, the accepted political tropes about it have hardened into history.

Guinness and the Park Royal Brewery serve as an exemplar for exploring these competing images and histories. In both the brewery itself and the wider company, a consensual, paternalistic management found itself increasingly at odds with wider economic forces, shareholder demands, and market pressures. In the period from 1975 to the early 2000s, Guinness moved from a niche beer-producing group with several small subsidiaries to a huge multinational beverage group. In the process, its management style and the theory underpinning it were radically transformed. During the 1980s, the company imported a different management culture and was caught up in arguably the biggest corporate scandal of the decade. It was an era of profound transformation for the workforce at Park Royal in terms of the content and nature of work and the fundamental relationships between workers and employers. This was so complete a reimagining of work that the more benign management and work culture of the thirty years of the long boom became unimaginable, impossible, and undesirable.

THE BRITISH BREWING INDUSTRY IN THE POSTWAR PERIOD

So how did Guinness fit into the wider context of the brewing sector in Britain from the 1950s and 1960s until the 1980s? Management in the UK brewing industry has been heavily criticized, with brewery leaders characterized as complacent, amateurish, and tradition bound.[5] The industry was run on "gentlemanly" lines, with little competition between companies. The sector comprised a few large regional or national players and a plethora of smaller, highly localized breweries that dominated particular towns or cities. In 1964, *The Economist* was damning: "Traditionalist, paternalistic, inbred, secretive—Britain's brewing industry slumbered through the nineteen fifties, hogging over £1,000 million of capital . . . A picturesque dinosaur. A declining industry."[6]

This paternalistic atmosphere was reinforced by the recruitment at management and board levels from the ranks of the landed gentry, senior military officers, and brewers' sons educated at private schools, a situation one commentator described as imparting a "squirearchical atmosphere in the board room."[7] During the 1950s, beer consumption had been static at around 25 million bulk barrels, but thereafter it began to grow to a high of 42.1 million by 1979, an increase of 71 percent or 2.5 percent per year.[8] This was part of a wider expansion in the consumption of alcohol in the period, including wines, spirits, and cider, reflecting population growth and greater postwar affluence. Most of the beer consumed in Britain was domestically produced. An important feature of the industry was its vertical integration, with brewers of all sizes acting as both producers and retailers of beer through the network of pubs they owned (known as a tied estate).[9] These could be small-scale local brewers, but increasingly the sector was becoming subject to mergers and takeovers. The number of brewing companies fell by 32 percent between 1950 and 1960—from 362 to 247—with the process accelerating toward the end of the decade.[10]

This trend was a result of a number of pressures on small brewers, such as greater competition from other chains, changing consumer demand, and especially sales of alcohol through off-license premises (liquor stores) and supermarkets. There was also a collective fear that if breweries did not expand, they would themselves fall prey to takeover or hostile merger. By the early 1970s, six big brewing companies emerged, formed out of multiple mergers: Allied (Ind Coope), Bass, Courage, Scottish and Newcastle, Watneys, and Whitbread. The largest of these by 1970 was Bass, with a market value of £330 million and a tied estate of 9,450 pubs.[11] A 1967 government Monopolies and Mergers Commission report found that the Big Six had a combined market share of approximately 68 percent; they operated around seventy breweries nationally (29 percent of the total). This same group owned 37,340 pubs, or 52 percent of the national total.[12]

During the 1970s, the dynamic within the industry changed even more as the Big Six expanded into other sectors such as food, drink, tobacco, and leisure and entertainment businesses. These trends were a recognition that pubs needed to be more than simply a place where liquor was sold. These mergers represented a huge shift from the traditional world of the brewers; the emphasis shifted from production to marketing. The creation of large conglomerates with considerable monopoly worried both government and consumer groups.[13]

Where did Guinness fit into this changed commercial landscape, and how did it develop in these years? Guinness was unique among the large brewers in Britain because it never attempted to create a network of pubs. It owned one pub near its hop farm at Bodiam, Kent, and its staff club at Park Royal.

Management had chosen not to create a tied estate because it wished to sell its stout to all of the other brewers, fearing that if it did own pubs, these would be seen as competition. Guinness, by any measure, was a large player within the sector: it was in effect the seventh member of the Big Six, enjoying 6 to 8 percent beer market share over the period.[14] It occupied its singular position through a combination of factors. Its stout was a popular product that sold well; hence, other breweries could stock it in their tied premises to complement their own range of beer. Guinness originally sold its product only in bottles, and often it allowed different brewers to bottle the beer themselves, therefore enjoying a further margin on sales.[15] Guinness was also positioned as a premium product with a greater margin than competitors' beers, making it an attractive line that had to be stocked by both brewers and pub landlords. This combination of factors gave Guinness many advantages but also made it vulnerable commercially, especially at a time when mergers and acquisitions were increasing the market power of the industry's big players. As far back as 1950, Park Royal managing director Sir Hugh Beaver (knighted in 1943) had warned his board that higher concentration in the sector would lead to greater competition from larger firms.[16] Jonathan Guinness, a family board member, explored this tension in his book *Requiem for a Family Business*:

> The core business was still stout-brewing in the British Isles. This always benefited from the enormous, though intangible, strength of the brand name; but at the same time it suffered from what I have nicknamed the Cuckoo Factor, the fact that most Guinness had to be sold in other companies' pubs. The way this affected Company decisions varied according to whether the Managing Directors were feeling confident or worried. When they were feeling confident it was regarded as if anything an asset; Guinness after all, got by without the need to run thousands of small catering businesses that tied up capital, required constant new injections for renovation and wasted management time.[17]

The other side to this equation was, as he went on to explain, that:

> The Company was to an important extent in the hands of its rivals, that every time it put up the price of its product, the other breweries which were its main customers could add more on for bottling and selling it. In theory there was also the nightmare that one of the bigger brewers might take it into its head to brew its own stout and push it in its pubs at the expense of Guinness, even exclude Guinness completely.[18]

Guinness attempted to head off this possibility by maintaining the attractive margins for its trade customers while spending large amounts of money strengthening its brand and, therefore, its status as a "must have" product in pubs. Indeed, the company spent far more per barrel on advertising than any of its rivals and was consistently the leading advertiser, ahead of the other Big Six brewers.[19]

Guinness was also vulnerable in two other related ways. First, with the development of draught Guinness in the 1950s, bottled Guinness became less important. Initially, the draught version of the stout was supplied only to pubs that were not owned by other breweries (freehouses). During the 1960s, draught keg beer became increasingly popular, and while sales rose, the margins the company had enjoyed fell.[20] Second, the 1960s saw important shifts in the consumption of beer: lighter, continental lager became more popular. Guinness had been at the forefront of this trend with the development of Harp Lager, which it introduced in 1961. Guinness formed a consortium to produce and market this new beer but once again was vulnerable to the "Cuckoo Factor" in that rival brewers could develop their own brands. From virtually no production and consumption of lager in the British market, sales grew steadily during the next quarter of a century. In 1971, 33 million barrels of ale and stout were sold but just 4 million barrels of lager, but by 1985, the figures were 23 million and 16 million, respectively, marking a significant shift away from traditional domestic beers.[21]

Guinness was, therefore, in a strange position. It was profitable, indeed highly so at times. Its core product, stout, continued to sell well, and it was involved in a fast-growing new beer in the form of the Harp Lager consortium. However, Guinness remained vulnerable to shifts in market demand and highly dependent on the goodwill of a small number of increasingly concentrated and powerful brewers who, at any time, could choose to stop selling its beer. While sales increased during this time, its margins were squeezed as the share of less profitable draught beer increased at the expense of the higher-margin bottled variety.

During the 1960s and 1970s, Guinness management chose to square this circle in a number of ways: the company maintained good relations with other brewers, allowing them healthy margins on its product; it did not attempt to build a retail empire by buying pubs; and it chose to share the brewing of its lager with other brewers. All these tactics were designed not to antagonize the Big Six. This strategy also led to a program of acquisition of companies and products outside of the brewing industry, including confectionery, newsagents (newsstands), health clubs, vacation companies, publishing, plastics, and pharmaceuticals. Some of these it acquired almost on a whim. In retrospect, this attempt to diversify, while sound in principle, was deeply flawed in practice: these various undertakings consumed a disproportionate amount of management time and capital in areas where the company had little or no expertise.[22] While some of these new undertakings contributed to profits, the core business of brewing was far and away the strongest and most successful part of the business.

In *Requiem*, Jonathan Guinness divided into four unequal parts the company's fortunes in the period from Beaver's retirement in 1960 to Ernest Saunders's arrival in 1981. During the early 1960s, there was progress, but profits tended to remain steady. From the late 1960s until 1972, this progress created profits. However, from 1973 to 1979, profits hid underlying problems with the business.

Finally, results in 1980 and 1981 were poor.[23] The problem for the company was that its core business needed new investment just as a recession struck in the late 1970s and as beer sales, which had risen consistently since the 1950s, began to decline. In part, this fall in demand was the result of increasing unemployment among blue-collar male drinkers, many of whom consumed Guinness.

ERNEST SAUNDERS AND THE TRANSFORMATION OF GUINNESS

The arrival of Ernest Saunders at Guinness in October 1981 was a pivotal event in the company's history, and nothing would really be the same after that date. His role in the organization's future shape and the changes he wrought laid the foundation for the creation of a global beverage firm in the late 1990s. But he was a controversial and divisive figure.[24]

The catalyst for Saunders's appointment was the catastrophic collapse in profits in the nonbrewing parts of the Guinness group. These results began to erode the company's position as a reliable blue-chip investment, making it vulnerable to a takeover. Guinness decided it would look outside the firm for a new man, and eventually they appointed Saunders, who had held posts in advertising and brand management roles in a number of large firms, including 3M, Schweppes, Beechams, Great Universal Stores, and finally Nestlé. According to his son James's book, *Nightmare*, Saunders was fairly damning of what he found when appointed; there is talk of his "salvaging the company."[25] Saunders related how his father began reading up on the company before he formally started in the post and was critical of what he was and was not sent to read:

> The documents turned out to be a mish-mash of unrelated material, ranging from a history of the Dublin brewery since the early years of the century to a philosophical treatise by Tony Purssell on possible ways for the company to move forward in the 1980s. What was missing was any factual data on how the group was doing now.[26]

The package given to Saunders included excerpts from *Guinness Time*, notes on the brewing process, and notable events in the life of the Park Royal brewery. It was clear that whoever had put the file together expected that this would be useful background material, essential reading for someone new to the business and the sector.[27] It also speaks to the corporate sense of the importance of the past and the clear expectation that this knowledge would be absorbed. The contrast between the expectation embodied in the file and Saunders's dismissal of it as an irrelevant "mish-mash" shows the gulf between the traditional Guinness management and a newer style of corporate governance interested squarely in financial figures.

Saunders's book is peppered with less-than-flattering accounts of the role of the Guinness family in the firm, especially at the board level:

His anxieties were increased by the first board meeting. He had only met a few directors before. "The family behaved as if it was still their private business, rather than being a public company with a Stock Exchange listing."[28] Lord Iveagh was the chairman. Simon Lennox-Boyd, later Lord Boyd, became vice-chairman after his mother retired from the board, Jonathan and Finn Guinness, two sons of Lord Moyne, a former vice-chairman, were directors. Edward and Peter Guinness, from different branches of the family, were also on the board, but not considered full family members.[29]

Nightmare is laden with metaphors of aristocratic decline; at one point the author likens the company to a crumbling stately home: "The Guinness Company that my father inherited was like a large, genteel family mansion that had been allowed to decay through neglect. Contrary to the public's image of the company, it was near to collapse."[30]

This impression, and its subsequent retelling, framed Guinness as being run by well-meaning, aristocratic amateurs out of touch with modern management techniques. And while they had made the mess, Ernest Saunders, according to *Nightmare*, felt that "my clear impression was that from that moment the company's many problems had been pushed clearly and squarely on to my lap. I was surrounded by the representatives of the major shareholders, but it was up to me to sort out the mess."[31] He quickly went about creating a new corporate strategy for the firm, appointing outside management consultants Bain and Company. He assessed what he called Guinness's "higgledy-piggledy string of diversifications" spread over the previous twenty-five years:

> In the earlier days there had been some production-based rationale behind some of the diversification decisions . . . but there appeared to have been no coherent strategy behind the non-brewing acquisitions in market terms, no real consideration of the expertise needed to manage businesses that were completely outside the board's personal expertise, and no thought of the difficulties in maintaining adequate control over such a large number of different activities with the unsophisticated systems in place at that time.[32]

Saunders's strategy was a dramatic slash-and-burn exercise in disinvestment, disposing of one subsidiary after another; during his first two years he sold off or closed 140 of its 300 subsidiaries.[33] One former Guinness employee remarked, "Not to put too fine a point on it—and Ernest Saunders certainly didn't—he came, he saw, and he kicked ass! We had never seen anything like it."[34] Profits began to dramatically improve from this point, but there was still the question of the historical underinvestment in the core brewing infrastructure of the business. A hundred million pounds was required to refurbish the Dublin brewery, and significant sums were also needed at Park Royal. Productivity at both plants was low compared to industry standards at the time. This was because not enough had been invested in the plants and because "management was also highly paternalistic and inefficient."[35]

Ernest Saunders's account of this time is revealing, if somewhat self-serving. He said that the Park Royal brewery "had been designed by the architect of Battersea Power Station—and looked it. The condition of the building was appalling, and so was the morale among its management and workforce. Someone remarked that the offices were more akin to a mental asylum."[36]

Saunders portrayed himself as a heroic savior of the business, recounting in *Nightmare* that he reshaped attitudes and galvanized the Park Royal staff singlehandedly. His narrative is peppered with anecdotes of how he persuaded and cajoled staff and management in the face of opposition. He described the relationships he built with key figures in management and labor:

> I consulted Maurice Freeman, the wise head of personnel. He was an old-timer who nevertheless was exceptionally helpful to me and keen to see the company survive. He had excellent relations with the unions, especially their leader, Larry Grogan, and started to prepare the ground. I met union representatives to explain the urgent necessity for action, and indicated my determination to do something about sales.[37]

Initially, Saunders remembered, his pleas were met with skepticism by the union, but Freeman talked them around to the point where the labor side had two questions for Saunders:

> They wanted to know whether Ernest would deal with Irish costs as well, because they had the natural union suspicion that the plan was ultimately to close Park Royal and import all the stout from Dublin. Second, the union representatives were unequivocally contemptuous of the management's lethargy in recent years; they wanted an assurance that Ernest would sort this out, and cut administrative and other costs as well. Ernest: "I gave them a positive response to both points, and even expressed my determination not to just keep Park Royal open but to get morale up and the place humming again."[38]

Saunders's strategy was undoubtedly successful in terms of increases in profit margin and the company's share price. When he joined Guinness in 1981, the share price stood at 49 pence, giving a market capitalization of £90 million. By 1984, shares were up to £1.20, giving a market capitalization of £200 million, a figure that still kept the firm outside the top one hundred listed companies in the United Kingdom.[39]

BUILDING A CONGLOMERATE

But Saunders was not content to just brew and sell stout at a greater profit margin. After divesting Guinness of many of its unprofitable subsidiaries, he embarked on an acquisition spree, this time in a more focused way and with greater success. This strategy was set against a wider background of corporate empire building based on mergers and acquisitions. The City of London (the financial district of London) was awash in "hot money" during the early 1980s, making financiers very enthusiastic to support takeovers, hostile or otherwise. This was driven by capital from Japan, Germany, the United States, and the United Kingdom. Investors seeking high returns and quick turnarounds were encouraged by loose regulation and eager merchant banks. Saunders's success in turning around Guinness's fortunes and in his positive initial forays into new areas such as leisure and spirits made him popular with investors.

This febrile City atmosphere meant that any company that was not expanding could become subject to a takeover bid. Guinness bid for Bells Whisky in June 1985. Bell's was a larger company, but after a protracted battle it became part of Guinness later that year.[40] The logic of the Bells takeover was partially driven by the Cuckoo Factor, as it allowed Guinness to win scale in a related business without antagonizing the rest of the brewing industry. This same logic lay behind its even more ambitious bid for the Distillers Company, which owned an extensive portfolio of famous spirit brands. The competition for Distillers was a bitter one between Guinness and the Argyll Group, with offers topping £2.5 billion. Although Guinness, in the summer of 1986, was finally the winning bidder, creating a far larger beverage conglomerate, it was at a huge cost in terms of finances and reputation.

The bid engineered by Saunders and a group of trusted lieutenants was achieved by artificially inflating the company's own share price by routing funds to friendly third parties. These companies and individuals would then purchase Guinness stock on the understanding that the company would buy it back if the third parties experienced losses. This was done without the knowledge of most of those working for Guinness or of other board members. In many ways, this was a very 1980s financial scandal involving some of the most famous names in the City of London and beyond, including Gerald Ronson, Sir Jack Lyons, and Ivan Boesky, the disgraced New York arbitrageur and insider trader turned FBI informant. Saunders himself was eventually sentenced to five years in prison for his role in the affair.[41]

A great deal has been written about the Guinness affair and Saunders's role in it. It was, and remains, one of the most high-profile examples of financial scandal, of the insider trading and corporate excess of the 1980s.[42] But it also is an important marker in a decade that changed the rules as to how companies were to carry themselves, shifting from what some might pejoratively describe as a more benign, even gentlemanly capitalism toward one driven by more narrowly defined and interpreted balance sheets; from stakeholder to shareholder capitalism.[43]

The 1980s also marked a shift from production-led organizations to a far greater emphasis on sales, marketing, and brand management, where the product itself was less important than the brand. In the case of Guinness, this change was reflected in the relationship between Saunders and Edward Guinness. Saunders rescued the organization from failing or becoming a takeover target and then oversaw exponential growth in the company in the mid-1980s. Guinness, by contrast, had been a manager and later a director of the firm for four decades. He was one of the last remaining family members on the board and the person chosen to tell Saunders, when the scandal became public, that he had to step down. But Guinness revealed ambivalence and a set of contradictory emotions toward Saunders and the latter's role in the company. On the one hand, he admired Saunders and his achievements at the firm, recognizing Saunders had turned Guinness from a relatively small brewing concern with a mixed portfolio of subsidiary businesses into a global beverage multinational, Diageo.[44] In an oral history interview, he looked back on the Saunders era:

> But it was so unfortunate what was happening. The confidence came back with Ernest Saunders; I mean, he really sort of got behind the marketing and that sort of thing and he just breathed new life into it. And, I mean, the extraordinary thing is because Ernest Saunders ended up at Ford Open Prison, and obviously it was very wrong what actually happened—but there's absolutely no doubt that it was he who really brought Guinness back, to being a force. And now it's gone on to be Diageo when it joined forces with Grand Metropolitan, as now I think it's the world's major drinks company. I mean, I think, looking back if I was asked to name five people who had come into my life other than my parents who had influenced my thinking, he would have to be one of those five. Because it was astonishing how he could face fantastic odds and still somehow pull through.[45]

He went on:

> Yes, I was loyal to him, because I could—I felt at that particular time, the only way Guinness was going to get out of trouble it was in, I mean the share price went down to about eighty, something like that. The only way we were going to get out was through him. His management style when he came in was to bring in Bains, the management consultants; suddenly the department were flooded with—they were called Bainites. They were sort of investigating every department and bringing in a lot of innovations that were improving the situation quite considerably. So I was loyal to him. I remained loyal to him right up to the sort of last stage when I had the unenviable task of final thing of telling him had to stand aside, because I was the senior executive director at that time. And yes, that was a memorable but highly distasteful evening.[46]

It is clear both from this interview and from his public statements that Guinness was conflicted in his reflections on Saunders: great respect was tempered with obvious regret. But there is also a tension at the heart of his own ambivalence, as Saunders in some ways took advantage of his sense of duty and morality toward the company, using an older way of doing business in a highly instrumental way to break down tradition.[47] Nowhere is this more clearly spelled out than when Guinness describes the way Saunders described him:

> Ernest Saunders said to me, and this was the fourth, I think, occasion . . . "I've always regarded you as the . . . conscience of the Company," and I hope I didn't sound over petulant on that last occasion I said, "Ernest, how could a conscience operate when it doesn't know what's going on?" Which I think unfortunately was true.[48]

In his interview this tension was nowhere more apparent than in Saunders's portrayal of Guinness as being on the point of total collapse before he was appointed. In part, Edward Guinness's motivation for editing and publishing of *The Guinness Book of Guinness*, an anthology marking the fiftieth anniversary of the Park Royal brewery, was to rescue and defend the reputation of the firm and those who had worked in it before the Saunders era As he noted:

> Yes, I mean, we had some very gifted people at that time and, as I say, starting off *The Guinness Book of Guinness*, it was partly that I was very anxious to sort of carry on with the research I'd been doing. But Ernest Saunders rubbished anything that happened in Guinness before he came in I was very anxious to show that there had been some wonderful [people] associated with Guinness over the years. And that was one of the motivations as far as *The Guinness Book of Guinness* was concerned.[49]

In his memoir, *A Brewer's Tale*, Edward Guinness goes into greater depth about the process of editing the anthology:

> Further it was coming very soon after the debacle and the timing might be considered questionable—indeed to my regret two good friends wrote expressing vehement disapproval. In fact I was only too well aware that Ernest had invariably disparaged the quality of past Guinness management and one of my aims was to portray the many people who had brought real success to the Park Royal Brewery through their technical, marketing and human resources skills.[50]

There is, then, both in his interview and autobiographical writing, a great sense of the importance of the historical record. As in his earlier editing of *Guinness Time*, Edward Guinness was attempting to capture oral history, memories, and simple anecdotes so that history would have an afterlife beyond the immediate events of a corporate scandal and a conscious and deliberate rewriting of history on the part of Saunders and his supporters.

Listening to his interview, reading his reflections, and dipping into the anthology itself, the reader is struck by the passing of an old order, the marking of events from a different time. While we are being invited to remember, these accounts are sealing a time off from the present, in part because the culture they describe seems so different from the present. So *The Guinness Book of Guinness*, even as it was published in 1988, was describing an altogether different corporate landscape, a culture made residual by changing markets, management trends, and fashion and by a transformation of the way work was organized and conceived. The Park Royal anthology becomes, then, an exercise in reflective and perhaps critical nostalgia, not in an overtly challenging sense but rather suggesting a different history and narrative.

REIMAGINING WORK AND THE ORGANIZATION IN THE 1980S

Events at Guinness, internally and externally, mirrored a much wider set of trends and contexts, regional, national, and global—a reimagining of work and organizations during this time. Park Royal had represented a common trend among UK businesses during the long boom era. With its vertical and horizontal integration, undertaking virtually all tasks in house, and its settled patterns of recruitment and promotion under a fairly benign paternalistic management, Guinness was not an unusual firm of the period. Certainly Park Royal was an extreme version of this pattern due to its size, profitability, and paternalistic roots, but many of these features were common enough in the period across the public and private sectors.[51] Significant change in work and organizations occurred during the 1970s and 1980s as a series of crises hit the international economy—the oil price shock of the early 1970s, growing levels of international competition, higher unemployment, and growing inflation all took their toll.[52] Organizationally, the response was a reconceptualization of work in the 1980s. In essence, firms increasingly shifted away from the kind of integration realized at Park Royal toward a model based on flexibility, outsourcing, and the creation of internal markets. A model of business as a unified entity, albeit one divided into divisions, was replaced by a different vision that fundamentally questioned the role and value of each part and purpose of the organization. Many companies adopted programs aimed at changing management culture, introduced greater flexibility in staffing, or simply pulled out of whole areas of the market.[53]

Another new pressure on companies was the far greater imperative to maximize shareholder value at the expense of the interests of all other stakeholders in a listed firm. Since the 1980s, the idea of maximizing shareholder value has overridden reinvestment, one of the main aims of corporate managers in the long boom. The previous policy of "retain and reinvest" reflected the far greater discretion open to senior managers during the long boom to decide how profits were allocated. During that period, corporations tended to retain both money they earned and the people they employed; these practices allowed companies to grow, retain staff, and provide attractive working conditions. This position was undermined through the 1980s by economic theory that privileged the power and interests of shareholders over those of managers and promoted debt-leveraged buyouts and takeovers to increase the value of stock shares.[54]

The previous strategy of retain and invest had laid the foundation for the creation of many of the good jobs for blue- and white-collar workers in corporations in the United States, the United Kingdom, and elsewhere.[55] By implication, the stress placed on shareholder value eroded that stable base for investment and with it one of the main incentives to share profits within organizations.[56]

These ideas on shareholder value need to be combined with a critical discussion of the use of market mechanisms within parts of the organization. These were designed to discipline managers, supervisors, and especially workers, making individuals and groups aware of their role in a supply chain or market relationship. Relationships based on a shared company or trade identity were first overlaid and then replaced by contractual ones based on roles of customer and supplier. Recently, US economist David Weil has written of what he labels the "fissured workplace," the way large corporations engage in a whole host of strategies that break up organizational structure through strategies such as outsourcing, franchising, and subcontracting. This is efficient in the sense that it enables large firms to reduce their liability for a whole host of aspects of their business, allowing them to concentrate on brand management and expansion, while the task of day-to-day management resides with subcontractors of various types.[57] All these aspects of corporate governance mark a profound shift in the way work and the corporation are managed and conceptualized—and many if not all of these features of the new capitalism were present at Park Royal.

CHANGE ON THE SHOP FLOOR

How did the work and careers of Guinness employees at Park Royal develop as a result of these reorganizations and restructurings, how did they experience change, and what did they feel about it at the time? Many of the workers were interviewed after the closure had been announced but before it actually took place in 2005 as part of an oral history project about the brewery. Memories of the Saunders period and subsequent events were framed by a longer-term understanding of what the reforms of the 1980s and 1990s had ultimately produced. There was an attempt to interpret the present through the past, but these narratives frame their understandings through *both* the pre- and post-Saunders eras. Each interview shares a complicated relationship with the multiple pasts being remembered. While the workers were critical of the Saunders period, and especially the methods he employed, they show more than a grudging respect for the strategies adopted by Guinness under his leadership, a concession that some form of change was necessary and inevitable. However, the interviews also demonstrate their continued attempt to find value in an older remembered past, a desire within the interview to make sense of change while not diminishing an older culture in which the workforce, individually and collectively, found value. There is a reflection on a process of disembedding, how workplace culture is disrupted and uprooted. This is evident in the process of job loss and the physical removal of former workmates but also in the narrowing of the spaces where the social networks and relationships can occur and thrive.

One of the most noteworthy things about the interviews is how little Saunders figures in individual narratives. In striking contrast to his own account in *Nightmare* of his supposedly singlehanded efforts to turn Park Royal around, those who worked there barely mentioned him. Henry Dawson remembered the period of austerity the Saunders era ushered in:

> He made a big bad impression, in the fact that he decided that things couldn't go on the way they were. I mean, we thought that we were still making money, good money. Our sales were good. We were selling more than Dublin, things like that. But all of a sudden the big children's thing that they had in the summer, the summer fête: canceled. "Not doing that any more, costs too much money." In the scheme of things it was a drop in the ocean. But it was the penny-pinching with him that upset everybody. He kind of wanted to do away with everything. He wanted to do away with meals in the canteen, where you had—instead of getting free meals you pay for them. And, to be honest, I think that at the time a lot of the people said, "That's okay, if it's gonna be subsidized." But it came out that no, you would pay the full price and all of this. Okay, fine: don't give us meals, we'll have sandwiches, we'll bring our own sandwiches in, if that's what you wanna do, but you won't get the respect of the work from the people that you used to get.[58]

Dawson's narrative displayed a defensive morality, a sense that the business was making money and yet an older set of values was being unraveled. He fatalistically accepted the withdrawal of established terms and conditions but at the cost of respect and good will. This morality was evident when he discussed Saunders's fate: "Yeah, he wasn't a very liked man, and when things developed and things come out of what he was doing higher up, I think a lot of people didn't have a lot of sympathy for him."[59]

Barry Hubbard touched on the same point, but his account reflected on some of the structural issues that Park Royal faced at the time:

> It went a bit haywire when Ernest Saunders took over, but that was probably a selfish reason, you know, because he tightened everything up, and if he hadn't of done, and some of the things he did do, perhaps we wouldn't have been here now. We might have gone under because I think the Guinness family weren't really running it properly. As I say, we were well over-staffed and I think it probably would have gone downhill, and it probably wouldn't have existed if someone had taken it over.[60]

This interview, too, is a complex narration of events, evidencing a dislike of some changes enacted by Saunders coupled with more than a grudging acceptance of their necessity in staving off the closure of the brewery for another two decades. It also offers a critique of previous management under the Guinness family, but this centers on their failure to properly invest in modern labor-saving technology.

David Hughes, a manager at Guinness, noticed the difference when he returned to Park Royal after an overseas posting: "Saunders was a new broom and was going to sweep them away, or sweep all the old traditions away, which they were terrified about, but many of the old traditions needed to go anyway. They were out of date and holding the Company back."[61]

Hughes is a fascinating character, embodying simultaneously a deep love of Guinness as an organization, its brand, and many of the people who worked there while highly critical of some individuals and the more general workplace culture. Frustrated by his lack of power to manage at Park Royal, Hughes took another post in the company. As he explained: "I went overseas then, I got fed up with the brewery, and went to Nigeria, tried to get out of the UK and leave it all behind."[62] But he contrasted the organization he had left with the one he found on his return:

> When I came back, Saunders was in. The new regime was in. He'd told the unions to tear up the rulebook. He'd emaciated the unions actually. He'd taken them on, head on, and said, "Look, I'll close the brewery unless you play ball here." When I came back as a manager in '82, I was allowed to manage. Personnel had stood back. Suddenly, I actually had responsibility and authority.[63]

He emphasized how important Saunders and the changes he had enacted at the brewery had been:

> '79, '79/'80 was a watershed. It's when Saunders came in and the whole thing was heading right down the pan. I mean, I think the company was close to closure. Oh yeah, I don't think it was too far away. I think it was close to probably to being bought out, you know, somebody would buy the brand, Heineken would take it over and brew it in a more modern plant. Park Royal was falling apart. Dublin was part-modernized but still had a lot of bad old areas. So it was an interesting period. I mean, Guinness has come way through now, so it's actually on a good footing now. But they were turbulent times, and it was the end of the old regime and the start of the new regime.[64]

Hughes contrasted that old regime with the new:

> Diageo is a modern company, with all the modern attributes—you know, that sort of slightly impersonal attitude to people, whereas old Guinness that I remember was very comforting to people, was very careful not to tread on toes, and didn't want people unhappy, and didn't want disputes, and wanted the union happy.[65]

Hughes's critique was largely based on what he perceived as the conservatism of more senior managers, what he described as "old brewing types" who while intellectually bright were limited in their knowledge and experience of wider management trends, often having joined Guinness straight from elite universities. Saunders, on the other hand, had a deliberate policy of bringing in outsiders. At one point, Hughes compared and contrasted these new arrivals with the old order:

> These were really competent people, and we respected them. Whereas the old out-going brewers, we loved them to bits and we liked them as people and admired them, but in terms of respect, I don't think managerially we respected them that much, because they were failing, and we could see where that failure was going.[66]

Changes to working practices after Saunders's arrival were driven by capital investment in plant and machinery with greater levels of automation. With each round of investment and reorganization came redundancies (or layoffs) and changes to the nature of work and how it was managed. Ray Snook, who began his working life in 1960 as a coppersmith, detailed the changes:

> I mean, we've gone from 220 people four years ago down to 80 now, if you go back to the '70s, there was a lot more. Like I said, every tradesmen had a mate, not only coppersmiths, every fitter had a mate, every electrician had a mate. Those roles have gradually dwindled. Automation has made a big hole in the workforce, but that is progress, I suppose.[67]

Snook was describing how this gradual process of change had fundamentally transformed the workplace culture that had socialized him and that he had valued, which he felt had *made* him. He wanted the listener to hear a balanced account of the past and to understand why the workforce looked as it did then and how it was efficient in its own terms and in the context of its time. He illustrated one aspect of automation and its impact on efficiency and levels of labor:

> Yeah, well, the automation has lost a lot of jobs. I mean, go to the kegging line over there now. We had two old kegging lines that probably did four hundred or six hundred [barrels] a shift, it's eight thousand and ten thousand a shift now, or more than that. The kegging line's capable of doing a thousand an hour; it's no-where near the four hundred an hour, the old lines. It's a massive difference, so that is automation.[68]

Snook stressed at the end of this quote that the efficiency was won by introducing new technology rather than simply stripping out wasteful, unproductive labor.

Dawson also spoke of the way the job changed both in terms of management and the increasing levels of machinery and computer control:

> I think in the '80s we started to get rid of the brewers and head brewers. I think the management structures changed, which meant that I was a supervisor then. And we took over the roles of the brewers and under brewers, done all the office work, which was quite a big challenge really. But it worked; it did work. And then, from then on, of course, computerization started to take over and things started to change slightly. The centrifuges we had, the old centrifuges, they started to be more modern, where you didn't have to do so much work to set them up and things like

that. And they were more controlled by small parts of computerization, and then they just got bigger.[69]

Dawson and several of his colleagues stressed that these changes were gradual, with waves of new technology, new management regimes, and layoffs occurring over the two decades beginning in the early 1980s. One of the managers on the site, Alan Mudie, described the succession of investments:

A lot of the old plant was falling apart so we had to do some quick fixes and some new plant to cover it. And that led to a £53 million project in 1993 called Project Robin, which involved a lot of new plant but also change in working conditions and a reduction in numbers from 500 down to 250 and basically changes in all the ways we worked, so elimination of demarcation lines, so all demarcation lines in the south have gone . . . so it's something that we're very proud of that we did, and we went through that process of change and there was big training issues because a lot of people had been working in the physical plant environment, either manual tasks of manually opening valves and pressing buttons to start plant. This was now moving into computerized equipment and full automation.[70]

For many of the process workers, this change in the content of work was a welcome one as it made their jobs more interesting and varied. One, John Woodgate, described the change he had experienced:

Definitely recently what has happened is the attitude of the blokes on the shop floor has changed, yes, definitely for the better because as they've been given more responsibility they've accepted it and taken it on and they're not having somebody looking over their shoulder all the time. I don't know how this compares with other industries, but it seems to have taken a long time to realize that you don't need three managers for every five blokes; it always seemed overmanaged to me. And that is the biggest change I've seen is the decimation of the management structure, more than like the shop floor, although that has been decimated. And the technical advances as well. I sit in front of computer screens now, whereas before I was having to hump and lift.[71]

Dave Bathurst's account is typical of the way workers elided many of the changes that had occurred at Park Royal over a twenty-five-year period:

Certainly in Saunders's time, in the early '80s, I think it became quite clear then to all of us that the sort of job for life, the family bit, was going. It was still there, but a lot of new people came in, turnover of staff increased, particularly on the sales, marketing, and finance side. Not so much on production because you made something, there you were, and heads disappeared but there wasn't new people coming in because you didn't replace, you were looking to reduce numbers. So by then I think people started to sense that it wasn't a job for life. Then, going on another ten years or so, certainly the emphasis has switched. There'd been numbers of redundancy programs and cost-cutting exercises. A lot of jobs were being outsourced.[72]

This sense of a continuing process of rationalization is reflected in the accounts of many of those who made it through to the final closure of Park Royal in 2005. The narrative of continual and gradual erosion is one that helps to contextualize the interviews themselves and the staff's acceptance of the closure. What is clear, however, is that they remembered the period from the early 1980s as a time of continuous change and insecurity. That decade was an uncertain one for many blue-collar manual workers, with similar stories of automation, redundancies, and industrial change replicated across the UK economy. The Guinness workers recounted that period at a time of even more heightened uncertainty—the closure of the brewery. The earlier parts of the interviews focused on more benign times; these were not static, certainly, but they represented a time of greater order and predictability in the workers' lives. It was these earlier times that they remembered fondly and that acted as a critical foil to the post-1980 changes to the working environment.[73]

The experience of being laid off was common in the interviews recorded around the time of the closure but was also present in discussions with those who had left the brewery earlier. Terry Aldridge worked at Park Royal from 1975 to 1995, when he was laid off in one of the waves of downsizing. Aldridge broached this topic having just described the culture of joking and fun in the brewery. Discussing what work meant to many of his former colleagues, he chose to explain it through the layoffs of the time and the impact they had on some:

> Excuse the pun, but it's like they not only make Guinness, they drink Guinness, they live Guinness, it's in their blood. And of course when the redundancy schemes come up, blimey, I seen guys that are bawling their eyes out, because they'd been made redundant. They'd been there for years. And they didn't meet the criteria for the next—I don't know if you know that the original brewery was decommissioned, built a new plant at the back for making Guinness and when the old one was decommissioned they didn't need half the staff. This is the idea of it, if you can go auto[mated] you can get rid of surplus staff, and that's when the redundancy came in. And we were all told, bye-bye, there's your redundancy and you're off. Certain people were left to be trained up to work the new brewery which was all computer controlled. If you didn't reach that criteria through the training, you were out. I think I failed—I can't remember what I did fail on.[74]

Aldridge described the aptitude tests that he and his fellow workers had to take as part of the assessment of who was to stay. These assessments took no account of seniority, disrupting another long-standing workplace norm.

Later in his interview, Aldridge returned to the topic of his own layoff:

> I knew that redundancies were on the cards, and I knew when the date was and obviously prepared myself for it. But when I left—again, as I was saying earlier

on—why me? Why not him? It's a kind of a stigma to be offmade redundant [laid off]—the thing is, you're not made redundant, it's the job that's redundant, isn't it.[75]

I asked him whether he felt angry at the time.

No, I wasn't angry. No, I didn't feel angry about it. There were some guys there that were in tears. Absolutely in tears! God, I mean they'd been here for years. Supervisors bawling their eyes out, I mean, it was very, very upsetting for them. But they had to go now to meet what was outside and get on with it. No, I wasn't angry, I was—all I can say is I was very proud to work for the company because they certainly didn't do me any harm, they looked after me.[76]

Another worker, Mick Costello, described in detail the gradual change in the atmosphere from the 1980s on. I asked whether he had expected his working life to change so much:

It might, it'll probably, sound naïve, but no. Because you were in such a nice, cuddly environment, you know you never envisaged the fact that things might just get harder. And to a certain extent, all that's happened is that we've just grown up with it. As the company's been forced to change, so have we. And you realize then for the first time that you've been put under pressure when you have to go through psychometric testing, et cetera, just to keep your job—just to prove you are good enough. I can remember at the time, when it first happened, I felt very, very much under pressure and I felt sorry for the people that were older than me at the time because they wouldn't have sat exams for maybe thirty years. So it must have been awful for them.[77]

Costello and others spoke about how alien this new way of being managed was and how different it felt from the workplace culture into which they had been socialized. All of the interviewees emphasized the continuous, open-ended nature of change after the first major rationalization in the 1980s, in stark contrast to the previous stability. As Costello explained:

I mean, psychometric testing is just part. I mean, to be put under that sort of pressure was incredible. The first major stuff would have been in probably about '88 and then it's been quite regular ever since; it's been a trimming process, gradually whittling down all the time.[78]

Most of the workers interviewed around the time of the plant closure mentioned having to reapply for their jobs through the various rounds of layoffs and rationalizations. It was striking how this process had been normalized by those who had undergone the experience; Hubbard's account was typical:

I mean, I've had a few ups and downs, you know, especially when . . . I think three times now we've had to reapply for jobs, you know, our own jobs, when they have been making redundancies. So, yeah, it's a bit nerve-wracking, but I always ended up with a job, so, you know, I wasn't one of the ones that didn't get a job.[79]

There were a number of aspects to the general sense of insecurity that the workforce at Park Royal had experienced over the two decades preceding the eventual closure. In essence, these were different aspects of a fragmentation brought about by the introduction of the market mechanism in the company. It was clear that the workers on site, even if they did not agree with these changes, had internalized the logic of such pressures. As Bathurst explained:

> There was then a huge investment program on the site ten years ago. So, in about 1991/92/93, a lot of the old plant was at the end of its useful life. Part of the quid pro quo was that a large number of jobs disappeared and there was a reorganization. It was fairly clear at that point that production jobs were going to go.[80]

While this sort of pressure on workers to accept changes in work practices in return for investment dated back to the 1970s, what was novel was how companies began to threaten closure on the basis of outsourcing core production altogether.[81] Bathurst remembered:

> Then, in 1999/2000, the last reorganization took place. Again, the choice for the site was quite stark. It was [Guinness management telling staff at Park Royal] "we can buy beer down the road at a significantly lower price." I think it was Scottish and Newcastle at Reading that said, "We will brew it at a significantly lower price" and the challenge was for the site: "Are you able to cut your costs? Because if not, we're going to close you." So, at that point, we went from three hundred or four hundred people down to where we currently are, which is about eighty people.[82]

What workers like Bathurst was describing were major shifts in the nature of the psychological or perhaps sociological contract between workers and employers. In addition to profound changes in technology, automation, and management, there was a fundamental transformation in the values and expectations underpinning the employment relationship in the brewery. In relating those changes, workers were lamenting not only the loss of former colleagues but also the erosion of a more secure and benign workplace culture and atmosphere they had highly prized.

As part of a process of internal marketization—the creation of competing cost centers, each with its own budget—the company split itself into various divisions and, most importantly, created an internal division between supply (production) and demand (sales). As Bathurst said:

> So I think when the supply/demand split came, that was very clearly marked out with this division between production and sales and marketing and other functions. It was made very clear to us that we were expected to stand on our own two feet, whereas not so long ago going down the road to contract through Guinness, you just wouldn't think of that. It became very clear that each site would be looked at under the microscope, costs would be examined, and if there was a more cost-effective option inside or outside of the company, that would be pursued.[83]

The workers viewed these relatively recent changes through a longer career perspective. They compared the totally integrated site of the 1950s to the late 1970s to the current situation:

> So the umbrella effect when I first joined 30-odd years ago of a total UK company that made something, marketed it, sold it, made a profit, that completely disappeared, so that now, I'd say in the last five to ten years, people have been very aware that there was no guarantee. If you weren't cost effective, then this site would go—and of course that's what's happened to us. So yes, there has been a big extreme change from where I was thirty-odd years ago to where it is now.[84]

What the new management created within the Park Royal site was effectively a series of semiautonomous cost centers, most notably the production/supply side and the marketing/demand side. In addition to this major divide, it outsourced many of the other functions of the site, such as catering, security, logistics, and the power plant. John Woodgate described this process of change in the distribution side of the brewery beginning in 1991, when he started at Park Royal:

> We had our own account fleet then, and so we were managing loads of drivers, mechanics, warehouse people, what have you. We contracted that out in '93/'94 to another company. As far as the warehousing of Guinness, we contracted out the warehousing in '95, so we then had no drivers and you were managing a contract as such. The company we gave it to failed to deliver miserably, so we terminated the contract with them in '96 and reissued a contract to the current people, TDG, who exist here at the moment, and that was for distribution only. So that was in '96; we extended that in the year 2000 to include the yard warehousing. That was contracted out, and it was added to the existing contract.[85]

Under this management strategy, the vertical and horizontal integration of an organization and the work that went on at one site is broken down, fragmented, or (to use Weil's term) "fissured." This fragmentation led to some of the workers managing relationships between the various subcontractors. As one manager observed:

> To me it's gone completely the opposite now, where it's gone from very, as I said initially, family orientated to totally impersonal. It's gone through the whole spectrum. Business does that, I understand, and change is good and I'll accept it and I'll go with it. The environment within this company at this moment in time to me is far too impersonal.[86]

When I asked about the qualitative differences this fragmentation had brought about, Ray Snook described the case of the scaffolders:

> Well, yeah, as you can see, it's not that easy to get hold of people when they're contracted out. I mean, we haven't actually got an appointed contract scaffolder at

this moment, because unless they are guaranteed a certain amount of work, they can't guarantee a certain response time, whereas a few years back, we had literally a scaffold firm on site, every day of the week. And we had lots of work going on, but that work dried up, so they weren't happy, obviously, and they said they can't afford to leave everybody here. It is hard now to get a response from a scaffold company.[87]

When I was interviewing Snook and many of the other long-serving members of Guinness staff, I kept wondering what they thought about these changes. In the case of someone like him, a time-served coppersmith who had begun his working life at Park Royal in the 1960s, I wondered how he felt about the job he now did. On one level, he had shifted to a supervisory or managerial position with less opportunity to do hands-on repair or maintenance. But on another, he was now even farther removed from the actual work, managing contractors and contracts. There was a general low-level lament in virtually all the interviews at the changes at Park Royal over the years and the deleterious effect they had had on the social atmosphere of the plant and its workplace culture.

MAKING SENSE OF CHANGE

How, then, do we make sense of the accounts given by those on or near the shop floor of their experience of two decades or more of workplace change? In the late 1980s, there was considerable skepticism among sociologists and other critical commentators on work about the scale and nature of organizational restructuring. It was clear that something was going on, but rightly there was caution about some of the more lurid claims about the changing nature of capitalism and how work was being reorganized. In particular, there was a great deal of skepticism about the idea of flexibility—the flexible firm and its associated features. In many ways, what the Guinness workers experienced was even more profound. Hearing the accounts of those who lived through this change is of critical value to historicizing these trends. All of the workers experienced one of the most extreme shifts in the way industrial work was organized and imagined. While the Park Royal site may have continuously brewed beer for nearly seven decades, the social organization of that labor and the assumptions surrounding it were, by the end of production, profoundly different from those of the 1930s.

If the earlier period, especially the thirty or so years after the end of the war, marked the high point of a more benign form of capitalism, then what unfolded after 1980 was different in almost every respect. In that earlier period, workers were treated as potential industrial citizens, subject to improvement and self-cultivation. They were encouraged to be part of the company, and they developed their own autonomous culture in and through the workplace. There were a whole series of hopes and expectations about what this positive engagement might develop, but the philosophy of work was underpinned by an unparalleled sense of optimism and a faith in coordinated collective effort. These local initiatives at Park Royal occurred within a wider expansive period in British society where real wages consistently rose and regions like London enjoyed virtually full employment throughout the period.

In that period, and extending back to the building of the brewery in the early 1930s, there was a clear sense of the need to establish, build, and reproduce a community. This ideal was designed into the very fabric of the built environment, the landscaping of the grounds that surrounded the brewery, and realized, however imperfectly, in the labor policies that governed the site. Money spent on the building, the landscaping, and the conditions of service were the acceptable price of fostering such a community. While the high hopes surrounding T. H. Marshall's "industrial citizens" or Edward Guinness's "Guinness Citizens" may have been scaled back over time, what Guinness created was a particular type of rich workplace culture that workers could embed themselves in, one that allowed them to develop a whole series of connections, cultures, networks, and values. What it created was an industrial culture, an industrial atmosphere, an industrial structure of feeling. To be sure, this culture had its faults, it marginalized and excluded, but it also allowed some workers to create a humanized space in which to work. What the oral histories allow us to do is to see elements of this culture. Rather like E. P. Thompson in his famous account of seeing class, these interviews give us privileged access to "the heat and the noise" of culture captured at work.[88]

The voices recorded here were not giving a rose-tinted account of a fictional past but one that critically evaluated that past both in its own terms and in historical context. This is a testimony that is fully aware of the shortcomings of the past but wants to rescue that past from an uncritical evaluation of the work of the long boom as simply wasteful, overstaffed, and indulgent. What they were individually and collectively describing was the process whereby the spaces for the social were being evacuated, atomized, or fissured. In part, this process is evident in the absolute loss of jobs in the plant, from a workforce of over fifteen hundred in the 1970s down to eighty on the cusp of closure. On one level, the erosion of the social is simply the gradual and sustained reduction in the critical mass of people at the brewery. However, there is another, arguably more profound sense of loss: the fissuring and fragmentation of the social relations of work. This is most obvious in the outsourcing and subcontracting gradually introduced at the brewery but was also evident in the newly formulated relationships between the remaining staff where interactions were based on contract rather than trust, a process of disembedding economic relations from their social contexts. What these interviews capture is the process by which an industrial structure of feeling is rendered marginal.

So is this simple nostalgia? Are these interviews an uncritical reflection on times past, a celebration of "back in the day," of warmly remembered youth? On the contrary: they represent a far more critical account, a critical, even analytic nostalgia. For what these older workers were doing in their interviews was questioning both the present *and* the past. They were mulling over profound questions about the nature of work and the quality of it. Like others I have interviewed for different oral history projects, these workers are not simply condemning younger, newer workers for not being like them. Rather, there is a deep consideration of what the industrial atmosphere of the past had allowed them to *be* and *become*. Further, there was an almost paternalistic concern about how younger workers would not be able to experience this quality in their working lives. This process of remembering, then, was a complex process of evaluating a whole series of social influences that had played out on them, that had created character, both individually and collectively. This industrial atmosphere and industrial structure of feeling is often something workers experience intuitively and a social background or context. It is only when this context is challenged or lost that people pause and consider its value. The impending closure of the brewery is an example of such a breach.

Henry Dawson sits in the mashing seat, from which he could mix hot and cold liquid in the mash tun. It was essential that the temperature was maintained neither too hot nor too cold. The operator would look at temperature gauges in front of him and adjust the temperature via valves on either side of the seat. *Photograph by Terry Aldridge, ca. 1985*

This photograph of a mash tun inspection, taken four decades after the painting by Terrance Cuneo, shows that very little had changed in the production process. Terry Aldridge captured this scene in 1985 before the brewery was modernized and much of the original plant was replaced. *Photograph by Terry Aldridge*

Hops arrived in the brewery in large heavy hop sacks, or "pockets," from Guinness-owned farms in Kent and were then added to the brew. *Photograph by Terry Aldridge, ca. 1985*

A blackboard is used to track details of each stage of each brew in the Vat House, about 1985. *Photograph by Terry Aldridge*

A worker fixes a pipe in place in the tanker bay. Much of the work of the unmodernized brewery was manual and labor intensive. *Photograph by Terry Aldridge, ca. 1985*

Terry Aldridge holds an image of the brewery and a maker's plate from a brewery mash tun vessel in 2015, a souvenir he took after the plant was modernized in the 1980s.
Photograph by Tim Strangleman

Workers chat in the process control room, about 2005. By that time, much of the brewery's work involved beginning, monitoring, and ending the brewery process electronically, as so much of the work was automated. *Photograph by David McCairley*

Testers participate in the daily Guinness taste test carried out as part of the quality control process, about 2005. They sipped multiple samples from different batches to check for consistency in taste, aroma, and appearance. *Photograph by David McCairley*

Henry Dawson supervises the grain roasting process, which helped to give the stout its distinctive color and flavor. Dawson was one of the final workers at Park Royal and had begun his career at the site more than thirty years earlier. *Photograph by David McCairley, 2005*

An abandoned part of the brewery in 2005. In the last few years of production, many of the parts of the site were no longer in use. *Photograph by David McCairley*

A blackboard lists the names, numbers, and duties of workers at Park Royal, about 2005. The numbers refer to the telephone extensions where they can be contacted. This was in a part of the brewery that was no longer in use in the last phase of the plant's life. The chalked names mix the names of departed workers and those about to be made redundant by the final closure. *Photograph by David McCairley*

A production shift team poses for a photograph in May 2005. The size of the team illustrates the dramatic impact of automation on the workforce. From the 1950s through the early 1980s fifteen hundred people worked at the brewery, many of them in production; by the end, there were seventy-eight Diageo workers employed on site. The name of each one was recorded on the bottle label of the final commemorative brew produced to mark the end of production at Park Royal in the summer of 2005. Such teams would work twelve-hour shifts in a rotating pattern with three other similar groups. *Photograph by David McCairley*

Workers in the refrigeration plant in 2005 serve as a reminder of how self-sufficient the plant once was, with virtually everything carried out on site by workers directly employed by Guinness. By the time the plant was closed, almost all functions apart from the core brewing process were undertaken by contractors, including these workers who were now employed by a separate company. *Photograph by David McCairley*

A cartoon depicts architectural historian Gavin Stamp's attempts to save the brewery buildings. Stamp is shown clutching a copy of Nikolaus Pevsner's guidebook to historic buildings. The cartoon illustrates the debate between the architectural community and the company. *Louis Hellman, artist; Architects' Journal, June 2005.*

The Malt House building was demolished in February 2006. In the background at the left is the new Diageo HQ building, which was built on the former brewery sports ground. *Photograph by Adrian Sturgess*

The demolition of the brewery exposed the interior steel frame of the buildings (March 2006). The image illustrates how solidly the original 1930s blocks were constructed. As such, it took much longer to demolish them than had originally been planned. *Photograph by Adrian Sturgess*

The brewery buildings stand, though the connecting walkway had been removed, in March 2006. The distinctive brickwork specified by Giles Gilbert Scott was still in excellent condition, "designed to last a century or two." *Photograph by Adrian Sturgess*

The restrained ornamentation designed by Gilbert Scott was still evident during demolition in April 2006, echoing his earlier work on the Battersea and Bankside power stations. *Photograph by Adrian Sturgess*

A crane grabber was used to pull down the brewery buildings. "They just chomped and chomped. The machines—I compared them to dinosaurs," recalled Diageo worker Adrian Sturgess. *Photograph by Adrian Sturgess*

Advertising for the new buildings at the Park Royal site announces, "The Future Starts Here," summer of 2015. *Photograph by Tim Strangleman*

6

THE GHOST IN
THE MACHINE

In his 2005 BBC television play *Friends and Crocodiles*, Stephen Poliakoff tells the story of a group of friends caught up in the late 1990s tech bubble. Toward the end of the drama, there is a pivotal scene in and around an old factory. In the speedy pans and quick cuts, the factory looms large; the sound of heavy machines in the background frames the visual action. Everything about the sequence seems chosen to emphasize an industrial era rapidly being eclipsed by the "new economy." The site is used as a backdrop for a meeting between corporate executives planning to shift the focus of the company away from its manufacturing past and present toward information technology products and services of the future. On their way to the meeting, the senior managers pass the mass ranks of vacuum cleaners the plant is currently manufacturing, brushing by them with obvious disdain.

Entering the canteen, the executives are met by a row of eager-to-please older waitresses, eager to serve them tea and currant buns, further emphasizing the antiquated nature of the space. Anders, the fictional CEO, dismisses the attendants from the room before turning to address his executives:

> I have to say this now because it is all the more powerful while we are in amongst it. This is the past, everybody! This is *over*! We will be ridding ourselves of all these factories—we make everything from these vacuum cleaners to lampposts, from soap to helicopters—it's ridiculous! It will all be shed. The terrible load we've been carrying is going to be off our back at last.[1]

Anders's strategy is to sell off the company's manufacturing base, using it as "a huge cash cow" he intends to "milk well and truly!" in order to buy every internet and telecom company he can lay his hands on.[2] The play's conceit is that Anders's strategy is to jump into the dotcom bubble of the late 1990s just as it is about to burst, jettisoning "boring" tangible products for the allure of something mysterious and more exciting.

Poliakoff has explored late-twentieth-century political economy in a number of his plays, and *Friends and Crocodiles* is one of the best at capturing the willful neglect of the past alongside the uncritical embrace of the future. As he says,

"My picture of the recent past will have collided with their imaginations and their memories."[3] The drama stands as a powerful critique of the restructuring of the economy away from traditional industries toward the service sector during the 1980s and 1990s. In 1950, despite the ravages of the Second World War and postwar austerity, Britain's share of world manufacturing exports stood at 25.4 percent. The country still had a huge manufacturing base producing steel, ships, cars, domestic appliances, and heavy machinery. 1955 was the peak year of industrial employment, when it represented 48 percent of all those employed. By 2009, its share of world exports of manufactured goods was just 2.9 percent, with just three million workers employed in the manufacturing industry.[4]

In the 1980s, there was a collective political concern about these trends, with the word "deindustrialization" increasingly used to highlight the loss of industrial capacity. For some, this was evidence of the long-standing weakness of the UK economy, with its roots in the eighteenth and nineteenth centuries' aristocratic culture, which lacked an entrepreneurial spirit. Others saw the deindustrialization of Britain alongside other developed economies as evidence of "creative destruction," the old economic order being wiped out by the growing tertiary economy and especially sectors such as telecom and financial services.[5]

Also present in political discourse from the late 1970s onward was a concern for those made marginal by industrial change and closure. Beyond the grim unemployment statistics, seemingly reported on a daily basis during the 1980s, there was a gradual realization that the old economic order was changing quickly, while the places where traditional industries had been practiced for generations were left isolated and seemingly abandoned to decay, their fate of interest only to academics and journalists.[6]

Though *Friends and Crocodiles* is a piece of fiction, it nonetheless manages to ask questions of the value of work and the industrial culture created by manufacturing. The play allows us pause to think about what the loss of this sort of work means to us as a nation. The twist, unintended by Poliakoff, was that the play's industrial backdrop was the soon-to-be-closed Guinness brewery at Park Royal. The plant's variety of spaces made it the ideal setting for this and other works of drama just as it closed its doors in 2005.[7] Park Royal again acts as a venue for exploring many of the themes of the 1980s, 1990s, and early 2000s, issues such as job loss, rationalization, closure, and deindustrialization.

NARRATING CLOSURE

As the process of deindustrialization has unfolded, more sophisticated accounts have emerged, moving away from the idea of a crude "body count" of lost jobs and blighted communities toward a focus on subjective experience, cultural meaning, and memory. Some commentators have pointed out the dangers of "smokestack nostalgia," the uncritical romanticization of the industrial past that ignores issues such as workplace injury, ill health, and pollution.[8]

Studies also show the range of individual and community responses to plant closure. Early examples captured the anger, resistance, and sense of betrayal felt toward large corporations when they pulled out of areas. Some communities reacted by turning in on themselves in a cycle of blame, shame, and self-immolation.[9]

Later worker narratives of job loss reflected anger mixed with resigned acceptance. By the late 1990s and early 2000s, closures could be seen as part of a two-decade-long process of gradual decline. Many employees by then had experienced a series of often brutal plant reorganizations, job redesigns, and buyouts that preceded closure. Individuals, families, and communities could be angry while recognizing that they were subject to a far wider set of forces over which they had little or no control. In other words, workers had normalized the waves of job losses and plant closures. Imagined along a continuum, deindustrialization narratives would have at one end the response of shock and fighting back. Toward the middle would be a sense of regret and passive acceptance. At the other extreme, workers would be, if not "happy," at least resigned to bidding "farewell to the factory," then using their severance pay to begin new, potentially more rewarding careers.[10]

Context matters in understanding how deindustrialization is experienced. That is obvious in many ways, the when, where, and how of plant closure. Those confronting the collapse of various industries in the mid- to late 1970s or early 1980s were pioneers in a growing army of laid-off workers, responding to closure in the best ways they could, writing the script they enacted as they went. Those workers may have been too close to the situation to fully appreciate its scope and scale. As time passed, workers facing similar events, however traumatized by job loss, did have models of a kind to follow so they could put their own individual and collective experience into perspective. The location of deindustrialization matters, too, of course; there is a huge difference between the experiences of workers laid off in a company town with no alternative sources of employment compared to others living in a dynamic city with a buoyant economy. Therefore, the time, the place, and the way in which industries collapse all count.

Who is being laid off also makes a difference. The skills and knowledge workers possess, the options for work they have, their health, their age and life stage, and their partners and their children all figure in how they experience change. Attitudes to job loss and wider deindustrialization are complex but intelligible.

Finally, closing narratives reflect on the value and values of the work and community being lost. Job loss, plant closing, and wider deindustrialization act as a breach in the day-to-day, taken-for-granted life people lead. Loss imposes space for reflection. The absence of work and the communities and cultures that surround it reveal hitherto hidden networks, social relationship, and unspoken connection.

CLOSING TIME

On Thursday, April 15, 2004, the multinational beverage group Diageo announced it would be closing its Park Royal brewery and transferring production to its St. James's Gate facility in Dublin. While Guinness was still the fifth-best-selling beer in the British market, a market that was itself the company's largest, sales had been in decline. Guinness consumption had actually grown globally by 3 percent, but in the United Kingdom, it had fallen by the same amount in the second half of 2003 alone, and by 7 percent in the Republic of Ireland. Gerry O'Hagan, director of Diageo's UK brewing business, said, "Between the breweries in London and Dublin, we have more capacity than we need. The right decision for the future of the Guinness brand is to invest in Dublin."[11]

Diageo's decision must be placed into a wider context of the brewing industry in the United Kingdom and globally, as well as the dramatic changes taking place in alcohol consumption patterns. Between 1989 and 2009, total beer consumption in the United Kingdom declined by 28 percent, with beer sales in pubs falling by 53 percent. This decrease occurred against a massive restructuring of the brewing industry in which large multinational groups took over significant parts of the market, and the ownership structure of pubs also changed dramatically.[12] The closure decision was also informed by the greater land value of the London site compared to that in Dublin, as well as the more intangible value attached to Irish-based production, with all its historical resonance in comparison to London. Clearly the "Irishness" of Guinness stout was an important part of the brand, one that would have inevitably been diminished by a Dublin closure.[13]

I first went to the brewery in 2004 for a project on older male workers. By this time, the closure announcement and a timetable for shutdown had already been made public. Park Royal was still a hugely impressive site, dominated by the original buildings dating from the 1930s. The grounds were still well tended and maintained, green and lush against the light-brown brick of the old brewery. Among the clipped lawns stood many of the mature trees and bushes planted over the previous six decades. Inside the plant, many of the original spaces were no longer in use; they had gradually been marginalized since the 1980s as production was reorganized and brewing methods evolved. Walking around, I noticed the quality of the original materials, the parquet flooring, the brass fixtures and fittings, that spoke of a different age and a different set of corporate values. The other striking quality of the site was just how deserted it was. There were few people around, and often those who were present were not the "core" Guinness workforce but rather contractors undertaking the numerous outsourced tasks that kept the brewery operational. At times, it felt as if the site was haunted by its past, its original purpose, and the many hundreds of workers who had once populated it.

I had lunch on several occasions with a small knot of Guinness workers in the now near-empty canteen; the space was by then ridiculously large for the residual staff employed on site. Listening to their accounts of working life, I got the real sense that this was a type of group therapy; retelling old stories about the brewery and those who had worked there was as much for their own benefit as for mine. These were a series of narrations that repopulated the brewery with workmates, friends, and relations—a landscape with figures. Through these mealtime discussions, they exchanged immediate news on the closure and the progress of negotiations over financial packages employees were expecting. But there was also a sense of people on the point of losing their jobs trying to understand what was happening to them and, more deeply, what their working life had meant. They were being forced to confront their own individual and collective careers within the trajectory of closure, and, in the process, comparing and contrasting what for many had been a benign environment with the relatively unknown labor market that awaited them beyond the brewery's gates.

An element of the Park Royal oral history project was to work with photographer David McCairley to produce a record in words and pictures of the last six months of production at the brewery. At the beginning of this process, McCairley asked me what type of images I needed. I said that I wanted portraits that showed people at work and that reflected all of the labor of the brewery. The images and the process of taking them revealed some fascinating issues about contemporary work. McCairley came back to me after his initial time on site and explained that it was often difficult to capture "work" as so much of the remaining labor consisted of monitoring processes rather than the active physical effort of previous generations, the type captured so beautifully in the Tanner images taken in the 1940s for publicity purposes. The attempt to reveal all the labor that went on in the site resulted in his taking photographs of many of the contractors in the brewery, including some Portuguese migrant workers employed as cleaners. One of the managers asked why we wanted to take images of this group, as they weren't "Guinness workers." What McCairley's photographs reveal is the emptiness of the site toward the end of its life; some of the images contain no workers, not necessarily through deliberate framing and choice but simply because so much of the plant was deserted. Even where workers were centrally present, as in the posed pictures of each shift group, these merely emphasized the small numbers of core Guinness staff on site at any one time—a dozen or so in each team. Even given my initial impression of the emptiness of the place, I should not have been surprised when, in my formal interviews, the remaining Park Royal workers experienced the closure as but the bitter end of a longer, even more lamentable process.

We turn now to the shop floor and the Guinness workers' experience of closure. These are voices of people who had survived up to the point of closure but who were mostly interviewed prior to the final end of production. Their stories reflect this situation and the tensions and expectations about what was to follow. The events around closure are refracted through a longer-term experience of working in the brewery and the waves of change over the years. Impending closure and its announcement clearly had a big impact on workers. Graham Bayford's experience was typical:

> We got a letter at work or at home asking us to come in at a certain time to a meeting, and they brought somebody in, way above, product supply director, as they call them, and he gave us the spiel that it was—I think his words were "There's nothing wrong with us but we're going to close you." Economics says the beer market is obviously not growing as fast as they'd like; they've got spare capacity in Ireland; with a few modifications or investment, they can brew it all in Ireland and ship it over and supply the UK[14]

Workers like Bayford reflected a fatalism about the decision and the way it was announced; both were recounted as impersonal, driven by economic circumstances and remote market forces. His colleague Dave Bathurst emphasized how memorable that day had been for all workers at the brewery:

> It's one of those dates, I suppose a bit like when Kennedy was assassinated; you know the day that it occurred. April 15th was when it was announced. Meetings had been arranged a day or two before. The first one was when the night shift finished at seven in the morning. We had a staff meeting, which I attended, at about nine-thirty or ten. There was then a day shift meeting later on, so everybody was covered very quickly. It was a fairly brief announcement—we all knew the review had been going on for some time—to say that a review had been completed, there were some comments about reduced volumes, site efficiencies, but the conclusion was that it had been decided Park Royal site should close.[15]

Many workers talked about how they half-expected closure, but as Barry Hubbard expressed it: "I think it was still a shock when it actually comes out of someone's mouth. They say, 'It's going to shut down, and this is the date'."[16] Les Woodgate was one of the shop stewards on site and was pulled aside to be briefed before the more general announcement:

> Well, I was the shop steward, so I had heard about five minutes before the rest of the staff. But it wasn't a surprise. They'd got the four shop stewards and take them into a room and a Frenchman, John Pierre, come in. I couldn't understand what he was saying. "Sorry, lads, basically we've made a decision, sales are dropping here and in Ireland and the decision's been made to shut Park Royal." I heard that five minutes before everybody else, and he went and told everybody else. And he had done it out of politeness to tell the shop stewards. That's how I heard.[17]

In the interviews there was an overwhelming sense of fatalism and acceptance about closure. However, in an article about the decision in the left-wing newspaper *Socialist Worker*, it was reported that "workers have reacted with anger to huge multinational Diageo's announcement of the closure of the Guinness brewery in Park Royal in Brent, North West London." The article quoted a worker at the plant:

> According to one union rep, "For a number of years management have used the threat of closing either Park Royal or St. James's Gate as a way of pushing through cuts and rationalisation in both plants. We gave concession after concession. We were told to "modernise" and we did, but it just meant more work and now they do this. Park Royal was set up by Guinness in the 1930s to avoid paying import tax. They're closing us down to get tax breaks."[18]

How, then, did the workers feel about the prospect of closure after it had been announced and the news had settled in? There was some variation in attitudes, but broadly there was a deep sense of passive acceptance. The quality of this attitude emerged across the interviews, although the workers expressed it in different ways. Woodgate noted: "Because I was a shop steward, I was involved in negotiations, which I suppose we come up with a fair deal. We've had heated discussions with the branch about redundancies and things like that, but that's being a shop steward, I suppose, and we have mud slung at us."[19]

Another union steward explained the divisions within the workforce over the decision to close: "Within the branch, to be truthful, there was a few people— well, I'm not saying a few, a sizeable minority who were happy to see it close. In 2000 they applied for a job but they didn't know what twelve-hour working was going to be like. After a time quite a few had got fed up with twelve-hour working."[20] These new shift patterns had clearly intensified the time spent at work and had proved detrimental to social and family life, over and above "normal" shift work. The same steward went on to describe the divisions within the workforce, but mostly these seem to have been over the closure package rather than an overt desire to fight closure.

The quarter of a century or so from the early 1980s had been marked by a gradual decrease in staff numbers through successive, often dramatic waves of rationalization. This had clearly inured people to job insecurity and continual change. As Bayford explained:

> The general feeling was that it nearly closed four years ago, and everybody [who] survived that "cull," as we call it, said, "How long have we got?" And the general opinion was five years, five years is what it is, so nobody was surprised. They might have thought we were surprised, but nobody was surprised because of the lack of investment on this site. Everyone just presumed they were just going to make it tick along as they needed it to tick along without having to plow a lot of money into it, and the price of land in London![21]

It is clear from this statement and from others that the staff had a sophisticated understanding of the complex business decisions being made about the future of the plant. Interviewees appreciated the need for new investment and the potential real estate value of the brewery site. On a day-to-day basis, workers like Graham knew what the implications of investment decisions, or lack of them, meant. There was a clear understanding of the market conditions in which Park Royal traded, as Hubbard explained:

> So it was just the decline in sales, really. And that's why most people took it okay. Because we all know we're good at what we do, we know that this is the flagship of all the breweries. They all look at Park Royal and say that we've done it. And that is why I was a bit sort of miffed while we were shutting down, because we hadn't done anything wrong. I don't think anybody was really very angry. They were disappointed, but I don't think anybody was angry and bitter because it just wasn't anything that we'd done ourselves.[22]

Many interviewees demonstrated this sense of pride mixed with disappointment: satisfaction that the workforce had done what had been asked of it in terms of efficiency but regret that this had not been deemed sufficient. As Ray Snook explained:

> I think the workforce have been very good. There's been one or two that, you know, are a little bit upset. They're upset because of what's happened here in the past with redundancies rather than because we're actually closing. The majority of the workforce has been—they've taken it better than I thought, and the plant, touch wood, is running very, very well, because I thought there might have been some—not sabotage, but would have thought people wouldn't care and be just, "So what? Let it run until it breaks," but they're not. They are still taking pride.[23]

Underlying many of the interviews was a complex set of emotions about the immediate closure but also the much longer context of rationalization. The staff understood closure was the result of a series of events and factors outside their control. The workers had delivered on their part of the bargain but had been let down nonetheless. Bathurst articulated these sentiments well in his interview. Bathurst was in his midfifties and couched his attitude to closure within the context of several waves of rationalization:

> A slight sense of disappointment but, equally, again, most of the people, they will have been through this in some shape or form. I've been through it probably now about three or four times. Well, a closure's different because there isn't any choice. Most people, as I say, will have been through this process three, four, maybe five times. So no great shock or particular issue with it; I didn't feel angry or upset or anything.[24]

Bathurst contrasted his attitude to the announcement of final closure with a previous round of rationalization:

> Funnily enough, five years ago, part of the deal we did then was, everyone was made redundant or could have been made redundant and everyone had to reapply for their job, or a job. I actually felt much more under pressure then with my sons

at university and things like that, thinking, "Bloody hell! If I don't get a job, I'm going to have to find another job and this could be a bit painful." So actually, five years ago, going for a job interview then for this job and waiting to hear the result two or three weeks later really was quite stressful. This time, no, I think I can genuinely say I didn't feel any stress—yes, okay, another two or three years would have been nice. I wouldn't say I'm not bothered, but I wasn't upset about it. I was more upset four or five years ago with the program then.[25]

This was a common sentiment among Guinness workers I interviewed around this time. At the time of closure, many of the staff were in their fifties, and a significant number saw their futures involving work, but not necessarily full-time employment. This gave workers some sense of certainty, but it also speaks to a wider and deeper sense of erosion of their identities as Guinness workers. Bathurst's account was by no means unique and reflected a certain detachment from his work. This was not an active choice but rather, as he said, the result of a process that had seen him having to apply and reapply for his post multiple times. Each cycle of this process was disruptive of a career narrative, the ability to be able to tell a coherent story about one's self and the place of work in one's life. Each round of rationalization further eroded, or corroded, one's ability to attach, connect, or embed oneself in one's work to the point where the final closure announcement came almost as a sense of relief, individually and collectively. This was in part because the final redundancy brought a level of certainty, another sort of closure.

There was a stark contrast between these attitudes and those reported by the same workers reflecting on work in the past, when they described a genuine quality of embeddedness. This was a combination of enjoying job security coupled with an individual and collective self-confidence in their employment, one that allowed a fundamental sense of ownership or moral responsibility for work to emerge. Both in the case of Guinness and in previous research, I have sought to understand this state of embeddedness, as well as the process of disembedding. We could think of it as a state where workers feel they have a grip on their jobs. What we have seen since the 1990s, however, is a process whereby gradually, finger by finger, that grip is loosened to the point where it is no longer present. This is, therefore, the loss of a broad-based industrial culture, an industrial structure of feeling that underpinned manual work over a number of generations.[26]

It is worth quoting Bathurst again at length to fully appreciate how he described his experience of this process. Asked if he would miss anything about working at Park Royal, he replied:

It's quite sad in a way. I suppose if I'd left about ten years ago, even then it was the Guinness Company. It was self-contained on this site, there are a lot of people that had been around for a long time in all sorts of functions, and I think I would have missed then that aspect of the company. It wasn't quite a family company even then, but it was more how I knew the company twenty, thirty years ago. What would I miss now when I go next June or whenever it is? As I say, it's rather sad to say. I am not sure I will miss an awful lot. I think after thirty-five years I almost feel slightly guilty making that statement, but the company has shrunk down so much.[27]

There is a lament here that speaks to the shifting ground of relationships within work, what could be described as a sociological contract between workers and their organization. Bathurst felt "guilty" and "sad" about his attitude to an organization he clearly still had great affection for while simultaneously acknowledging that the plates on which that trust was built have moved beneath his feet. He recognized that his affection was for something that had disappeared.

Bathurst went on to explore why this was the way he felt about the present when compared to various points in his career:

> You're probably aware that on this site all the non-production people moved over the way to the new office block about a year ago. So in that sense, the site now only has at any one time, when I'm here, perhaps thirty Guinness people on it. There are a number of contractors, some of whom I know, some of whom I don't. So in that sense, when I walk out of the gate in a year's time or whenever it is, we will have had a year or so, eighteen months, two years, of very few people on the site. A lot of the buildings are empty. Those other functions aren't around. So I don't actually feel that I will miss an awful lot. As I say, I see a very clear thing in my mind of how I would have felt ten years ago, or even five years ago, to how I do now.[28]

This sense of disembedding is at once highly personal and simultaneously extremely social in that an individual feeling of attachment is implicated in the presence of others. The previous experience of embeddedness was to a large extent rooted in being part of a larger community of familiar faces, a shared culture of ritual self-knowledge built up over time. Another worker imagined himself back in the 1970s to make the point about attachment:

> If you came in the seventies, I don't know the exact figures but a large proportion of people then would have only worked for Guinness as it was, and that would have been their intention until they retired. You'd have long service, a long service profile in the company, certainly greater than 50 percent, probably significantly greater.[29]

This passage reflects the way workers understand what had been lost, in this case a rootedness in work that was unremarked upon at the time but is revealed through the process of restructuring both in the organization and more widely in the economy. This same worker compared his early working life with his more immediate surroundings:

> I'm talking Diageo across the road, but I would imagine that more than three-quarters have less than three to five years' service. So the job for life that people

thought of then has long since gone. I'm not saying that's a bad thing or a good thing; it's just a fact of life. But certainly people are—it's a phrase I've heard people say—are "passing through." It's a notch on the belt that possibly says, "Yeah, I worked for Diageo," which would still be perceived as an excellent company to have worked for, but it, it is different. People would not now expect to work for many years.[30]

Like Bathurst, this interviewee expressed feelings of being marginal or marginalized in terms of an identity around work. What workers had valued in the past was precisely that notion of being rooted, embedded in the firm, whereas what they now appeared to experience was a more contractual and fugitive relationship with work and coworkers. The phrase "passing through" strongly suggests a transient relationship with work and by implication with those one works with. The "notch on the belt" likewise speaks to a more individualized desire for self-achievement rather than a collective endeavor or identity.

In his 1998 book *The Corrosion of Character*, American sociologist Richard Sennett addresses this question directly. This quality of work-based relationships and of character is a central one, he thinks, for modern capitalism. As he puts it, "There is a history, but no shared narrative of difficulty, and so no shared fate. Under these conditions, character corrodes; the question 'Who needs me?' has no immediate answer."[31] In their responses to my questions, Guinness workers were in their own way reflecting on this question themselves.

WHAT NEXT?

As part of the interview, workers were asked what they intended to do after the plant closed. This was revealing in a direct way, as some had firm plans, but it also uncovered a broader set of ideas and questions about work, past, present, and future. Being laid off acted as a breach, disrupting taken-for-granted attitudes about the meanings and identities surrounding what they did and the relationship between their economic and social life. Context and individual circumstances played a huge part in how interviewees framed their hopes and fears for their futures. Many who had survived successive "culls" were of an age where, with the help of a lump-sum payment and an early pension, they were happy to retire. For others who were younger and had younger children or even second families, their sense of the future looked less secure.

For those who were financially secure, getting a "little job," often a "little driving job," was an aspiration and showed that, after a lifetime of work, they wanted to continue to be socially active while stepping down from full-time employment. This was the idea of a gentle decline into retirement rather than dropping off the cliff edge of work/no work.[32] Snook talked of the possibility of acting as a consultant using his knowledge of the software he had worked with at Guinness: "So I'm quite hopeful that we will get some work in that area; if not, I wouldn't be too proud to stack shelves in Tesco. I'll find something. I'll go back working in a pub; I worked in a pub before. I've worked in a betting shop."[33]

Snook here was both emphasizing the software skills he possessed and reinforcing his narrative of himself by showing willingness to engage in less-skilled, even unskilled work. Work mattered to Ray, but his sense of self-worth was bound up not with *what* he actually did, but rather from doing *something*. This may reflect a dignity and self-confidence rooted in having been embedded in a strong occupational culture. Even when that original source of identity is lost, it still has a residual presence in workers. Industrial citizenship, therefore, has a half-life.

Bayford made it clear that he, like Snook, wanted to work, but less intensively than he currently was:

> A little driving job, if it's available. Whatever was around, it wouldn't worry me; picking up rubbish doesn't bother me. I've done shift work for thirty-four years, so I'm not sure whether I can do anything else. Because I shouldn't get a bad pension, it won't be a fantastic pension, but it should be a lot better than a lot of people.[34]

In these and many other interviews, there was a strong sense of a work ethic, a desire to do "something useful," not simply relax into leisure. Bathurst was typical when he noted, "I'll be fifty-six next year. I could just put my feet up, but in a way, after thirty years, there's almost the work ethic and the discipline of it. Call me boring, but I quite like it, actually getting up in the morning, going to work, things to do, busy, new experiences and things."[35] He later joked, "There's not enough gardening and painting and DIY and golf to do at home. My wife would kill me, anyway."[36]

Some of those about to be laid off were in a different position in that they had long-standing health problems. Although Guinness had accommodated their requirements at Park Royal, life in the external labor market looked a good deal more uncertain. As one worker explained:

> When it closes, I'll be fifty-one years of age with heart trouble—not the most em-
> ployable, I wouldn't have thought, so it does worry me what's going to happen.
> I definitely want to work. I couldn't stay at home; it'd do my head in completely.
> I mean, after the heart trouble, I just stagnated indoors. I mean, it's like I could
> basically feel my mind just being sucked away, absolutely shocking. My mind'd be
> sort of thinking about any old thing, just to occupy me, I was only too relieved to
> get back to work. So I know what sitting at home's going to do to me. I can't do
> shift work. Who's going to employ me, really?[37]

Being laid off for some workers would therefore reveal health issues that had been accommodated at Guinness. Here again, we hear how important work and the work ethic is in a personal narrative. Employment and returning to it after illness has a redemptive quality, over and above drawing a wage. Woodgate touched on this when asked about his plans for life after Guinness:

Obviously, because I've been at work since I was fifteen, sometimes the thought of taking time out does appeal to me, but probably only appeals to me for a short while. After about six weeks, two months, I think I might think, I've got to get a job, I've got to do something. I need something that is going to keep me active because there is a social thing about work as well, isn't there. That's the thing, like we was talking about it the other day, one of the worse things we could do is go somewhere where they're all sad, miserable people, because we do have a good laugh here, I must admit, we always have a good laugh, and we do have a social life with it. That's one of the things I would miss, the social side of it.[38]

Here, then, the social aspects of employment combine with a strong personal work ethic, recognizing a distinctly masculine way of doing the social. The community at work is performed shoulder to shoulder while doing things rather than through face-to-face activities. This passage also reflects a complex account of both work and leisure. The simple bifurcation between work on the one hand and leisure on the other does not easily operate here. Rather, Woodgate is expressing an understanding of employment as a more rounded environment, where labor overlays leisure and vice versa. Les saw the importance of taking pleasure in work rather than seeing work and leisure as separate spheres of life. The pleasure people take in work is precisely in those social spaces afforded by labor itself.[39]

Toward the end of their interviews, I asked the workers about their children, what they did, and how they saw their children's careers unfolding. This again was revealing, not only about the next generation and their work ethic but also because it entailed further reflection on the complexities of the labor market for the soon-to-be-laid-off Guinness workers themselves. While many of the interviewees' children had enjoyed a better education and had significantly higher qualifications, there was no guarantee that this would see them into secure employment. Woodgate, with two adult children, reflected on his own family experience:

Well, my son is twenty-eight; he's out of work. He finds it very difficult to get a job. He's been made redundant twice. My boy's attitude to work is that it has to fit around his social life. That's half the problem, because he is quite a good footballer, so if it means working Saturdays and that, he don't want to know; he wants a Monday-to-Friday job. And what I've seen, they're not easy to come by.[40]

Woodgate related both his own fatherly frustration with his son's work ethic, but also his understanding of his son's options in the labor market:

He had a job at Smiths Industries in Bushey. He was in the stores there, and they had a couple of redundancies and they had to pick on him; I think he was the last one in, so he was the first one out. Then, after a period of unemployment, he got a job in a store in Watford, in the warehouse, and that lasted eighteen months, and they shut that down. So that's two jobs he's lost. So he has had various bits and pieces, but he can't seem to get a permanent start. But these things happen, don't they. And there's not a lot of industry around Watford now; it's all shutting down.[41]

In the interview, Woodgate was clearly thinking about his son's circumstances through the lens of his own, relatively stable, employment history with Guinness. His own career, while later involving rounds of rationalization, had provided a stable environment in which to raise a family on a blue-collar wage.

Bathurst's two sons were in a slightly different position, having both trained and qualified as engineers. One had found employment with Nestlé as an apprentice before eventually becoming an electrical engineer, but his son's post had been eliminated:

> His experience, I suppose, is the same as mine but a bit earlier. He did eleven years at Nestlé, and they've been doing almost what we've been doing, which has been cutting numbers year after year. So he was made redundant in February this year. We talked about it a fair bit because Nestlé, again, even then there was a culture of you join the company and you not quite stayed forever but you were in and that was it.[42]

His other son studied engineering at university before struggling to get a job. When he did get a position, he stayed only eighteen months before getting "itchy feet" and moving on, gaining another post, which he left after another year and a half. Reflecting on his own work history, and that of his two sons, Bathurst observed:

> So, yes, I have quite long conversations with them, but one of the things I've tried to encourage them to do is not quite get stuck in the groove. Robert has been forced to think about that because he was made redundant from Nestlé. With Steven, it's the other thing. I wish he would stay a little longer with each company. But, yes, we talk about work, we talk about redundancy.[43]

There is a lot going on in this passage, indeed in the whole of Bathurst's interview, in terms of his own biography and his narrative of employment. Through his appraisal of his own working life, he struggled to make sense of his own fortunes and those of the next generation. He recognized his own experience in his elder son's layoff, raising questions about the long-term nature of corporate commitment and stability. By contrast, in the case of his younger son he was concerned about a *lack* of personal commitment. In both instances, we can see questions of embeddedness, or lack of it, appearing in his narrative. Redundancy seems to be the reward for commitment, but he still wants his younger son to embed himself in his work. While this tension is being played out, he wants to warn his sons, based on his own experience, to "not quite get stuck in the groove." The inclusion of "quite," subtly qualifying his advice, is fascinating. It is the recognition of not taking one's career for granted, to always be in the position to move to something else or at least be prepared for that eventuality. Bathurst was reflecting Richard Sennett's point that "the old work ethic revealed concepts of character which still matter, even if these qualities no longer find expression in labour." This observation highlights the importance of self-discipline that is voluntary rather than merely passive submission to the power of the employer. There is, therefore, a residual value in an older work ethic being recognized just as it seems to be becoming fatally undermined by contemporary attitudes to work.[44]

This type of reflection on the changing nature of work was common in the interviews, which showed a broad concern with the values that were animating the contemporary labor market, the attitudes of employers and employees. Mick Costello had two school-aged children from a second marriage. He talked about his own working life compared to those his children were likely to enjoy:

> Coming from Ireland, my parents sort of idolized the word "Guinness." It has a great reputation in Ireland as well as it did over here. I would recommend Guinness to anyone; I didn't like the change to Diageo and also I have learned that if you're in a comfort zone, be very careful because it might not last for too long. I've learned a lot here over thirty-five years. If I say to my kids, if I could give them one reasonable piece of advice, it would be never become complacent because if you do I think you'll be in for a shock.[45]

This need to guard against complacency was rooted in an understanding of the profound and deep-seated changes in the economy. As Costello said, "But I think in the whole industrial era I've worked, during that time there was a hell of a lot of change. The industrial world as we know it has changed a hell of a lot in the last thirty years."[46]

CLOSING THOUGHTS

Most of the interviews at Park Royal took place in 2004 or 2005, and a smaller number were undertaken in subsequent years. In the final part of all these interviews, the workers were asked about their reflections on working at the brewery, and the responses often revealed fascinating insights into both their careers and work more generally. They almost always contextualized the period preceding closure by comparisons with the past. What these passages reflected was a critical nostalgia, a weighing up of the relative value of what they had enjoyed in the past and what they were about to lose. Memory here was a powerful evaluative mechanism by which the present could be judged. Asked if he would miss anything about working at the brewery, Snook observed:

> I shall probably miss some of the people, not all of them. Yes, it's a bit like an institution, really; I think my car won't know which way to go in the morning if I don't come here. I can't say I'll miss the social side of it now because it's not like it used to be. It's going to seem strange not coming here.[47]

Costello reflected on the changes he had experienced with the company: "I know I'm going to be out of a job. I'm not bitter about being out of a job. I just feel very, very sad at seeing the Guinness name almost vanishing into oblivion, certainly in Great Britain, whereas I've been extremely proud to have worked for this company as long as I have."[48] This pride was infused with a strong sense of morality, informed by a feeling that Park Royal was subject to forces outside the control of individuals or of the workforce as a whole. Costello and many of his colleagues embodied a sense of responsibility and engagement, a sense that they had done their best, but through no fault of their own, this had not been enough to save the brewery from closure. Reflecting on what he would miss, Mick noted the camaraderie of the site:

> I get to see the team as it comes round, and at meal breaks, it's quite a social event. I'm going to miss it greatly. I live locally; I could probably walk home in five minutes. If I end up selling and moving, it's going to be thirty-five years of my life gone. Yeah, I've got a very, very strong bond with this place. I'll shed a tear or two, I think, when it goes. I'll find it difficult to break. I know nothing else, basically.[49]

The feeling of ambiguity over closure was present in virtually every discussion with workers; the features of work that had once been of value were now greatly diminished. Here an interviewee reflected on loss:

> I don't think there's anything about Diageo now as a company that I'm particularly going to miss. Again, go back a few years, I would have missed the security that a big company brings; the salary at the end of the month, some of those other benefits and things like medical insurance, the conditions that go with it. That doesn't bother me anymore. Go back thirty years, there was lots of other things— sports facilities, clubhouse facilities, all sorts of Guinness-related outside-of-work-time activities. All sorts of things. Because they've disappeared over the last few years—the sports have been cut back, the sort of extracurricular activities have disappeared—they're not there to be missed anymore. I don't mean it in a sort of disappointed way, but there aren't many things I will miss of Diageo/Guinness as it is now. It's—I guess the last few years it's been the work thing and, of course, it generates a salary.[50]

It was clear that as the rationalization and restructuring processes had been implemented, many of the intrinsic aspects of work had been greatly reduced or had disappeared altogether; as this worker confided, those intrinsic rewards were simply "not there to be missed anymore." So the sense of loss many did indeed feel was complex, consisting of a mourning for many of the features of work that had long since disappeared. While many would have wished to have continued working at Park Royal, the loss of the work itself held few regrets.

I interviewed Henry Dawson both in 2005, before the brewery closed, and again in 2015. In our earlier discussion, he made a powerful link between the brewery in the past compared to the present:

Yeah, a colossal part of my life, if you think, when I first started here, with all the blokes we had on shift, once you got integrated into the shift you were on, you were actually with those blokes longer than you were at home with your wife and children each day. So they became like a family. You knew all about their families. You knew when they had problems. You knew if their kids were sick because all those problems got brought to work with them. And that seemed to die off throughout the years because you don't have that close contact because there are not so many people working together.[51]

This ambiguity became more apparent when Dawson discussed the brewery buildings after being asked about being attached to work. He said that he was and he was not, explaining, "If you had seen the buildings when they were full of equipment, when they were actually a working brewery, they were striking. Empty, they're ghosts."[52] He was capturing an important aspect of work, the way it is situated within place and time. Dawson was not simply nostalgically wallowing in the past, however close or distant. Rather, he was thinking through the quality of working life and how it had changed, in particular how the social aspects of labor, the proximity of working groups, had been reduced over the years. But he was also clear that what he would miss was the way this social quality had animated interaction and the physical space of the brewery. In his mind's eye, he was picturing a landscape with figures. Empty, the buildings were full of ghosts.

THE FINAL BREW

In early June 2005, Edward Guinness was asked to start the final brew at Park Royal, which was due to close later that month. A week later, there was an event to mark the bottling of this commemorative brew, and he was again present. In his autobiography, *A Brewer's Tale*, he said:

> Having seen the brewery in the course of construction at the age of twelve and starting my career there in 1945, it was sad to see its finish as an active and flourishing entity sixty years after I had entered its gates. At that stage I was amazed by its immensity and modernity—so unlike the grimy mills in Lancashire . . . and I never lost that sense of awe in the forty-four years where it was my base. Familiarity never diminished this sense of wonder. . . . Perhaps it was the memories of the people that hit hardest. . . . It was great to be reunited with some old friends, many as it proved, for the last time, but it would have been difficult for the young hosts and hostesses to appreciate the depths of feelings for the Old Times.[53]

Many of those interviewed would have undoubtedly shared these sentiments about the final closure and especially about the memories of friends and workmates. How do we make sense of these ideas and attitudes toward work in the wider context of closure processes and bigger questions of deindustrialization?

How does Park Royal fit with other accounts of industrial loss, and what can it tell us more widely about work?

Other stories of plant shutdowns and deindustrialization over the years make it possible to detect a range of responses, attitudes, assumptions, and feelings. Often workers report distress and rage at what they confront; they feel anger or betrayal at the news of closure. At the opposite end of that continuum are those who are happy to bid "farewell to the factory."[54] What all of them have in common—and this is one of the signatures of this genre of economic and social research—is the way closure reveals a whole host of the patterns and structures around work. Specifically, plant closure as well as the wider process of deindustrialization uncovers not just the immediate visceral attitudes to redundancy but a much deeper sense of loss associated with industrial work. The oral histories from Guinness are no different.

Deindustrialization and closure can be thought of here as a breaching experiment: the end of production creates a space for reflection, whether individuals or groups like it or not. Revealed in the process are many of the taken-for-granted attitudes, identities, assumptions, and attachments associated with work. Closure and its associated redundancies start a search for meaning both about the present and future but, more especially, about the past. What was good and bad about the past, why did I enjoy it, what do I retrospectively see as important? These are just some of the questions posed if not always fully answered. What the workers revealed is not straightforward or simple nostalgia. Instead, they laid bare an ambiguous attachment that they narrated across interviews as they reflected upon a working life. Their enjoyment of being embedded is double-edged; to stay connected is to be rooted, for better or worse.

The interviews also revealed how employment for many industrial workers has changed radically over time. Workers at, or after, the point of loss reflected on the experience of their younger selves while considering the radical rupture in the quality of work and working life itself they have undergone. What they related in terms of their past is an atmosphere of relative predictability and order, where work structures and people were intelligible and knowable. They described a moral order of the workplace in which they discovered value and gave shape to their working lives and to those of others. This sense of intelligibility, what I have called a type of embeddedness, is subject to change over time. In the Guinness example, a broad feeling of attachment and ownership gradually dissolved as a result of a number of separate but related developments. This disembedding process, this erosion of a feeling of ownership, can explain some of the mixed reaction to the news of the closure. There was a general sense of resignation that closure was inevitable, that given the market conditions and the company's situation, it made corporate sense to close Park Royal. But underpinning this resignation was the sentiment that workers had drawn back from investing too heavily in their jobs for their own self-preservation. As a number of them explicitly said, they had been through a number of restructurings over the previous decade and a half, which had involved them having to apply for an ever-diminishing number of posts—a sort of macabre version of musical chairs. In this context, the plant closure came as, if not relief then as certainty, a fixed known around which life could be reoriented. What was being lamented at the point of closure was not what was, but rather what had been. While the loss of salaries and enduring friendships were sources of regret, what the workers fondly remembered was a different quality of work and working life they had enjoyed earlier in their careers. This was a more rounded sense of employment embedded in social relationships, as well as a broader understanding of the structures that allowed and enabled people to mature over time, an "industrial citizenship" of sorts.

Finally, what was revealed in the interviews at Park Royal was a deeper understanding of orientations and attitudes to work. This was manifest in how workers discussed their own working lives and what the future held for them, but it became especially apparent when they spoke of their adult children's experience of employment. While most of the Guinness workers' children were better educated and qualified than their parents, their experience of work had not usually been as positive. This next generation had to confront instability, precarity, closure, and layoffs themselves—and at earlier stages in their careers. In trying to make sense of their children's experiences, Guinness workers were inevitably reflecting on their own lives and the values they had absorbed along the way. What resulted was never a simple retreat into the past; indeed, what they narrated was a very clear sense that the models that had informed their working lives held little or no value for the next generation; the advice was to "not get stuck in a groove," to keep one's options open, to "never be complacent."

When the last brew was completed, it was bottled with a special label to mark the occasion. The label read "GUINNESS COMMEMORATIVE BREW: TRADITIONALLY BREWED, PARK ROYAL BREWERY LONDON." On the reverse were the names of all seventy-eight members of the Park Royal operations team. A workforce that had once, not so long ago, numbered over fifteen hundred people could now be listed comfortably on the back on a bottle of stout.

7

THE RUINED GARDEN

In his 2010 book *A Guide to the New Ruins of Great Britain*, architectural critic Owen Hatherley cites J. B. Priestley's *English Journey* as one of his principal influences. Hatherley's aim was to offer a critique of postwar architecture, especially that which had emerged since 1979. He reflected back on the "three Englands" of manmade structures that Priestley had uncovered on his 1934 travels: the countryside, one that had "long since ceased to make its own living"; a second England of the Industrial Revolution, a place of "iron, brick, smokestacks and back-to-backs"; and a "commercial world of arterial roads, Tudorbethan suburbia, art deco factories and cinemas; cheap and ersatz, but without the brutality of the second." Hatherley sought to extend and update Priestley's typology by adding a fourth and fifth England to the mix: the "country of the postwar settlement, of council estates, Arndale centres and campus universities" and the "post-1979 England of business parks, Barrett homes, riverside 'stunning developments,' out-of-town shopping and distribution centres." Hatherley wanted to explore the way this latter vision of England had decimated both the architectural and political collectivism embedded in the former.[1]

Hatherley's observations provide a useful stepping-off point for thinking about many of the issues considered here. One aspect of industrial decline lies in ruins and ruination; loss is embedded and remembered in material structures, objects, and images. Ruins, especially industrial ones, have excited a range of responses and interventions from a variety of groups. Workers, for example, often collect mementos of their former workplaces, sometimes a brick or piece of rubble that acts as proof that they were there.[2] As one witness noted of laid-off factory workers returning to their former place of work: "There are people who walked in and out of these gates for thirty-five years. They come by and point and say, 'I worked at that window up there,' then they pick up [a] brick or a piece of stone and go away."[3]

A second way to think about ruination is through the aestheticization by cultural theorists, photographers, and urban explorers. Urban explorers in particular are "fascinated primarily in the flotsam of capital. They engage in a practice intensely interested in locating sites of haunted memory, seeking interaction with the ghosts of lives lived."[4] All of these interventions in different ways speak to a contest over memory, over the past, and by implication a vision for a yet unrealized future. Ruins lend themselves to visual imagery; the huge number of coffee-table books about the ruins of Detroit and other deindustrialized cities attest to this widespread fascination.[5]

And yet this gaze is not unproblematic; it is often described as "ruin porn" or deindustrial voyeurism, and photographers and artists are accused of riding roughshod over the memories and dignity of former workers to provide titillation for hipsters wallowing in rustbelt chic. In another register, images of industrial decline are seen as part of a "smokestack nostalgia," conjuring up of an imagined past that compensates for the absence of meaningful employment today while downplaying industry's negative impact on the health of communities and the environment. As one commentator observed, "Recent years have seen photographers, artists, urban explorers and (yes) scholars flood into deindustrialized cities like Detroit, prompting a public backlash against 'ruin porn' and the hipster commodification of misery."[6]

In the reflection on industrial closure and on industrial ruins, there is a profound consideration of the meaning of industrial work both to those who carried it out and to the wider communities who were, for a time at least, the beneficiaries of the prosperity it brought. Ruins, just like the loss of work, break routines; they force us to confront change and the taken-for-granted past. Ruins and the process of ruination reveal the attachments, the meanings, and sense of loss associated with the past.

The Park Royal brewery affords us another privileged occasion for exploring many of these issues. Memories were defined and attached to buildings, physical objects, and the places in which they are located. The battle over the former brewery buildings and their importance as industrial heritage was fought on the wide canvas of the press. The redundant brewery buildings were entered by urban explorers, and the site was subject to reimagination as part of urban redevelopment. Former workers and a variety of others found meaning in images of ruin and destruction, illustrating how memory was stimulated by a variety of images; pictures become part of a mourning process, a form of industrial obituary.

THE DEMOLITION OF PARK ROYAL

If, in the 1930s, Park Royal and its environs could be seen as the Silicon Valley of its day, by the 1990s it offered an altogether different prospect. Many of the factories planted there in the interwar years were, like Guinness, subject to rationalization and often closure. Some of the iconic buildings of the era were demolished, like the Firestone Building, or were repurposed, like the Hoover Building, which was converted into a supermarket.[7] The Guinness brewery buildings had come under the shadow of demolition even before their ultimate closure. In 1998, plans were unveiled to redevelop the valuable West London site. The spring issue of *Park Royal London*, the quarterly magazine of the Park Royal Partnership, noted, "The majority of the buildings on the [Guinness] site are over 60 years old, with many standing empty and no longer required for modern brewery production."[8] The glossy publication's details of the plan included new roads, "high quality" office development, five acres of open public space, improved transport links, a hotel, new leisure facilities, a "wildlife corridor," and housing. Bright color photographs showed a radical reimagining of the site, through architect's models and artists' illustrations of the proposed redevelopment. However, the £350 million design ran into opposition, most prominently from the architectural pressure group the Twentieth Century Society, which lobbied hard for the existing brewery buildings to be spot listed.[9] In one letter to the Listing Branch of the Department of Culture, Media and Sport, the case officer for the society wrote: "The Guinness factory captured a moment in British manufacturing when factory buildings were being used quite self-consciously to convey a message about the company and the product."[10]

In later correspondence from the society to the planning officer at Brent Council,[11] the tone was more urgent, as the listing had been rejected by the secretary of state, against the recommendation and wishes of English Heritage. As the letter put it, "The Society is therefore convinced that the buildings on this site are clearly of national architectural importance, but have not been recognised as such due to considerations other than their architectural and historic importance being allowed to influence the listing decision."[12]

Urging Brent Council to stand up for the buildings, the society pointed out, somewhat backhandedly, "It is clear that the Borough of Brent is not so overwhelmed with historic buildings of this standing that it can afford to sacrifice the Guinness site in the proposed manner."[13] The letter concluded by informing the council that the Guinness site was one of fifty twentieth-century buildings to be included in the society's *Buildings at Risk* report, emphasizing its national importance. The "other" considerations seem to have been that Diageo wanted the flexibility to remodel the site in line with new investment. The company had also commissioned a report that poured cold water on the idea of seeking new uses for the existing buildings.

Two years later, Diageo proposed a slightly modified plan to build a 1.25-million-square-foot office park called Firstcentral, consisting of nine corporate headquarters buildings, of which Diageo's would be one. A 2000 article in the *Financial Times* reported the rundown nature of Park Royal, describing it as "a jumble of ageing factories and warehouses . . . in the heart of a declining industrial area." What was proposed in their stead was seen as "transformational," the article noted: "They will be stunningly different." The developers "will be seeking occupiers squeezed out of central London by rising rents, traffic congestion and sheer lack of new buildings." The article trumpeted the development's green credentials, noting it would be one of the first "major urban regeneration projects to match government demands for 'sustainable' development."[14] The eventual result was the Diageo HQ7 building on the site of the former Guinness athletics ground.

By the time the closure of the brewery was announced, things had moved on, and Diageo made plans to demolish the entire site, generating a huge amount of attention in the mainstream media and the specialist architectural and heritage press. Under the headline "End of era for work of pure genius; Plans to demolish brewery that is hailed as modern masterpiece," *The Guardian* reported that "to some it is a bland brick box; to others, a modernistic masterpiece on a par with such temples of industrial design as Battersea power station." The piece described how the planned destruction was part of Brent Council's regeneration plans and that the brewery buildings had a certificate of immunity from listing granted by the government. The Twentieth Century Society described the scheme as "pure architectural vandalism": "To sweep away such structures without serious discussion and good reason would be irresponsible and philistine." The article recorded that Gavin Stamp, chair of the society, "has appealed to Diageo to allow architectural experts to inspect the brewery and urged Brent Council to come up with a more imaginative use for the buildings." This position was further supported by SAVE Britain's Heritage, whose secretary stated, "The Guinness factory is [Gilbert] Scott at his most powerful and monumental, it is almost unbelievable that these buildings cannot be economically used."[15]

Stamp was one of the most vociferous critics of Diageo's decision to demolish the brewery through his position as chair of the Twentieth Century Society, in his column in the satirical magazine *Private Eye* under the pen name Piloti, and eventually in a chapter about the brewery in a book of his collected essays, *Anti-Ugly*. Here he rehearsed many of his objections to the plans and the importance and aesthetic quality of Scott's buildings but went further to encompass a more ecological perspective: "No serious attempt has been made to see if the brewery buildings can be re-used while, with growing consciousness of the 'embodied energy' in built structures, demolishing such superb masonry seems to me wicked."[16] In the conclusion to this same chapter he warmed to this environmental theme:

> Surely politicians and bureaucrats should learn to think more holistically, more intelligently? As for me, I will lament the fact that, in future, my Guinness will not emanate from those magnificent brick blocks at Park Royal but will have been imported from Dublin—thus wasting more energy as well as wasting those millions of special 2⅝-inch Wellington facing bricks separated by ⅜-inch flush joints of carefully tinted mortar. Nobody is building walls like these anymore.[17]

But this story became more complex still. In defense of its decision to demolish the buildings, Diageo began to dispute just how central Gilbert Scott's involvement had been to the overall design. Under the strap line "Brewery Heritage Denied," the *Architects' Journal* reported that "global drinks corporation Diageo has refused to accept that Gilbert Scott was responsible for one of

London's most significant industrial buildings—so that it can justify its demolition."[18] An official spokesperson from the firm stated: "It's important to understand that the buildings were designed by Alexander Gibb and Partners—with Sir Giles Gilbert Scott acting as a consultant to add some decorative features, particularly the brickwork."[19]

Rob Sharp, an architectural journalist, pointed out that Nikolaus Pevsner's guide to the architecture of North West London attributed the design to Scott, while Gibb and Partners acted as consultant engineers. Sharp suggested that sketches in the Royal Institute of British Architects library provided evidence that Scott was "concerned with the modelling of the masses of the building, as well as all of the external detail and the choice of brick."[20] Later in the same issue, there was a cartoon of Stamp carrying the Park Royal buildings on his head after one of the famous John Gilroy Guinness advertisements; Stamp proclaims "Gilbert Scott," while in the second panel a wrecking ball labeled "Diageo" crashes through the buildings as a startled Stamp looks on. Another speech bubble, from an unseen third party, declares: "No, It's Not!"[21]

When I interviewed Stamp in the book-lined study of his South London home in 2009, he was eager to stress just how important Scott was as an architect and by extension the Guinness brewery: "As far as I'm concerned, it's a major work by Sir Giles Gilbert Scott, who[m] I regard as one of the great architects of the twentieth century, in his sort of industrial style that he'd rolled out for Battersea Power Station."[22] When I put to him Diageo's suggestion that Scott was merely a consultant on the buildings, Stamp laughed: "So what? I mean, he made the outside of the buildings matter, and he made a very good job of it. I thought those blocks looked splendid. As I say, he had terrific brickwork. I mean, that's why it's so wicked to see such beautiful masonry destroyed that could have been retained."[23]

Later in the interview, Stamp described more fully the importance and nature of the contribution the architect had made and why this was key to understanding what was lost at Park Royal:

> Yes, it doesn't need to be there, no. No, it could just be plain, plain brickwork, but his job was to make that brickwork interesting and introduce a bit of—I mean, he regarded himself as an artist, an artist architect, and so elements like those vertical piers were introduced just for architectural effect, but they don't disguise the nature of the big blocks underneath. I mean, some people would say it's just cosmetic. No, it's more than that: it's giving a proper architectural treatment to what otherwise might be just very ungainly, ugly blocks—just what he did at Battersea[24]

The buildings at Park Royal clearly meant a lot to the architectural community, or at least elements of it. But what did these same structures mean to those who worked there, and how did the built environment figure in their memories?

BUILDING MEMORIES

Almost all of the workers interviewed before closure talked at length about the buildings and their memories of working in them. These reflections included their initial impressions of the site when they had begun their careers and significant events in their lives and those of their coworkers. But more poignantly, their reflections returned to the fate of the buildings just before the closure and their impending demise after production finished. They voiced a mixture of sentiments, an almost universal regret for the projected fate of the site, tempered by an overwhelming pragmatism at the prospective destruction.

Peter Maher's interview was a good example of this mix. He had not worked at Guinness for long when he was interviewed, starting in 2000; he had worked for twenty years at a Heinz plant close to Park Royal. What was fascinating about his account was the way he compared and contrasted the experience both of closure and demolition at the two sites. Maher kept drawing on the similarities between the two workplaces, the culture of work, the paternalistic management, and the general industrial atmospheres. His reflections on his previous job at Heinz constantly merged with his thoughts on Guinness: "That [atmosphere] gradually went out of it over time, though, as I think it's happened here in Guinness. So they were quite good, I think big companies are quite good like that, or at least they were."[25] When pushed to elaborate, Maher almost took on the role of an anthropologist, casting himself as an outsider who had come to the brewery trying to understand what it had been like prior to the changes of the previous two decades:

> They were more similar, I think—well, a lot of the social end of it was gone—but I do ask people about the history of the place and the way it worked here, and go into old buildings and you say, how many people worked in here, and you think, that sounds like exactly the same, and they didn't need that bit anymore. The same thing happened to us [at Heinz].[26]

Like Guinness, the Heinz factory had been highly efficient but was closed, as Maher lamented, because it had been in the "wrong place at the wrong time and the wrong size." It was, he said, a "good factory." Maher's reflections continued to mix his feelings toward his old employment with that of his current position. He had returned to the now-demolished Heinz site, and while denying being nostalgic, he said he felt "quite sad every time I walk there. I really do. As I say, twenty-odd years is a long time. I will admit I still miss that, you know. I miss the people that I worked with."[27]

Maher used his experience at Heinz to come to terms with his current loss and those of his workmates who had been employed at Guinness for much longer than he had. He reflected on what was to happen to the buildings, describing the parallels between the fates of the two sites as "uncanny": "Yes, I think it'll be more so here because this place is a landmark, isn't it. Anybody that comes in and out of West London knows the Guinness brewery. It's going to look very strange to see that [demolition] done."[28]

There was a strong strand of pragmatism running through the interviews carried out in 2004 and 2005, an overwhelming sense of the need to let go of the physical site, in the same way that a more general attachment to work discussed in the previous chapter was being eroded. In my interview with Henry Dawson in 2005, he spoke about his mixed feelings toward the buildings:

> They're like ghosts, being empty. They were actually beautiful buildings when they were full because everything was copper and brass and it was all clean and shiny, because that was the way it was kept, you know, polished up. Seeing the brew house as it is now, an empty shell with nothing in there, it's dead, finished, gone. So, no, I won't be sad to see them go like that, but I'm sad that they're empty and all the vessels are gone.[29]

I asked Dawson if he were going to take any souvenirs of the plant to remember it. "No, I don't think so," he replied. "I've got all my memories in my head."[30] There was a similar pragmatism in an interview with Dave Bathurst:

> When I drive to work each day over the years, I've seen on, on my route plenty of buildings that are exactly like this one that have come down over the years and other things have been built on them, sometimes better, sometimes worse. I don't feel any great emotion. From my local station at Hampton Court, I can take the train up to Waterloo. It grieves me every time I go up there to see Battersea Power Station in its sorry state, and it angers me almost. That's the same architect that built the brewery. It would grieve me enormously if in fact the buildings were listed, which they're not, and they were allowed to moulder away into a sort of derelict unpleasant decrepit sight. To a certain extent, if they ever do anything with Battersea Power Station, which they did with Bankside,[31] I can always go and look at those to remember what the brewery looked like but, no, I think it's the right thing to do [demolition]. You can't convert the buildings. So, yeah, the plant should go, the buildings should come down and something else built on it. As I say, I go past lots of sites over the years that have gone through that transition. On the Great West Road, I look at things like the old Trico building, which was knocked down and has now become that, I think, wonderful GlaxoSmithKline building.[32]

It was better for Bathurst and some of his other colleagues that the site had a "clean death" rather than a drawn-out decline and ruination. As he went on, he made clear he would want memories of how it *had* been:

> So, no, I think a few photos that remind of the buildings will do fine. It should come down. It will be a great pity if it just deteriorated because no one could agree what to do with it. So it's probably a good thing it's not listed because I think it would just sit here and decay. No, it'll be good. No, I shan't feel any great sadness.

I'll probably come and drive over occasionally, or if I happen to be this way and see at what stage it's got to.[33]

The workers' attachment to the buildings is somewhat different from scholarly and artistic approaches. For employees, the brewery buildings prompted memories, but they were not sufficient to hold these memories. As with Dawson, I asked Bathurst if he planned to take any mementos of his working life at Guinness:

I probably will. Down in my little health and safety cupboard, I've got the road signs, they had signs down there, that say Oast Way. So I suspect no one will want them. I may take those home with me. Would I want a little memento or something? Yes. I'd want something that's just on the mantelpiece or wherever to just say, "That reminds me of where I worked for thirty-odd years." But no more than that; I won't be at the gate with placards saying "Do not demolish these buildings." No, they must come down, but I will certainly take some sort of memento, more than a brick. I gather the bricks are quite valuable.[34]

There was real affection for the buildings and the material surroundings of work. Most of the employees interviewed felt a connection with the plant as a whole and the various individual spaces where they had worked. The built environment had helped to frame memories of both work and those they had worked with; the buildings helped to shape both the form and content of those memories. There was, too, a sense of awe at Park Royal as a place to work, one that for most of their careers they perhaps had largely taken for granted. Closure and the imminent demolition of the buildings acted as a breaching experiment in which workers were forced to consider consciously, perhaps for the first time, their attitude toward, and relationship with, their physical environment.

I was surprised at the time of the plant closure just how much historical knowledge the workforce had of the buildings' origins. In some ways this reflects an oral tradition within the brewery whereby details of the past were exchanged over time. This had been aided and underpinned by the historical nature of the staff magazine, *Guinness Time*. Many of the older workers on site at the point of closure had, earlier in their career, read the magazine, even though its last number had been published some three decades before. Some interviewees still had copies in desk drawers and lockers or had rescued discarded copies from waste skips.

Workers secured their memories by taking material objects as mementos of work. Photographs were important, but time and again people talked about taking something tangible as a reminder of where they had worked. While these objects had little if any extrinsic value, they had a great deal of intrinsic meaning for those who took them. In this way, we can make sense of the potential contradiction here of being resigned to seeing the buildings destroyed and yet valuing them and what they represented. There was a pragmatic fatalism about what was to happen, which the workers felt powerless to prevent, in much the same way they had accepted the news of the closure itself. However, there was also an attachment to the buildings and the memories they represented that meant some would rather see the factory destroyed than have it "moulder away" and become a ruin, however picturesque and aesthetically rich it might be.

EXPERIENCING DEMOLITION

The demolition of the brewery in 2006 revealed more meanings embedded in the built environment, often through visual means. Here images record events, capture memories, and stimulate deeper reflection on industrial change. After Park Royal closed in 2005, I was contacted by a Diageo employee, Adrian Sturgess, who worked in the company's headquarters building, HQ7, next to the brewery. A clerical worker offering support to wholesale customers selling Guinness, Sturgess had begun work in the brewery's offices in the late summer of 2001, and as he said himself he had "fallen in love" with the buildings. He had seen pictures taken by David McCairley as part of the original project and had been inspired in turn to record the demolition of the buildings. An eager and talented amateur photographer, Adrian took thousands of images of the plant's dramatic fate over the period of a year or so. I interviewed him in 2009, sometime after the brewery buildings had finally come down. In his West London flat he showed me his huge collection of visual material and talked at length both about the choreography of demolition and what the buildings had meant to him.

During the interview, we looked at the photographs he had taken, with each new image sparking more memories of the site. He described the demolition machines at work while he was taking pictures:

> They just chomped and chomped. The machines—I compared them to dinosaurs. They sort of went in and grabbed and grabbed and crushed, and then sort of pushed and pushed and pushed. I was getting closer and closer, and the guy that I was with was, "Come back, get back—you're going to get hit by something!" And the whole sort of thing sort of went, waah, down.[35]

Often Adrian would begin to reminisce about the buildings when they had been whole, pointing out architectural features or instances in his working life at the plant. Gaining official permission had been difficult, but after numerous attempts he got a break:

> One lunchtime—it was winter, freezing cold—standing pointing my camera through the railings at the malt store, the bits of bricks coming off, and this guy just came up to me, and said, "Oh, are you interested in what we're doing?" I explained that I worked at the brewery, and he said, "Well, I'm the site foreman—do you want to come inside?" I said, "Well, I'd love to, if I can." He said, "Oh, just come over and contact us and you can come in."[36]

After being issued a hardhat and a fluorescent yellow jacket, he was allowed on the site, as he explained excitedly:

And then having to try and fit it in around my shifts was quite difficult, because I couldn't just take two hours out. The first time I went, I took an extended lunch break and I was gone for three hours, and I got a telling-off for being away for three hours. I said to my boss, "It's a once-in-a-lifetime opportunity—I was shown around the whole site, from top to bottom." He said, "Oh. If you want to go again, you have to do it outside work time." So if I was on the late shift, I'd make an appointment for the next morning to be there at 8:30, so go 'round till 11:30, and then go and get ready for work to carry on. I just couldn't wait to see what the pictures looked like [laughing]![37]

I was intrigued at his motivation for undertaking what had become such a mammoth project. His reply reflected both a personal desire and what he saw as a public duty to record the process for posterity:

Oh, I was just fascinated. I didn't think anybody else was doing it. I don't know why, but I just had a passion for that building. A lot of the people that had started after me, they didn't even know. They didn't work there. I suppose it could be because that's the only place I'd ever worked in London. That was the first job I had in London, and I've been there ever since. It just was a special place. I didn't think anyone was recording it, and I wanted to, and eventually I ended up taking thousands and thousands and thousands of photos [laughing]![38]

When I pushed him to explain his attachment to the buildings, he remembered looking over at the brewery from the HQ building:

I don't know what it is. There was just something about the building . . . whether it was the detail, whether it was the brick . . . I just found it fascinating, and I used to love walking 'round there. You know, you'd come up the stairs, every morning, when I'd come up the stairs, I always used to stop at the top before I'd go in and look over the side.[39]

He compared his own feelings about the loss of the buildings with those of his colleagues, some of whom, like him, had actually worked on the old site when the offices had been located there:

The people in my section, I sat next to—I still sit next to—my friend Margaret, and she also worked there, and it was a sense of sadness that it was coming down, but a lot of people just couldn't be bothered, just like, "Oh, well." You'd be working away, and all of a sudden, the whole floor would just go [makes noise], and you'd think, okay, they've pulled down a wall, and you'd look over and this cloud of dust would come over.[40]

A narrative of loss haunted this interview, but this was at times mixed with anger at the sheer waste of what he had seen. This was especially apparent when he showed me images from the former office block, Apollo House. Talking about the reception area, he said: "I watched them smash the reception desk with sledge hammers. It was a beautiful oak desk, and these two guys were having so much fun."[41] This indifference on the part of some was in stark contrast to his own deep sense of attachment. This was best illustrated while he was showing me his own former workplace being demolished:

> It was just after five o'clock, I was told it was coming down. That was the part of the brew house that I worked in, and that wall actually came down on my birthday. I remember standing on the road, in absolute floods of tears, thinking, "Oh, my building's coming down! My window—there it goes, into pieces!"[42]

Although he had worked in the brewery buildings for only a relatively short period, he had become as attached to them as many of the production workers had, most of whom had known the site for much longer. His bond has a moral quality to it, an ethic of care for the site, which is revealed not just in his general account of the structures being demolished but in those passages where he perceived disrespect for their fate—be it the indifference of his colleagues, or especially the demolition workers gleefully setting about their destruction of a desk. His images do more than simply record the process of demolition; they reveal in pictures the construction of the building, showing how the surface fabric of the building related to what lay underneath. Collectively, they make a grim bookend to the photographs in the Guinness archive of the blocks being constructed in the 1930s.

However, Sturgess was not the only person taking images of the site at this time. When I interviewed Terry Aldridge, a former production worker, in 2015, he revealed that he, too, had visited the site to bear witness to the demolition. He had left the brewery under one of the previous downsizing schemes, in 1995. A keen photographer, as he showed me the images he had taken of the destruction, he told me about the impact of what he saw:

> I was very saddened by that. I was a bit angry in some ways because I thought they were going to [deep inhalation] use bit of it, maybe the brew house, as a museum. I went up there during the time that they were demolishing the place, and it's a bit of a lump-in-the-old-throat job. You're looking at this poor old building, the way you see it, and you can see all the floors—I got a picture in here—you can see all the floors and you say, "Oh, that's where I stored the bucket there, when I was wetting that" [laughs]. God! It was sad. Yeah, very sad.[43]

Aldridge made several pilgrimages to his former place of work, but by the final visit there was little to record:

> I went back again at a later date and there was absolutely nothing left; there was just these pyramids of rubble. And I'm standing there thinking, "Wait a minute, where was it? Was it slightly that way or this way?" Because you've lost it [bearings]. Really odd, to see it like that. Yeah, it was sad.[44]

I was fascinated to understand why Aldridge, who had not worked at the plant for over a decade, would make the long trip from his South Coast home to record the fate of a former place of work. After a long sigh, he told me:

> Curiosity, I suppose. Can't help but go back up there. You work there all those years, and you just—it's funny, I wouldn't go back and see Lancia's [his former workplace] be demolished. And they did demolish that building. No, it was something about the brewery, the people in it, the work, the camaraderie of all the people that you work with. You couldn't help but go back. It's almost the last tribute.[45]

A little later that summer, I interviewed Dawson in his North West London home, ten years after I had initially talked to him, while the brewery was open. I asked him if he had returned to the site during its demolition. He said simply: "No, I stayed away. I didn't want to see it being knocked down. I've been back up the headquarters now and I look at it and think, "What used to be there was an iconic building. Now there's nothing, there's just a hole."[46]

I asked him if he had seen any of Aldridge's photographs of the demolition: "Yeah, I know Terry did. He's tried to get me to have a look at the pictures—oh, no. Don't particularly want to. I've seen a couple of odd pictures, but I don't particularly want to see it."[47] As he explained to me, "I'd rather remember it how it was working . . . and people smiling while they were at work."

There are some fascinating things going on in the observations of Sturgess, Aldridge, and Dawson. In their different ways, each man showed a great love of his former site of work, each saw great value in it, and each was sad, and even angry, to witness the buildings destroyed. But while Sturgess and Aldridge felt compelled to take photographs of the ruination process, to record the events *because* of this attachment, Dawson could not bear to look at these same images, precisely because he wanted to remember attachment in a different form. Through images, memories can be stored and regenerated but also perhaps eroded. These images allow a complex range of emotions to surface and circulate.

EXPLORING RUINS

In 2005, the brewery became the site of urban exploration by *Forbidden Places* author Sylvain Margaine. Based in Belgium, Margaine is one of Europe's most high-profile photographers and urban explorers, managing to monetize his hobby through a popular website and a series of bestselling coffee-table books recording his travels through abandoned spaces. The page on Margaine's website dedicated to Park Royal describes the brewery as an "incredibly beautiful site completely untouched" and details how he also "managed to explore: labs, silos, rooftops, demolition machines, offices, radio room, hair salon . . . A king-size urban exploration in an incredible place, protected from vandalism."[48] There are twenty-three images of Park Royal on the *Forbidden Places* site, both internal and external shots, as well as the eventual demolition of the brewery.

On one level, these images qualify for the "ruin porn" category of urban exploration critique. Little, if anything, is said about those who used to work there, although there is an explanation of the brewery's abandonment. However, the pages devoted to Park Royal confound simple dismissal as indulgent aestheticization when one examines the comments section. When I visited the website in the summer of 2016, there were fifteen posts commenting on the Park Royal images, the majority of which were written by former workers or their family members. The commentators were clearly grateful for the chance to see inside the brewery again, if tempered by regret at the fate of the buildings. Some told stories of working at the plant and mixed these with a broader reflection on the nature of work. One of the latest posts was from former worker David Warr:

> . . . joined the company in the summer of 1974. I went into the Boys' Scheme which meant over a two year period you got to work for a month or two at a time in one of the many departments in the brewery. What an eye opener that was for a still wet behind the ears boy of sixteen. Guinness as an employer was fantastic, good pay, free pension, free food and beer, brilliant sports club and social scene plus the company had a real family feel to it. It was like a little world of its own. It is very sad to see the pictures now as they bring back so many great memories. Mostly though you remember the people and the characters you worked with and met. There are some really good stories to tell about this place and the people in it but I would be here for at least a week if I went into them all.

This text could have come straight from one of the interviews I recorded, reflecting as it does on the nature of work at Guinness and its "family feel." It is overwhelmingly positive, some might say nostalgic, for days of youth. This positive account is then tempered by the same person's use of that account of his own past to reflect on the present condition of employment:

> I can't help but think that companies nowadays would benefit by taking the approach Guinness did to their employees and still make good profits as Guinness did. Although there was close to 1500 people working there when I started, everyone seemed to know everyone else and that included the directors. I remember getting into a lift one day in the malt store not long after I started and a chap got in who I didn't know but he asked my name and then went on to explain he knew my father who was still working at the brewery at the time. It turned out to be Edward Guinness.

There is a longing here for a different type of capitalism, one in which people in positions of power could remember the names of their subordinates. This is a desire for simple recognition. In another post, Carole Harris, whose father had worked at Park Royal, said of the buildings: "I recall being in awe of this magnificent building. Such a shame, but unfortunately business does not survive on sentiment."[49]

Clearly, then, urban exploration is capable of more than simple aestheticization of abandonment. These images can also spark memory and, by extension, a critique of both past and present. They allow the viewer to ponder change on an individual and collective level.

RETHINKING THE RUINS OF PARK ROYAL

How, then, do we make sense of Park Royal through its abandonment, ruination, and ultimately complete demolition? How can we think about the way that workers respond to material and visual reminders of their former workplaces, and what can it tell us about work now and in the past? In her fascinating book on the obituary, sociologist Bridget Fowler wrote:

> The obituary offers the rare accolade of public recognition, the first step towards posthumous memory. Yet it is not just a *store of value*, it is also a *measure* of value: the obituary as a biographical form illuminates the social reality of dominance and distinction, whilst only rarely shedding light on the world of subordination.[50]

The larger genre of highly aesthetic deindustrial literature can thus be read as a form of memorialization, a collective recognition of value, and therefore is something that might be welcomed. But Fowler is also right that obituary is always selective. Thus Fowler's analysis, derived from French sociologist Pierre Bourdieu's concepts of dominance and subordination, reflects the ways in which some urban explorers produce a certain type of account that is devoid of a critical discussion of class relations and processes. The urban explorers' focus on aesthetics and the beauty of ruins acts as a selective obituary that is in danger of ignoring the people who once populated those spaces. Further, there seems to be a class disconnect between the urban explorers and photographers, whose emphasis is on pleasure, exploration, and discovery of the self, and those people for whom the ruins were once workplaces. From this perspective, there is something unseemly or even objectionable about middle-class urban explorers gaining pleasure from sites of working-class loss. Spelunking can be read as akin to dancing on a grave, an unthinking act in what, for some, is a deeply meaningful, almost sacred space. Anger directed against urban explores is inspired by class antagonism meted out to the working class, twice, by middle and upper-class people: first in the process of closure and second as postindustrial necrology. In both cases, violence is being done, one class on another, whether by design or accident.

However, it is wrong to read the literature and imagery of industrial ruins only in this narrow sense. These interventions can also be thought of as mourning in a more extensive and expansive way, one that is more inclusive and one with a more open class dynamic.

In guarding against the danger of "smokestack nostalgia," it is important to listen to the way workers talk about their past, to acknowledge the real value they discovered in their work and how this in turn allows them to reflect critically on both their former employment and work now and in the future. The Guinness workers' interviews about the process of ruination at Park Royal suggest a complex picture of engagement and disengagement, celebration and mourning, embedding and disembedding. It allows access to an industrial structure of feeling once more, a way to elicit a deeper, more profound understanding of the tensions and contradictions that underpinned industrial work. The Guinness workers are capable of lamenting the rationalization, the closure, and the destruction of their former workplace while simultaneously accepting that loss as part of a process of change over which they have little if any influence. There is an imperative to remember the past through memories but also through images and material objects that may elicit such memories. Obituaries celebrate a life but also help in the mourning process; they offer a degree of closure after loss. But obituary is also about the facilitation of memory, to frame and remind. The process of writing obituaries can be the work of many hands, from urban explorers, to photographers, to workers, to companies themselves. Even a decade after the closure of the brewery at Park Royal, the reminders of this industrial past keep popping up. To use American sociologist Avery Gordon's evocative phrase, they keep "haunting" the social in the present.[51]

Dramatic change acts as a breaching experiment, a rupture in the normal everyday routine that allows, however uncomfortably, reflection on change or loss. It is only at these moments that we start to recognize what we once had and have now potentially lost. The story of Guinness acts as a privileged occasion in understanding some of the contemporary trends within work and corporate life. It epitomizes many of the broader themes in economic life of the last thirty years, as a company closes down one part of its operation and seeks to reimagine its site along very different lines. Older narratives and ideas of sustainability and landscape are overridden by new ones that promise to deliver stunning new places to work and enjoy leisure, to replace the older vista of an industrial economy. The story of Guinness also maps out in microcosm many of the debates over the value and nature of the past in material culture. What counts as development and change? Are change and heritage in conflict? What is the role of monuments to an industrial culture rapidly being eclipsed in a new economic setting? Can new uses for redundant buildings be found, or should they be knocked down to make way for the new regardless of their architectural pedigree?

Guinness is part of a wider story of the nature and meaning of the industrial ruins and material culture from a bygone age. For some, the aestheticization of the industrial past is at best trivializing and at worst disrespectful, the flood of coffee-table renderings of abandoned factories ignoring wider social and economic questions about the past and present. For others, such visualizations are provocative and challenging, subverting taken-for-granted notions of progress and change. The visual and material rendering of abandonment also elicits a range of memories about work. Here history is both marked and celebrated alongside more critical reflection both of that past and of the "now" of the early twenty-first century. If the ruins of Park Royal were memory spaces, in the complete eradication of any trace of those structures, visual images and material artifacts continue to elicit a range of recollection. Industrial culture has a half-life.

CONCLUSION: RETURNING TO PARK ROYAL

On a hot sunny day in mid-August 2016, I returned to Park Royal after a ten-year break. In 2006, I had visited Diageo worker Adrian Sturgess in the HQ7 building that overlooked the brewery, which at that point was in the early stages of demolition. As I walked up from the Tube station at Hanger Lane, the traffic was as heavy as usual. I was conscious that, wide as the footpath was, few pedestrians ever used it now—most were sensible enough to avoid the choking fumes of eight lanes of traffic and the constant deafening noise of cars, buses, and trucks making their way to and fro in West London. As a bus passed me, I thought of J. B. Priestley's 1933 *English Journey* and speculated whether any of the passengers were planning to write a book based on what they saw from their seat; what would they report as their England? An oasis of vegetation and relative calm ran for much of the distance from Hanger Lane to the old brewery grounds; here, nature flourished in its abandonment.

At Park Royal, I descended the path to cross over the railway bridge and then on to the former brewery site itself. Sporadically, over the intervening years, I had tried to keep abreast of what was happening there, scanning Google Earth for evidence of change. On one occasion, I had seen the complete brewery flattened; however, as I moved my cursor around the site, parts of the former buildings made a ghostly reappearance, only to disappear again as I moved on—an older image still haunting the site. Other clues were found on fan webpages of BBC television's *Doctor Who*, for enthusiastic Whovians had returned to the location where a 1968 series had been filmed; their "after" images showed no sign of the brewery's existence.[1] Later still, there was evidence of new structures promised as part of the area's redevelopment; buildings in various states of readiness appeared among the dereliction.

As I emerged from the underpass, a new landscape presented itself, one that, while not finished, had seen extensive development in the intervening decade. Deciding to do a counterclockwise circumnavigation around the footprint of the old brewery, I set out, guided by the old familiar road names—Coronation Road, Rainsford Road—and my memories of what had been. Passing giant real estate posters promising new "mixed use accommodation," illustrated with artists' impressions of what was to come, I made my way past some low-rise industrial units that housed a mixture of distribution companies and food assemblers. The air was filled with the not unpleasant smell of cooked bacon, a contrast to the former pungent aroma of hops. While neat and smart enough in their own way, the industrial sheds that had replaced Gilbert Scott's design offered little for architectural enthusiasts.

What would Priestley have made of these new arrivals? They were functional gray sheds designed to last no more than a couple of decades before being rendered into something else. If it were not for the bright upbeat signage outside the plots, the casual observer would have no idea what went on in those places. As I continued my walk, I passed a group of contract gardeners, trimming the grass of the verge, collecting litter that had blown there from the nearby unloved gyratory road system, and tidying up the neat corporate shrubbery. Their van was poised to move off to their next contract elsewhere in London. Watching them, I was reminded of the scores of Guinness gardeners and arborists who had worked there in the three decades or more after 1945. Although much of the work stayed the same, there were huge differences between these itinerant contractors and the rootedness of the Guinness staff of decades earlier.

Turning the corner onto Twyford Abbey Road, I found plenty of reminders of Guinness. The company housing in Iveagh Avenue, Bodium Way, and Toucan Close was still intact and attractive in its own way. The big difference from the images in *Guinness Time* that had celebrated the opening of the housing estate in 1951 was the number of cars parked outside each house: the uninterrupted vista of pleasant crescents of yesteryear was now a sea of vehicles. Turning back toward the south and Park Royal station, I noticed a faded enamel Guinness sign on the side of a new Romanian restaurant, but it mentioned Dublin as the site of production, not Park Royal. A great deal of construction was going on in this part of the former brewery land, as billboards attested to the "luxury waterside urban living" that buyers would soon be able to enjoy.

Deciding to walk through the gardens of the relatively new office park, with its ponds and bamboo maze, I emerged into a clearing outside the office buildings themselves. Shirt-sleeved management and clerical workers, identifiable by the brightly colored lanyards hanging around their necks, enjoyed their lunch in the late summer sun. Before returning to the station for my journey home, I came across a large billboard, again advertising the plot for a mixed-use development. Behind it, there was almost no evidence that the brewery had ever stood here. The only trace, apart from the Guinness-inspired road names, was the impressive wrought-iron fence that ran down the side where the buildings had been. The sign announced "The Future Starts Here."

Park Royal continues to act as a privileged occasion or arena for understanding contemporary Britain and many of its economic and social structures. That brief tour around the footprint where the brewery once stood offers an important sense of the nature of contemporary capitalism. This is embodied in the plant and buildings of this new world, with anonymous metal-clad industrial units that could be placed anywhere in the country, from Cornwall in the very southwest of England to John O'Groats in the north of Scotland, if not beyond. Quick and cheap to build, they can be erected and dismantled with relative ease, and while they may require an architect, it probably does not need to be one who is the president of the Royal Institute of British Architects or who is concerned with marrying traditional and modernist language in their design.

The types of labor found in the area, too, speak volumes about the changes wrought over the years. Rather than one large employer, the space is dotted by a multitude of smaller undertakings, often branches of larger conglomerates. These are hubs of activity designed to lock into the complex logistics demands of the 24/7 economy. These are often firms that act as subcontractors to larger undertakings whose workers will be on a mixture of permanent and temporary contracts. Some will be part of that newly labeled group the "precariat," enduring a series of contracts through their working lives, fitting in as best they can to the new forms of labor that the new economy demands. Each of these units will be serviced again by a multitude of subcontractors: cleaners and caterers, gardeners for the modest plots of landscape now deemed to be sufficient, and security guards on duty at the gates. These workers, too, will probably be on modest wages, and like their counterparts who work directly for the firms they serve, few if any will be able to enjoy trade union membership.

LANDSCAPES

Park Royal can be read as a rich set of landscapes. It is a landscape of organization, a corporate space, a palimpsest where capitalism has been ordered and reordered with changing fashion and taste. With the building of the brewery in the 1930s, what emerged was a highly rationalized landscape, one designed to transcend the problems of the original brewery in Dublin with all its cramped, messy compromise. Its buildings embodied a very particular vision of how the organization saw itself—one that wanted to make a powerful, if a little understated, claim about itself, projecting in its buildings values of tradition, solidity, stability, and calm within a forward-looking long-term project. This was a set of structures that spoke of being rooted and transcendent. But this sense of corporate identity went far beyond the buildings themselves. The brewery was set in more than a hundred acres of land, and this was no accident; it was a deliberate active choice to create a vast estate of landscaped parkland, gardens, leisure facilities, pasture, and farmland. Importantly, these features—the twelve hundred trees, three thousand shrubs, bushes, and plants added over the decades—were understood as what a contemporary large profitable company *should* do, not only for the workers directly employed on the grounds but also as a neighbor. These features of the Park Royal landscape were considered long-term investments in a common good and were not calculated as a cost to the balance sheet; they were seen as benefits that would pay back in multiple ways down the years.

This same corporate landscape began to be reshaped during the 1980s, with the rationalization of the site, the abandonment of some parts of the brewery, and the new building in others. The Park Royal site itself became decentered from the larger corporate entity being created from the core. The brewery's profits, made from the tangible production of stout, underwrote the creation of what would eventually become one of the largest multinational beverage firms in the world. In this changed corporate landscape, Diageo saw the Park Royal brewery as one asset in a much wider portfolio of brands. Brewing became a cost to be controlled by efficiencies on site or by subcontracting ancillary labor. In this corporate landscape, the real estate and its structures were mapped on a spreadsheet as costs and assets. In the changing economy of the 1980s, the brewery looked increasingly out of place and time. Like the owners of many of the other manufacturing plants of West London that had been built in the interwar period, Guinness sought a new solution to its problems and decided to move production altogether.

The brewery at Park Royal is also a landscape of labor; of construction, of brewing and all of the supporting trades, to its destruction, demolition, and redevelopment. Most importantly, the story of Park Royal demonstrates the dramatic differences in the way labor has been organized, treated, and fundamentally conceived of over the seven decades of the plant's existence. Guinness began by recruiting its workforce from its own staff in Dublin, from its immediate contractors who had been involved in building the brewery, and the local labor market of West London. From the beginning, almost all of the labor undertaken at Park Royal was carried out by workers directly employed by the company itself. The only exceptions in the early days were the transport workers, who themselves had "Guinness Citizenship" extended to them during the 1950s. From that point on until the 1980s, every single worker on the site—from management, supervisors, brewery, truck drivers, bricklayers, and scaffolders, to pastry chefs, cleaners, and security guards—enjoyed stable permanent employment with relatively high wages and a range of fringe benefits such as pensions and the encouragement of management to join a trade union.

But this landscape of labor changed as well. By the 1980s, many firms began to outsource what were viewed as ancillary functions; as these moves proved successful and were judged more efficient, the balance shifted so that increasing proportions of what was previously considered the "core" work was tendered out to contractors who were willing and able to take on all sorts of tasks, from building maintenance to cleaning, catering, and gardening. As the logic of labor reform unfolded, that previously large stable core of workers shrunk to a fraction of the once fifteen-hundred-strong workforce, ultimately reduced to the seventy-eight names that made it onto the commemoration brew label in 2005.

Park Royal is also a landscape of imagination and reimagination over the years before, during, and after the brewery was built and demolished. The principal way in which we can conceive of this imaginary landscape is through the notion of industrial citizenship. In the wake of the Second World War, Guinness management made a conscious and deliberate attempt to consider the purpose of work and what it could be. This was not a prosaic job-redesign program or an efficiency drive, although these were elements of personnel management at this time. Nor was it simply an extension of the paternalistic management for which Guinness was renowned, from its Irish origins in Dublin. There was a genuine drive to create something new—social spaces in which people could develop and grow as workers and, more especially, as human beings. This was a profound and at times touching humanistic appeal to the better angels of the human condition, the sense that staff had to be helped to be all that they could be.

Evidence of this was most notable in the ideas and philosophy behind the training program for young entrants in the brewery, the Boys' and Girls' Scheme—fondly remembered by those who had gone through it as a challenging and richly rewarding system. Written accounts of these programs clearly show that, intellectually, they were underpinned by a clear moral purpose about the nature of work and the human condition. Workers had to be developed through their experience of different aspects of the labor of the brewery to be sure, but their character was also to be stretched and molded by a social and cultural milieu that included sports, outdoor pursuits, and intellectual engagement. The aim of this program, and of other aspects of "Guinness citizenship," was not to produce a pliable, biddable set of automatons; rather, it was to create individual capacity in the subject. This citizenship avoided stressing individualistic traits, aiming instead at creating a conscious reflexive awareness of the role and moral responsibility of workers to others in their society—whether on the immediate grounds of the brewery or in the wider community at large.

Part of the reimagining of work in the period of the long boom was the way the company actively introduced sports and social facilities. This was not unusual for organizations of the era. What was perhaps distinct was the sheer range of this provision and the way it meshed with this broader attachment to autonomous citizenship. In the early 1960s, Guinness employees could enjoy more than thirty different sports and social clubs on site. They could engage in football, rugby, swimming, running, hockey, and lawn bowls, among many other pastimes. They could join one of the two theatrical groups that performed in the 120-seat Guinness theater, or they could simply drink in the Toucan Inn. The point is that they had the choice, time, and resources to do as they wished with their leisure time and some of their work time. Their employment was not in any simple way just about the money.

But Guinness was also imagining its brewery and its environs in a far more developed way. It committed time and considerable resources to landscaping and improving the 134 acres of muddy building site left by the construction contractors, transforming it into a carefully and thoughtfully cultivated space. This husbandry went beyond planting a few trees and shrubs. The company took considerable pride in employing noted arborists and award-winning landscape designers to improve the grounds. Management had a vision for "an estate in factoryland" that was every bit as ambitious as a Georgian aristocrat's vision. Guinness did not need to pay this level of attention to the environment, but they wanted to create something beautiful and desirable that would grow organically and would be enjoyed by visitors and on a day-to-day basis by those who worked there—just because it seemed like a good thing to do.

It is easy to dismiss and even mock the improving tone of the articles in *Guinness Time* and other documents that sketch out such citizenship. It is clear that by a point in the 1960s, this type of project had run its course in a conscious way. But equally apparent is that workers—blue- and white-collar alike—actively created their own autonomous culture within the space and opportunities created by the company and the wider postwar economy. It was this group of men and women who entered the brewery and were socialized into identities of work, trade, and union. They learned patterns of interaction and in turn reproduced and reinvented their own form of industrial citizenship, culture, and atmosphere—an industrial structure of feeling. To be sure, this had many elements of the type of Guinness citizenship desired by company management, not least an autonomous confidence underpinned by the era of full employment, job security, and regular pay raises. Life in these postwar years got noticeably and measurably better year by year, decade by decade. While Guinness as an organization changed and expanded in many ways, there was an intelligibility and order about it. Work structures were underpinned by a set of rules that, while not everyone agreed with them, were largely seen as fair. This space was then reimagined by workers and bent into a form where a working life could unfold for skilled, semiskilled, and unskilled staff, one where individuals could be part of a community and allow themselves to enjoy and humanize even dull, repetitive processes of labor.

In the immediate postwar period, there was a vision and a will to reenchant the workplace at Guinness, and this was part of a wider humanistic impulse in British society, the triumph of the Herbivores over the Carnivores. Recorded in the pages of *Guinness Time* is the clear recognition that the trauma and disruption of the war had had a profound effect not only on veterans but also on those who had lived through the conflict on the home front. As the house journal noted, there was a need to reanchor people in their place of work, to reanimate the social so that they would better understand one another and what they did together. In other words, the aim was to reembed staff into the social fabric of the brewery, with the recognition that these social bonds needed attending to and would not simply spring from people working in close proximity.

From the 1980s onward, Park Royal was reimagined in a very different register. Organizational structure and work were utterly transformed by rationalization, job redesign, and automation, but more profoundly, the essential relationship between an organization and its employees was recast. Here the ambition to create citizenship was sloughed off and employees were reimagined as human resources, if not simply costs to be reduced. The nature and content of the employment relationship became fragmented and fissured. Provision of extra-work facilities became calculated as a cost rather than as a more diffuse public good. In places of work far beyond Park Royal, this same process occurred, radically diminishing an important sphere for the nurturing of culture. What was inevitably lost in the process was the broader, deeper understanding of the human condition and the importance of allowing time and space for people to mature as part of a collective social project.

Whether by design or by accident, the reimagining of work since the end of the long boom has meant that many of the lessons of the war and subsequent years have been forgotten. There seems at times to have been a willful attempt to disembed workers by way of job redesign, labor churn, or corporate fissuring. The result is a detachment from a broader vision of the workplace as an arena of legitimate extra-economic activity, a social space one where it is possible to enjoy oneself in the company of others and to grow. This detachment may have positive outcomes for employers. Workers' ability to confront and resist management's right to manage may be reduced, but it simultaneously corrodes a sense of responsibility, commitment, and trust. This is where the critical nostalgia of my interviews is vital in weighing up what has been lost as a result of corporate change. Here, acceptance of the necessity for change is tempered by the desire to remember what was lost in the process. In the absence of any alternative historical record, these oral histories provide a compelling account of the past and the process of historical change.

The British people have now voted to leave the European Union. While there has been a torrent of political commentary on why the nation opted for "Brexit," one of the constant explanatory themes to emerge has been the deindustrialization of Britain since the 1970s and with that the decimation of the kinds of traditional jobs that once gave identity and meaning to working-class people and their communities, exactly like those at Park Royal. Crucially, while the economic importance of such a loss is clear, there is also space in such narratives for other aspects of change around identity and meaning, attachment and belonging. Quite rightly, what the political and journalistic classes are discovering is that work once provided an important arena for people above and beyond being a source of income; in other words, work matters in multiple ways.[2]

When we look back to the era of the long boom and remember wistfully the ways we used to work, are we engaged in smokestack nostalgia? Are we choosing to forget some of the more problematic aspects of the postwar settlement? The period from the end of World War II until the 1970s was one of growing real incomes across much of the industrialized world, especially for working-class people; it was an exceptional period in the history of capitalism. If we are to endeavor to fundamentally change the way capitalism works, we cannot simply return to the model of the New Deal in the United States or the era of consensus politics of the post-1945 settlement in the United Kingdom, compromised as both were with all manner of contradictions and historical specificity.[3] The type of organization, and the nature of work, characteristic of the long boom era has largely gone and is not going to return. But perhaps now is the time to examine in greater detail how it was that that era has come to be so fondly remembered. To be sure, it was underpinned by sustained rising living standards over those thirty years from 1945 to 1975. But the potential of that period was about much more than just rising wages; it was also a time when working people enjoyed a sense of stability and a degree of security as never before. It was this atmosphere that allowed them to enjoy themselves inside and outside work, to benefit from an unprecedented degree of autonomy and control over their economic lives and a confidence about their future and those of their families.

I will never forget one interview I did with a Guinness worker. At the end of a long interview, the interviewee came out with pure gold (after I had turned the microphone off, as was so often the case). Reflecting on his early working life at the brewery in the late 1960s and early 1970s, he said, "Can you imagine what we used to have here?" The preceding interview had drawn up a whole series of memories and reflections on a working life, the conditions of service, the sports and social clubs, the vertical integration of the site, and the workplace camaraderie. The tone of disbelief in his voice was vivid, as if he had enjoyed some illicit pleasure, and that even remembering and admitting enjoying those features of working life was somehow wrong. There was a profound sense that the types of conditions of service, and indeed the other forms of corporate investment, were illegitimate extravagances that were bound to end sooner or later. He spoke for many of his peers in voicing an obituary for a lost world of work. Striking, too, is just how deeply neoliberal ideology has penetrated our collective consciousness, to the point where it has completely delegitimized a more expansive, progressive, and humane vision for capitalism. In short, contemporary culture and politics seems to have restricted our imaginations so completely that we cannot see alternatives to the current state of affairs.

In a speech at the 2005 Labour Party conference, Tony Blair, then the prime minister, said:

> The pace of change can either overwhelm us, or make our lives better and our country stronger. What we can't do is pretend it is not happening. I hear people say we have to stop and debate globalisation. You might as well debate whether autumn should follow summer. The character of this changing world is indifferent to tradition. Unforgiving of frailty. No respecter of past reputations. It has no custom

and practice. It is replete with opportunities, but they only go to those swift to adapt, slow to complain, open, willing and able to change.[4]

Blair's speech testifies to the rhetorical power of this dominant vision of the present and future. There is no need to think or reflect, just passively accept and run that bit harder to keep up.

This is where memory, history, and especially oral history are vitally important. The voices recorded for this project in their own modest way sought to recall and defend the legacy of the long boom. The workers realized they were the beneficiaries of a more expansive vision of work, as well as experiencing its reversal. This is an account of being embedded in one's employment with all that entails, but this is not simple nostalgia; rather, it is a more complex reflection on workplace cultures and appreciation of what was good and what was not in the past. Above all, the voices of Guinness are a series of meditations on change and what this may mean for themselves, their children, and for wider society. Although the buildings and the physical presence of the brewery were lost over a decade ago, the images and memories of what went on in Park Royal remain as a testament to that lost world—a time capsule waiting to be dug up, its contents discovered anew to offer guidance into an uncertain future.

It seems to me that this is the way we can think of Park Royal and thousands of other places of work like it in the postwar era: offering signposts to different destinations. We need somehow to reimagine them into existence. The voices of Guinness, as well as the images of other kinds, help in this process of reimagination, increasing our capacity to think more critically about the past, present, and available futures. These images help us see; they act as a breaching experiment, showing that the structures of contemporary working life are not fixed and immutable. The legacy of Guinness at Park Royal is to remind us that we are able to imagine something different, new, and better for the world of work. Can you imagine?

Notes

Introduction

1. See David Hughes, *Gilroy Was Good for Guinness* (Dublin: Liberties Press, 2013).
2. It is not my intention to write a conventional corporate or business history of Guinness; this has been done elsewhere. See, for example, Patrick Lynch and John Vaizey, *Guinness's Brewery in the Irish Economy 1759–1876* (Cambridge, UK: Cambridge University Press, 1960); S. R Dennison and Oliver MacDonagh, *Guinness 1886–1939: From Incorporation to the Second World War* (Cork: University of Cork Press, 1998). Later history is told in a number of books, including Jonathan Guinness, *Requiem for a Family Business* (Basingstoke, UK: Pan Books, 1997); Derek Wilson, *Dark and Light: The Story of the Guinness Family* (London: Orion Books, 1998).
3. Bill Bamberger and Cathy Davidson, *Closing: The Life and Death of an American Factory* (New York: Norton, 1999).
4. Most of the records relating to Park Royal are held in the company's Scottish archive, while those relating to Dublin are held in the archive at St. James's Gate. Inevitably there is some duplication and crossover between the archives and what they hold.
5. My doctoral studies involved the evolution of workplace culture and management on the railway; see Tim Strangleman, *Work Identity at the End of the Line? Privatisation and Culture Change in the UK Rail Industry* (Basingstoke, UK: Palgrave, 2004)
6. See Tim Strangleman, Emma Hollywood, Huw Beynon, Ray Hudson, and Katy Bennett, "Heritage Work: Re-representing the Work Ethic in the Coalfields," *Sociological Research Online* 4, no. 1 (1999); Tim Strangleman, "Networks, Place and Identities in Post-Industrial Mining Communities," *International Journal of Urban and Regional Research* 25, no. 2 (2001): 253–67.
7. Jefferson Cowie and Joseph Heathcott, eds., *Beyond the Ruins: The Meanings of Deindustrialization* (Ithaca, NY: Cornell University Press, 2003).
8. There are clear commonalities in the oral history narratives collected around deindustrialization. See, for example, Tracey K'Meyer and Joy L. Hart, *I Saw It Coming: Worker Narratives of Plant Closing and Job Loss* (Basingstoke, UK: Palgrave, 2011); Tom Juravich, *At the Altar of the Bottom Line: The Degradation of Work in the 21st Century* (Amherst: University of Massachusetts Press, 2009); Steven High and David Lewis, *Corporate Wasteland: The Landscape and Memory of Deindustrialization* (Ithaca, NY: Cornell University Press, 2007).
9. Harold Garfinkel, *Studies in Ethnomethodology* (Englewood Cliffs, NJ: Prentice-Hall, 1967). See also the way Ezzy uses this notion in terms of individual experience of unemployment in Douglas Ezzy, *Narrating Unemployment* (Aldershot: Ashgate, 2001).
10. Barry Bluestone and Bennett Harrison, *The Deindustrialization of America: Plant Closings, Community Abandonment, and the Dismantling of Basic Industry* (New York: Basic Books, 1982).
11. See, for example, Cowie and Heathcott, *Beyond the Ruins*; Steven High, *Industrial Sunset: The Making of North America's Rust Belt, 1969–1984* (Toronto: University of Toronto Press, 2003); Steven High and David Lewis, *Corporate Wasteland: The Landscape and Memory of Deindustrialization* (Ithaca, NY: Cornell University Press, 2007); Kathryn Marie Dudley,

End of the Line: New Lives in Postindustrial America (Chicago: University of Chicago Press, 1994); Sherry Lee Linkon and John Russo, *Steeltown USA: Work and Memory in Youngstown* (Lawrence: University of Kansas Press, 2002). For a review see Tim Strangleman and James Rhodes "The 'New' Sociology of Deindustrialisation? Understanding Industrial Change," *Sociology Compass* 8, no. 4 (2014): 411–21.

12. See, for example, Judith Modell and Charlee Brodsky, *A Town without Steel: Envisioning Homestead* (Pittsburgh: University of Pittsburgh Press, 1998); Linda Fine, *The Story of Reo Joe: Work, Kin, and Community in Autotown, USA* (Philadelphia: Temple University Press, 2004); S. Paul O'Hara, *Gary: The Most American of All American Cities* (Bloomington: Indiana University Press, 2011); Daniel Sidorick, *Condensed Capitalism: Campbell Soup and the Pursuit of Cheap Production in the Twentieth Century* (Ithaca, NY: Cornell University Press, 2009).

13. See, for example, Michael Burawoy, *Manufacturing Consent: Changes in the Labor Process under Monopoly Capitalism* (London: University of Chicago Press, 1982); Richard K Brown and Peter Brannen, "Social Relations and Social Perspectives amongst Shipbuilding Workers: A Preliminary Statement," *Sociology* 4, no. 1 (1970): 71–84.

14. Sherry Linkon, "Navigating Past and Present in the Deindustrial Landscape: Contemporary Writers on Detroit and Youngstown," *International Labor and Working-Class History* 84 (Winter 2013): 38–54.

15. See Richard Sennett, *The Corrosion of Character: The Personal Consequences of Work in the New Capitalism* (London: Norton, 1998); Guy Standing, *The Precariat: The New Dangerous Class* (London: Bloomsbury, 2011); Carrie M. Lane, *A Company of One: Insecurity, Independence, and the New World of White-Collar Unemployment* (Ithaca, NY: Cornell University Press, 2011); Ulrich Beck, *The Brave New World of Work* (Cambridge, UK: Polity, 2000); Zygmunt Bauman, *Work, Consumerism and the New Poor* (Buckingham, UK: Open University Press, 2000); David Weil, *Fissured Workplace: Why Work Became So Bad for So Many and What Can Be Done to Improve It* (Cambridge, MA: Harvard University Press, 2014); Tim Strangleman, "The Nostalgia for Permanence at Work? The End of Work and Its Commentators," *Sociological Review* 55, no. 1 (2007): 81–103; Tim Strangleman, "Work Identity in Crisis? Rethinking the Problem of Attachment and Loss at Work," *Sociology* 46, no. 3 (2012): 411–25.

16. Pierre Rosanvallon, *The Society of Equals* (Cambridge, MA: Harvard University Press, 2013); Thomas Piketty, *Capital in the Twenty-First Century* (Cambridge, MA: Harvard University Press, 2014).

17. Jefferson Cowie and Nick Salvatore, "The Long Exception: Rethinking the New Deal in American History," *International Labor and Working-Class History* 74 (Winter 2008): 3–32; see also Jefferson Cowie, *Stayin' Alive: The 1970s and the Last Days of the Working Class* (New York: The New Press, 2010).

18. André Gorz, for example, says: "Even in the heyday of wage-based society, that work [modern work] was never a source of 'social cohesion' or integration, whatever we might have come to believe from its retrospective idealization. The 'social bond' it established between individuals was abstract and weak, though it did, admittedly, insert people into the process of social labour, into social relations of production, as functionally specialized cogs in an immense machine."
André Gorz, *Reclaiming Work: Beyond the Wage-Based Society* (Cambridge, UK: Polity, 1999), 55. See Strangleman, "The Nostalgia for Permanence at Work?," for a summary.

19. When I was doing fieldwork before the closure in 2005, several employees at Park Royal told me of things they had rescued from the waste skips, and during visits to the archive I came across things that had been donated in this way.

20. The majority of these have not been fully transcribed and seem to have been undertaken for the internal publication—Edward Guinness, *The Guinness Book of Guinness 1935–1985: An Anthology Based on the First 50 Years of The Park Royal Brewery and Its Connections* (London: Guinness Publishing, 1988).

21. *Guinness Time* was the Park Royal staff magazine that ran from 1947 to 1975. It was published to a high standard and featured impressive amounts of photography and other visual

media It seems to have been superseded in 1975 by various papers and magazines. Edward Guinness, *A Brewer's Tale: Memoirs of Edward Guinness CVO* (Croydon, UK: CPI Group, 2014); Guinness, *Guinness Book of Guinness*; David Hughes, *A Bottle of Guinness Please: The Colourful History of Guinness* (Wokingham, UK: Phimboy, 2006).

22. There are a number of important volumes that look at corporate identity, image making, and public relations in the late nineteenth and early twentieth centuries. Interestingly, these draw on material—often visual—for both internal and external audiences. See David Nye, *Image Worlds: Corporate Identity at General Electric* (Cambridge, MA: MIT Press, 1985); Roland Marchand, *Creating the Corporate Soul: The Rise of Public Relations and Corporate Imagery in American Big Business* (Berkeley: University of California Press, 1998); Elizabeth Fones-Wolf, *Selling Free Enterprise: The Business Assault on Labor and Liberalism 1945–60* (Chicago: University of Illinois, 1994); Allan Sekula, "Photography between Labour and Capital," in *Mining Photographs and Other Pictures: A Selection from the Negative Archives of Shedden Studio, Glace Bay, Cape Breton 1948–1968* (Glace Bay, Nova Scotia: NSCAD/UCCB Press 1983), 193–268. With regard to the use of corporate staff magazines, see Michael Heller, "Editorial Introduction Company Magazines 1880–1940: An Overview," *Management and Organizational History* 3, no. 3-4 (2008): 179–96, and also some of the articles in that special edition

23. See Carol Quirke, *Eyes on Labor: News Photography and America's Working Class* (Oxford: Oxford University Press, 2012).

24. *Guinness Time* 4, no. 3 (1957).

25. I have also been lucky in being able to access a doctoral thesis written by London School of Economics student Ian Gledon in 1977. This study of industrial conflict at an anonymized Park Royal from 1969 onward gives an insight into conflict and consensus within the brewery and adds context and color to a wider picture of a period of considerable industrial disquiet. Ian Glendon, "The Participant Observer and Groups in Conflict: A Case Study from Industry" (unpublished PhD thesis, London School of Economics/University of London, 1977). Though awarded in 1977, the initial fieldwork dates from 1969.

26. A R Tanner's life is worthy of greater research I have been able to find very little on him in public records. He was taking photographs for *Picture Post* before the Second World War and then joined the army during the war and is mentioned in Fred McGlade, *The History of the British Army Film and Photographic Unit in the Second World War* (Solihull, UK: Helion, 2010), 59 and 107. I could track down little about him in the Guinness archive other than the stamp on the rear of his images.

27. For more on Gilroy, see Hughes, *Gilroy Was Good for Guinness*. For more on Cuneo, although it does not mention his work for Guinness, see Terence Cuneo, *The Mouse and His Master: The Life and Work of Terence Cuneo* (London: New Cavendish, 1977).

28. There is a wealth on writing on visual methods and approaches. For general discussions, see Gillian Rose, *Visual Methodologies: An Introduction to the Interpretation of Visual Materials*, 3rd ed. (London: Sage, 2012); Clarice Stasz, "The Early History of Visual Sociology," in *Images of Information: Still Photography in the Social Sciences*, ed. John Wagner (London: Sage, 1979), 119–37. For more focused discussions on the visual representation of work and labor, see Elizabeth Brown, *The Corporate Eye: Photography and the Rationalization of American Commercial Culture, 1884–1929* (Baltimore, MD: Johns Hopkins University Press, 2005); Tim Strangleman, "Ways of (Not) Seeing Work: The Visual as a Blind Spot in WES?," *Work, Employment and Society* 18, no. 1 (2004b): 179–92; Tim Strangleman, "Representations of Labour: Visual Sociology and Work," *Sociological Compass* 2, no. 4 (2008): 1491–505; Tim Strangleman, "Visual Sociology and Work Organization: An Historical Approach," in *The Routledge Companion to Visual Organization*, ed. Emma Bell, Samantha Warren, and Jonathan E. Schroeder (London: Taylor and Francis, 2013), 243–58.

29. Michael Saler suggests that this suspicion of the visual is deeply embedded in the Protestant Reformation Michael Saler, *The Avant-Garde in Interwar England: Medieval Modernism and the London Underground* (Oxford: Oxford University Press, 1999).

30. Raphael Samuel, *Theatres of Memory*, vol. 1, *Past and Present in Contemporary Culture* (London: Verso, 1994), viii.

31. Douglas Harper, "Meaning and Work: A Study in Photo Elicitation," *Current Sociology* 34, no. 3 (1986): 24–46.
32. Samuel, *Theatres of Memory*, 373.
33. Ibid., 375.
34. Humphrey Jennings, *Pandaemonium: The Coming of the Machine as Seen by Contemporary Observers* (London: Picador, 1985).
35. Ibid., xxxv.
36. Studs Terkel, *Working: People Talk about What They Do All Day and How They Feel about What They Do* (New York: Pantheon Books, 1972), xxv.
37. Jennings, in addition to being a writer, was an artist and poet and is best remembered as a talented filmmaker. See Kevin Jackson, *Humphrey Jennings* (Basingstoke, UK: Picador, 2004); Philip C. Logan, *Humphrey Jennings and the British Documentary Film: A Re-Assessment* (Farnham, UK: Ashgate, 2011).
38. *Guinness Time* 13, no. 1 (1959): 16.
39. Raphael Samuel and Paul Thompson, *The Myths We Live By* (London: Routledge, 1990), 7.
40. Alessandro Portelli, *The Death of Luigi Trastulli and Other Stories: Form and Meaning in Oral History* (Albany: SUNY Press, 2001), 2.

Chapter 1

1. J. B. Priestley, *English Journey* (London: Penguin, 1934), 10.
2. Ibid.
3. Ibid.
4. For a broader consideration of Priestley's influence and thinking in the 1930s, see John Baxendale and Christopher Pawling, *Narrating the Thirties: A Decade in the Making: 1930 to the Present* (Basingstoke, UK: Macmillan, 1996).
5. George Orwell, *The Road to Wigan Pier* (London: Penguin, 1937), 19.
6. Paul Swann, *The British Documentary Film Movement 1926–1946* (Cambridge: Cambridge University Press, 1989), 88.
7. As Denis Linehan has argued: "In the Britain of the 1920s, a new space for political and moral consideration emerged: the declining industrial region. The fate of districts in South Wales and the North of England, which were characterized by mass unemployment, industrial unrest and declining industry, gripped the national imagination. These industrial regions, with their 'armies of unemployed', summoned up notions of danger and distress." Denis Linehan, "An Archaeology of Dereliction: Poetics and Policy in the Governing of Depressed Industrial Districts in Interwar England and Wales," *Journal of Historical Geography* 26, no. 1 (2000): 99–113, 99.
8. Denis Linehan, "Regional Survey and the Economic Geographies of Britain 1930–1939," *Transactions of the Institute of British Geographers*, New Series, 28, no. 1 (2003): 96–122, 102.
9. O. Stanley, *Hansard* 14th November 1934, col. 2093. Cited in Linehan, "Archaeology of Dereliction," 103–4.
10. For a broader discussion of the place of northern England see Dave Russell, *Looking North: Northern England and the National Imagination* (Manchester: Manchester University Press, 2004). As Peter Scott suggests: "The 'new' character of these areas (as centres for their principal interwar industries) appears to have been an important attraction to industrialists. There is strong evidence that manufacturers deliberately located in new industrial areas, partly to escape the great strength of organized labour in more established centres." Peter Scott, "Women, Other 'Fresh' Workers, and the New Manufacturing Workforce of Interwar Britain," *International Review of Social History* 45, no. 3 (2000): 449–74, 458. For another account of the growth of the female workforce in the interwar period, including material from the general West London area, see Miriam Glucksmann, *Women Assemble: Women Workers and the "New Industries" in Inter-War Britain* (London: Routledge, 1990).
11. Aldous Huxley, *Brave New World* (London: Grafton, 1932).
12. Baxendale and Pawling, *Narrating the Thirties*. For other general accounts of 1930s Britain, see Richard Overy, *The Morbid Age: Britain and the Crisis of Civilization, 1919–1939*

(London: Penguin, 2009); Malcolm Muggeridge, *The Thirties: 1930–1940* (London: Fontana, 1940); Julian Symons, *The Thirties: A Dream Revolved* (London: Cresset Press, 1960).

13. Patrick Lynch and John Vaizey, *Guinness's Brewery in the Irish Economy 1759–1876* (Cambridge, UK: Cambridge University Press, 1960).

14. Bill Yenne, *Guinness: The 250-Year Quest for the Perfect Pint* (Hoboken, NJ: John Wiley, 2007), 55.

15. Ibid., 56–57.

16. For a history of the various branches of the Guinness family, see Michele Guinness, *The Guinness Spirit: Brewers and Bankers, Ministers and Missionaries* (London: Hodder and Stoughton, 1999).

17. For details of labor relations in Dublin in the first three decades of the twentieth century, see Chapter 16 in S. R Dennison and Oliver MacDonagh, *Guinness 1886–1939: From Incorporation to the Second World War* (Cork: University of Cork Press, 1998).

18. Ibid., 256.

19. Philip Williamson, *National Crisis and National Government: British Politics, the Economy and Empire, 1926–1932* (Cambridge, UK: Cambridge University Press, 2003).

20. For general political histories of Ireland in this period, see Roy Foster, *Modern Ireland 1600–1972* (London: Penguin, 1988), chapters 21 and 22, and F. S. L Lyons, *Ireland since the Famine* (London: Fontana, 1971), part 4.

21. Dennison and MacDonagh, *Guinness 1886–1939*, 251.

22. Ibid.

23. Ibid.

24. For details of this company, see Godfrey Harrison, *Alexander Gibb: The Story of an Engineer* (London: Geoffery Bles, 1950); details on the firm's dealings with Guinness over Park Royal can be found on 144–45.

25. Owen Bulmer Howell, *The Park Royal Development Company Ltd.* (London: Guinness, 1959), 2.

26. Hugh Beaver, quoted in Edward Guinness, *The Guinness Book of Guinness 1935–1985: An Anthology Based on the First 50 Years of The Park Royal Brewery and Its Connections* (London: Guinness Publishing, 1988), 8.

27. Howell, *Park Royal Development Company*, 3.

28. Dennison and MacDonagh, *Guinness 1886–1939*, 255. See also Howell, *Park Royal Development Company*.

29. Hugh Beaver quoted in Guinness, *Guinness Book of Guinness*, 8. This anthology reproduces many of the articles initially published in *Guinness Time*.

30. *Daily Express*, November 10, 1932.

31. *Dublin Evening Mail*, November 10, 1932.

32. The kieve acts like a giant sieve to collect the extracted sugars and water while leaving the grain behind. This collected liquid is called sweet wort.

33. Mark Plumpton quoted in Guinness, *Guinness Book of Guinness*, 11.

34. Ibid.

35. Ibid., 12–13.

36. Copy of letter to Sir Giles Gilbert Scott from Hugh Beaver (Alexander Gibb and Partners), October 30, 1933, in Guinness archive, Dublin.

37. The guinea was equivalent to twenty-one shillings in predecimal currency, one pound and one shilling. It was still commonly used for professional fees and sporting prize money.

38. Letter to Scott from Beaver, October 30, 1933.

39. Hugh Beaver, "Obituary for Sir Giles Gilbert Scott," *Guinness Time* 13, no. 2 (1960): 8.

40. Gavin Stamp, "Giles Gilbert Scott and the Problem of Modernism," *Architectural Design* 10–11 (1979): 72–83, 73–76.

41. Ibid., 73–76.

42. Ibid., 82.

43. Unpublished briefing document from the Twentieth Century Society, "Guinness Brewery, Coronation Road, Park Royal, LB Brent," by Elaine J. Harwood (1990), 2. For a wider and more sympathetic treatment of the design of Wallis, Gilbert and Partners see Joan Skinner,

Form and Fancy: Factories and Factory Buildings by Wallis, Gilbert and Partners, 1916–1939 (Liverpool: Liverpool University Press, 1997).

44. Unpublished briefing document from the Twentieth Century Society, "Guinness Is Good for You!: A Visit to Park Royal and North Ealing" (May 1995), 4.
45. Beaver, "Obituary for Sir Giles Gilbert Scott," 8.
46. Ibid.
47. Howell, *Park Royal Development Company Ltd.*, 6.
48. Unfiled photographs in the Guinness Archive.
49. Guinness, *Guinness Book of Guinness*, 18.
50. Rather confusingly for the reader, this piece was written by Howell himself in the third person.
51. Howell, *Park Royal Development Company Ltd.*, 5.
52. Ibid.
53. Derek Wilson, *Dark and Light: The Story of the Guinness Family* (London: Orion Books, 1998), 201.
54. Dennison and MacDonagh, *Guinness 1886–1939*, 256.
55. *Middlesex County Times*, March 23, 1935.
56. Guinness, *Guinness Book of Guinness*, 18.
57. Ibid., 23.
58. Wood in ibid., 18–19.
59. These names refer to the different sizes of barrels in use in the trade.
60. Guinness, *Guinness Book of Guinness*, 34.
61. Dennison and MacDonagh, *Guinness 1886–1939*, 261.
62. Betty Mears quoted in Guinness, *Guinness Book of Guinness*, 28.
63. Ion Commiskey quoted in ibid., 34.
64. Bob Nichol quoted in ibid., 38.
65. John Webb quoted in ibid., 48.
66. See Philip Williamson, *Stanley Baldwin: Conservative Leadership and National Values* (Cambridge, UK: Cambridge University Press, 1999). For a flavor of Baldwin's speeches and writing of the interwar period, see Earl Baldwin, *On England* (London: Penguin, 1937).
67. Beaver, "Obituary for Sir Giles Gilbert Scott," 8.

Chapter 2

1. T. H. Marshall, *Citizenship and Social Class* (London: Pluto, 1992; first published, 1950).
2. John Baxendale and Christopher Pawling, *Narrating the Thirties: A Decade in the Making: 1930 to the Present* (Basingstoke, UK: Macmillan, 1996).
3. Jim Mortimer, "The Changing Mood of Working People," in *Labour's High Noon: The Government and the Economy 1945–51*, ed. Jim Firth (London: Lawrence and Whishart, 1993), 244.
4. Paul Addison, *The Road to 1945: British Politics and the Second World War*, 2nd ed. (London: Pimlico, 1994), 15.
5. Ibid.
6. Michael Frayn, "Festival," in *Age of Austerity*, ed. Michael Sissons and Philip French (Oxford: Oxford University Press, 1963), 308.
7. Addison, *Road to 1945*, 278.
8. David Hall, *Working Lives: The Forgotten Voices of Britain's Post-War Working Class* (London: Bantam Press, 2012), 1.
9. Richard Hyman, "Praetorians and Proletarians: Unions and Industrial Relations," in *Labour's High Noon: The Government and the Economy 1945–51*, ed. Jim Firth (London: Lawrence and Whishart, 1993), 168.
10. Ibid., 166.
11. Ian Roberts, *Craft, Class and Control* (Edinburgh: Edinburgh University Press, 1993); Alan Fox, *History and Heritage: The Social Origins of the British Industrial Relations System*, (London: Allen and Unwin, 1985); J. E. T. Eldridge, *Industrial Disputes: Essays in the Sociology of Industrial Relations* (London: Routledge and Kegan Paul, 1968).

12. See Nicholas Comfort, *Surrender: How British Industry Gave Up the Ghost 1952–2012* (London: Biteback Publishing, 2012); Bruce Collins and Keith Robbins, eds., *Debates in Modern History: British Culture and Economic Decline* (London: Weidenfeld and Nicolson, 1990); Martin Wiener, *English Culture and the Decline of the Industrial Spirit 1850–1980* (Cambridge: Cambridge University Press, 1981); Theo Nichols, *The British Worker Question: A New Look at Workers and Productivity in Manufacturing* (London: Routledge and Kegan Paul, 1986).

13. See Nichols, *The British Worker Question*, for an excellent dissection and rebuttal of this argument.

14. See Richard Hoggart, *The Uses of Literacy* (London: Penguin, 1957); for an intellectual overview of the period from the point of view of the social sciences see Mike Savage, *Identities and Social Change in Britain since 1940: The Politics of Method* (Oxford: Oxford University Press, 2010).

15. *Guinness Time* 1, no. 1 (1947): 3.

16. Edward Guinness, *The Guinness Book of Guinness: An Anthology Based on the First 50 Years of The Park Royal Brewery and Its Connections* (London: Guinness Publishing Ltd., 1988), 115.

17. Ibid. Bodiam was one of the staff houses built on the brewery site. They were named after the Guinness hop farms in Kent.

18. Ibid.

19. Elizabeth Brown, *The Corporate Eye: Photography and the Rationalization of American Commercial Culture, 1884–1929* (Baltimore, MD: Johns Hopkins University Press, 2005).

20. Ibid., 137.

21. David Nye, *Image Worlds: Corporate Identity at General Electric* (Cambridge, MA: MIT Press, 1985), 33.

22. Roland Marchand cites a Pennsylvania Railroad executive's formulation of the lament and its solution: "The Old Era of Personal Contact"; "Passing of the Intimate Touch"; "Seeking an Effective Substitute." Roland Marchand, *Creating the Corporate Soul: The Rise of Public Relations and Corporate Imagery in American Big Business* (Berkeley: University of California Press, 1998), 102.

23. Brown, *Corporate Eye*, 137–38.

24. Marchand, *Creating the Corporate Soul*, 216. For two very different accounts of the corporate fight against state control and labor power, see S. Jonathan Wiesen, *West German Industry and the Challenge of the Nazi Past, 1945–1955* (Chapel Hill: University of North Carolina Press, 2001); for the United States, see Elizabeth A Fones-Wolf, *Selling Free Enterprise. The Business Assault on Labor and Liberalism 1945–60* (Urbana: University of Illinois, 1994).

25. Brown, *Corporate Eye*, 138.

26. Ibid.

27. Ibid., 120.

28. Ibid., 142.

29. Nye, *Images Worlds*, 83.

30. Marchand, *Creating the Corporate Soul*, 110; Brown, *Corporate Eye*, 136. Brown quotes one critic on the topic: "The more contributors there are, the better. Every contributor is an earnest reader; his friends and acquaintances and even his enemies are also attentive readers." Brown later reinforces this point by quoting another commentator on the importance of domestic news of workers' families: "It means absolutely nothing to an art critic to see a picture of the Jones' baby boy, but to the members of Tom's department it does mean something, for haven't these people heard for months all about Junior's wonderful ability to do that which no baby has ever done before?"

31. JoAnne Yates, *Control through Communication: Rise of System in American Management* (Baltimore: Johns Hopkins University Press, 1993), 195, cited in Marchand, *Creating the Corporate Soul*, 110.

32. Nye, *Image Worlds*, 84.

33. For an account of the complexity involved in the creation and reproduction of photographic material, see Barbara Rosenblum, *Photographers at Work: A Sociology of Photographic Styles* (New York: Holmes and Meier, 1978).

34. Brown, *Corporate Eye,* 146, gives an example of a striking New York transit worker refusing to supply images of his family for a company magazine. Also Nye has a detailed discussion of the passive resistance he detects in some of the GE photographs. Nye, *Images Worlds,* 92; see also Carol Quirke, *Eyes on Labor: New Photography and America's Working Class* (New York: Oxford University Press, 2012).

35. *Guinness Time* 1, no. 2 (1948): 15.

36. *Guinness Time* 1, no. 1 (1948): 14.

37. *Guinness Time* 16, no. 4 (1963): 4.

38. Ibid., 8.

39. Ibid.

40. *Guinness Time* 3, no. 3 (1949): 3.

41. Émile Durkheim, *The Division of Labor in Society* (New York: Free Press, 1964; first published, 1893), 372.

42. See David Hughes, *Gilroy Was Good for Guinness* (Dublin: Liberties Press, 2013). Hughes discusses the cover illustrations Gilroy undertook for *Guinness Time* and the portraits he did of Guinness directors and senior staff over the years.

43. See Terence Cuneo, *The Mouse and His Master: The Life and Work of Terence Cuneo* (London: New Cavendish, 1977).

44. This type of commercial representation was not unusual during the postwar period— Cuneo, for example, produced poster work and paintings for many large UK companies, including Ford, British Railways, British Petroleum, and Laing Engineering. This reflects a wider corporate confidence of the time that aimed to project positive images about industry, not simple company propaganda This artistic expression spans painting, poster art, documentary film-making, and photography. For a broader discussion of postwar documentary film-making by both private and public-sector bodies in the United Kingdom, see Patrick Russell and James Piers Taylor, eds., *Shadows of Progress: Documentary Films in Post-War Britain* (London: BFI/Palgrave, 2010).

45. Documentary and industrial photographers of this era certainly did create images of female laborers, often portraying them in a positive, even a heroic, light; see, for example, Juliet Gardiner, *Picture Post Women* (London: Collins and Brown, 1993), and the rendering of female subjects by an industrial photographer can be seen in Maurice Broomfield, *Maurice Broomfield Photographs* (London: Foto8, 2009).

46. Nurnberg, cited in John Ward, "The Walter Nurnberg Photograph Collection at the National Museum of Photography, Film and Television, Bradford," in *Presenting Pictures,* ed. Bernard Finn (London: Science Museum, 2004), 149–50.

47. Peter Stebbing, "Industrial Image 1918 to 1986," in *Industrial Image; British Industrial Photography 1843 to 1986,* ed. Sue Davies and Caroline Collier (London: Photographers' Gallery, 1986), 45.

48. Ibid., 49.

49. Walter Nurnberg quoted in Ward, "Walter Nurnberg Photograph Collection," 154.

50. *Guinness Time* 3, no. 1 (1949): 17.

51. Ibid.

52. *Guinness Time* 5, no. 4 (1952): 12.

53. Roger Bannister trained for his record attempt on the Guinness running track at Park Royal. *The Guinness Book of Records* was also conceived of at the site, but that is another story.

54. *Guinness Time* 7, no. 3 (1954): 3.

55. Richard Hoggart was famously concerned with the influence of American popular culture on British youth during this time; the threat came mainly from coffee and milk bars. Hoggart, *Uses of Literacy.*

56. *Guinness Time* 8, no. 1 (1954): 3–4.

57. *Guinness Time* 8, no. 3 (1955): 16

58. *Guinness Time* 13, no. 2 (1960): 11.

59. *Guinness Time* 16, no. 4 (1963): 27.

60. Guinness, *Guinness Book of Guinness,* 267.

61. Julia Parker, *Citizenship, Work and Welfare: Searching for the Good Society* (Basingstoke, UK: Palgrave, 1998), 161.

62. Bryan S. Turner, foreword to Émile Durkheim, *Professional Ethics and Civic Morals* (London: Routledge, 1992; first published 1957), xiii.

63. Ibid., 5.

64. Ibid.

65. Levy, in Broomfield, *Maurice Broomfield Photographs*, iii.

66. Frayn, "Festival," 308.

Chapter 3

1. These were a program of rationalizations carried out by the state-run British railways.

2. *The Titfield Thunderbolt*, Ealing Studios, 1953.

3. Barr gives a highly critical reading of the film: "It offers a fantasy of small-town life, of a cosy rural community. Timeless and self-sufficient . . . protected by the outside world." Barr compares and contrasts Titfield to other more progressive films from the studio, which were more radical, progressive, and antiauthoritarian. Charles Barr, *Ealing Studios* (London: Studio Vista, 1993), 159.

4. W. G. Hoskins, *The Making of the English Landscape* (London: Penguin, 1955), 298.

5. Ibid., 299.

6. Writers such as L. T. C. Rolt and John Betjeman, in their different ways, celebrated technological advancement but regretted the destructive trends in postwar Britain. Like Hoskins, both Rolt and Betjeman interpreted what was going on in the postwar period as threatening to British, especially English, culture. Organically embedded technologies, such as railways and the earlier canal system, were seen as endangered by the twin evils of modernization and rationalization driven by technocratic and centralizing impulses. Betjeman especially projected a melancholic nostalgia for a passing England, rapidly being pulled down, destroyed, or otherwise defaced. Rolt is a fascinating character and one who awaits a proper full-length study. A trained engineer, he wrote extensively about the various technologies of the Industrial Revolution and yet decried much of what had resulted from the impact of precisely that technology. His philosophy is perhaps best seen in L. T. C. Rolt, *High Horse Riderless* (Bideford: Green Books, 1947; republished, 1988). An example of melancholic Englishness by Betjeman can be found in John Betjeman, *Coming Home: An Anthology of Prose* (London: Vintage, 1997).

7. David Matless, *Landscape and Englishness* (London: Reaktion, 1998), 267.

8. Ibid.

9. Ibid.

10. Here again, Betjeman represents a key figure, most notably in London and his high-profile campaigns to save Victorian railway architecture, John Betjeman, *London's Historic Railway Stations* (London: John Murray, 1972). See also Raphael Samuel, *Theatres of Memory: Volume 1: Past and Present in Contemporary Culture* (London: Verso, 1994).

11. Howard Newby, *The Deferential Worker* (London: Penguin, 1977), 11–12.

12. Ibid., 14.

13. Tim Strangleman, *Work Identity at the End of the Line? Privatisation and Culture Change in the UK Rail Industry* (Basingstoke, UK: Palgrave, 2004a), chapters 3 and 4. See also Raymond Williams, *The Country and the City* (Oxford: Oxford University Press, 1973), for a much more historical account of the role of the countryside on the English imaginary.

14. For rural and agricultural life in England and the wider United Kingdom, see Alun Howkins, *The Death of Rural England: A Social History of the Countryside since 1900* (London: Routledge, 2003); see also Malcolm Chase, "'Nothing Less than a Revolution'? Labour's Agricultural Policy," in *Labour's High Noon: The Government and the Economy 1945–51*, ed. Jim Firth (London: Lawrence and Whishart, 1993), 78–95.

15. Edward Mills, *The Modern Factory* (London: The Architectural Press, 1951), 138. See also Peter Merriman, *Driving Spaces: A Cultural-Historical Geography of England's M1 Motorway* (Oxford: Blackwell, 2007).

16. I discovered these reels at the end of my time in the Guinness archives in Menstrie, Scotland, when one of the archivists handed me two DVDs labeled "Guinness Company Films." She had kindly digitized a number of long-neglected spools of cine film as she knew I might find them of interest. The first covered 1948 to 1951, the second 1951 and 1952.

17. *Guinness Time* 1, no. 3 (1948): 3.

18. Leo Marx, *The Machine in the Garden: Technology and the Pastoral Ideal in America* (Oxford: Oxford University Press, 1964), 13–14.

19. Ibid., 229.

20. Most of the material for this section comes from an anonymous typescript filed in the Diageo archives in Scotland.

21. *Guinness Time* 16, no. 2 (1963): 11.

22. Ibid.

23. *Guinness Time* 1, no. 1 (1947): 9.

24. Ibid., 10.

25. *Guinness Time* 4, no. 4 (1951): 8.

26. Ibid.

27. Ian Peaty, *Brewery Railways* (Newton Abbot: David and Charles, 1985), 38.

28. *Guinness Time* 10, no. 3 (1957): 6.

29. Ibid., 7.

30. *Guinness Time* 4, no. 3 (1950): 8.

31. *Guinness Time* 16, no. 2 (1963): 10. Le Sueur was an extremely well-regarded and talented arborist, plantsman, and landscaper. He had been appointed to several government advisory posts concerned with forestry and landscaping and held a number of awards for his achievements. He had also written a number of books on planting and screening. I am grateful to Charles Watkins (see n. 36 of this chapter) for his help with aspects of Le Sueur's career.

32. Various tree count figures were given over the years. The higher figure of 3,000 seems to include those examples already on site when the brewery was built.

33. *Guinness Time* 10, no. 4 (1957): 1.

34. *Guinness Time* 1, no. 3 (1948): 9.

35. Ibid.

36. For an extended discussion of the social and cultural meaning of trees and human intervention see Charles Watkins, *Trees, Woods and Forests: A Social and Cultural History* (London: Reaktion, 2014).

37. See http://www.gardenvisit.com/landscape_architecture/london_landscape_architecture/visitors_guide_1984/guinness_hills_jellicoe (accessed May 11, 2015).

38. *Sunday Times*, April 1, 1962.

39. Ibid. Geoffrey Jellicoe was a renowned landscape designer and theorist; influenced by the ideas of Carl Jung, he explored the role of the subconscious in landscape design. See Geoffrey Jellicoe and Susan Jellicoe, *The Landscape of Man: Shaping the Environment from Prehistory to the Present Day*, 3rd ed. (London: Thames and Hudson, 1995); Michael Spens, *Gardens of the Mind: The Genius of Geoffrey Jellicoe* (Woodbridge, UK: Antique Collectors' Club, 1992).

40. Merriman, *Driving Spaces*, 79.

41. Geoffrey Jellicoe, *Studies in Landscape Design* (Oxford: Oxford University Press, 1960), 74.

42. Jellicoe, *Studies in Landscape Design*, 75.

43. *Guinness Time* 11, no. 4 (1958): 1.

44. Ibid., 3.

45. Ibid.

46. Ibid.

47. Jellicoe went on to stress what his Park Royal/Western Avenue design meant to him: "This test case has certainly established in my mind the fact that it is neither cost nor design technique that is holding up good road landscape in this country, but solely the effort involved to get the ideas created and executed. Indeed I would like to see an obelisk erected inscribed with the names of all those who will have contributed to a landscape which will be purely romantic and have no function whatsoever; for it is the element of emotion

that is basically the motive power of all our actions, and in the modern world this is being slowly stamped out as being irresponsible and uneconomic. Soon, too, if we are not careful, our perceptions will be so dulled that we shall not be able to observe nature even when it is presented to us with all the ensnaring arts of landscape." Jellicoe, *Studies in Landscape Design*, 75-76.

48. *Guinness Time* 3, no. 3 (1949): 10.

49. Ibid., 11.

50. For a variety of examples over three centuries or so, see Humphrey Jennings, *Pandaemonium: The Coming of the Machine as Seen by Contemporary Observers* (London: Picador, 1985). See also Gillian Darley, *Factory* (London: Reaktion, 2003).

51. See Roland Marchand, *Creating the Corporate Soul: The Rise of Public Relations and Corporate Imagery in American Big Business* (Berkeley: University of California Press, 1998), especially chapter 1.

52. Stephen Marglin, "The Origins and Functions of Hierarchy in Capitalist Production," in *Capital and Labour—A Marxist Primer*, ed. Theo Nichols (London: Fontana, 1980), 237-254.

53. Louise Mozingo says, "Corporations of extraordinary power appropriate the symbolic forces of this ideal embodiment to portray a 'corporate soul' and to promote business as a purveyor of progressive values. The corporate campus humanized, sanitized, and glorified the corporate endeavor by invoking seductive American themes." Louise Mozingo, *Pastoral Capitalism: A History of Suburban Corporate Landscapes* (Cambridge, MA: MIT Press, 2011), 99.

54. Cultural historian David Nye has written extensively about the relationship between landscape, technology, and modernity; see David Nye, *American Technological Sublime* (Cambridge, MA:MIT Press, 1994); David Nye, *Narratives and Spaces: Technology and the Construction of American Culture* (Exeter, UK: University of Exeter Press, 1997); David Nye, *America as Second Creation: Technology and Narratives of New Beginnings* (Cambridge, MA: The MIT Press, 2003).

55. In her book about the Games, Hampton relates the following anecdote about events at Guinness: "The preliminary rounds were played at the Guinness grounds at Park Royal in west London. During one match, a man wearing a badge and an armlet claimed to be an Olympic official. He collected valuables such as watches and wallets from competitors for 'safe-keeping' and was never seen again. 'We were concerned, if not too downcast, to draw with Switzerland in our first [hockey] match,' said John Peake. 'Guinness laid on free drinks after the game. The first Guinness is delicious, the second is good; the third quite good, the forth a bit bitter and the fifth you can't remember.' Janie Hampton, *The Austerity Olympics: When the Games Came to London in 1948* (London: Aurum, 2008), 272.

56. *Guinness Time* 1, no. 3 (1948): 3-4.

57. *Guinness Time* 12, no. 3 (1959): 4-6.

58. *Guinness Time* 12, no. 4 (1959): 3. The house journals referred to were *Guinness Time*, which covered events at Park Royal, and *The Guinness Harp*, a shorter-lived and less successful staff magazine for the St. James's Gate site in Dublin.

59. *Guinness Time* 12, no. 4 (1959): 3. The foundation stone was indeed laid on General Election Day, October 8, 1959; the Conservatives won the election under Prime Minister Harold Macmillan, who had, during the campaign, used the famous phrase "Never had it so good," a reference to the general prosperity and growing affluence at the midway point of the long boom. The Labour Party, which had suffered its fourth successive general election defeat, was led by Hugh Gaitskell, who would be replaced, after his early death, by Harold Wilson. It was Wilson who would use another memorable phrase, "The white heat of technological revolution," to burnish his modernizing credentials. Finally, only a short distance from the Park Royal brewery, Margaret Thatcher was elected to Parliament for the first time for the seat of Finchley in the North London suburbs.

60. The prospect of nuclear war and the age of the atom bomb featured in *Guinness Time* from time to time. In 1952, a piece appeared about the establishment of a Civil Defence unit at the brewery. Under what appears to be a bombed-out scene of brewery buildings, the article

draws parallels with the ARP organization of the war years but notes that "it takes much longer these days to train a C.D. volunteer than it did in the last war, because more knowledge is available and new weapons have been devised, such as the atomic bomb and the nerve gases." Basic training consisted of lectures covering topics such as "the various types of warfare possible these days, such as high explosive, fire, atomic, biological and chemical, and the means of protection available against them—yes—even protection against the atomic bomb." *Guinness Time* 5, no. 4 (1952): 20–22. In a later editorial, a seemingly innocuous piece on the weather and seasons suddenly makes the point that "however much we may suspect that the atom bombs have changed the weather we feel in our hearts that this year will not be quite like the last and, if we are prudent, we plan our holidays." *Guinness Time* 11, no. 4 (1958): 3.

61. *Guinness Time* 1, no. 4 (1948): 4.
62. *Guinness Time* 5, no. 2 (1951): 6. Housing was an issue that regularly surfaced in the various parts of the brewery archive. Housing was an especially acute problem in the early postwar years. Guinness was reluctant to take on complete responsibility for the accommodation of its workforce. The development at Moyne Place took the form of forty-four semidetached two-story, three-bedroom houses. Allocation was based on need, size of family, and length of service. The properties were maintained by brewery staff.
63. *Guinness Time* 7, no. 1 (1953): 3.
64. Ibid., 5.
65. *Guinness Time* 8, no. 3 (1955): 3.
66. Ibid. This was also a topic that surfaced during the interview I carried out in 2013 and is a feature of his autobiography. See Edward Guinness, *A Brewer's Tale: Memoirs of Edward Guinness CVO* (Croydon: CPI Group, 2014), especially chapter 3, which covers this period. From these various sources, it is clear that this experience was a formative one for the young Edward Guinness both economically and socially. More work needs to be devoted to understanding fully the combined experience of the 1930s Depression *and* the war on the postwar generations, both shop floor and management.
67. *Guinness Time* 8, no. 3 (1955): 3–4.
68. Ibid., 4.
69. *Guinness Time* 26, no. 3 (1973): 11.
70. Hugh Beaver, "Obituary for Sir Giles Gilbert Scott," *Guinness Time* 13, no. 2 (1960): 8.
71. *Guinness Time* 28, no. 4 (1975): 29.
72. See Daniel Dorling, *Injustice: Why Social Inequality Persists* (Bristol: Policy Press, 2011).

Chapter 4

1. Ken Coates and Richard Silburn, *Poverty: The Forgotten Englishmen* (London: Penguin Books, 1970). Research for this book was carried on in the St. Ann's district of Nottingham in the 1960s and was seen as alerting a wider population to the problems associated with poverty in the midst of the affluent society.
2. John Goldthorpe, David Lockwood, Frank Bechhofer, and Jenifer Platt, *The Affluent Worker: Industrial Attitudes and Behaviour* (Cambridge, UK: Cambridge University Press, 1968); John Eldridge, *Industrial Disputes: Essays in the Sociology of Industrial Relations* (London: Routledge and Kegan Paul, 1968).
3. André Gorz, *Reclaiming Work: Beyond the Wage-Based Society* (Cambridge: Polity, 1999), 55.
4. Zygmunt Bauman, *Work, Consumerism and the New Poor* (Buckingham: Open University Press, 1998), 18.
5. Selina Todd, "Affluence, Class and Crown Street: Reinvestigating the Post-War Working Class," *Contemporary British History* 22, no. 4 (2008): 501–18, 514.
6. Richard Whiting, "Affluence and Industrial Relations in Post-War Britain," *Contemporary British History* 22, no. 4 (2008): 519–36.
7. See also Avner Offer, "British Manual Workers: From Producers to Consumers, c. 1950–2000," *Contemporary British History* 22, no. 4 (2008): 537–71.
8. Trevor Lummis, "Structure and Validity in Oral Evidence," in *The Oral History Reader*, 2nd ed., ed. Robert Perks and Alistair Thomson (London: Routledge, 1998), 255–60; Valerie Yow,

Recording Oral History: A Guide for the Humanities and Social Sciences (Plymouth, UK: Altamira Press, 2005); Harold Rosen, *Speaking from Memory: The Study of Autobiographical Discourse* (Stoke-on-Trent, UK: Trentham Books, 1998); Ken Howarth, *Oral History: A Handbook* (Stroud, UK: Alan Sutton, 1998); Martin Conway, *Autobiographical Memory: An Introduction* (Milton Keynes, UK: Open University Press, 1990).

9. Raphael Samuel and Paul Thompson, *The Myths We Live By* (London: Routledge, 1990), 7.

10. Ibid., 6.

11. Alessandro Portelli, *The Death of Luigi Trastulli and Other Stories: Form and Meaning in Oral History* (New York: SUNY Press, 2001), 2. See also Alessandro Portelli, "What Makes Oral History Different," in *The Oral History Reader*, 2nd ed., ed. Robert Perks and Alistair Thomson (London: Routledge, 1998, 32–42).

12. Samuel and Thompson, *The Myths We Live By*, 8.

13. Fred Davis, *Yearning for Yesterday: A Sociology of Nostalgia* (New York: Free Press, 1979).

14. Tim Strangleman, *Work Identity at the End of the Line? Privatisation and Culture Change in the UK Rail Industry* (Basingstoke, UK: Palgrave, 2004); Alastair Bonnett, *Left in the Past: Radicalism and the Politics of Nostalgia* (London: Continuum, 2010).

15. Henry Dawson, interviewed 2015: 1.

16. Graham Bayford, interviewed 2004: 2.

17. Les Woodgate, interviewed 2004: 2.

18. Dave Bathurst, interviewed 2004: 20.

19. Henry Dawson, interviewed 2015: 4.

20. Terry Aldridge, interviewed 2015: 2.

21. Ibid., 12.

22. Mike Thomas, interviewed 2015: 5.

23. Ibid., 4–5.

24. Ray Snook, interviewed 2004: 2.

25. Ibid., 4.

26. Mick Costa, interviewed 2004: 1–2.

27. Mick Costello, interviewed 2004: 1–2.

28. Mick Costa, interviewed 2004: 2.

29. Dave Bathurst, interviewed 2004: 2.

30. Ibid., 2.

31. Ibid., 3.

32. David Hughes, interviewed 2009: 3.

33. Mike Thomas, interviewed 2015: 17–18.

34. Ibid., 18–19.

35. *Hop backs* refers to the stage of the brew when the boiling wort is emptied from the coppers into the hop backs (hence they hold back the hops) and the wort is pumped to the coolers to cool.

36. Terry Aldridge, interviewed 2015: 7–8.

37. Mike Thomas, interviewed 2015: 19–20.

38. Ibid., 20.

39. Les Woodgate, interviewed 2004: 4.

40. Ibid., 5–6.

41. Dave Bathurst, interviewed 2004: 3.

42. Ibid., 6.

43. Mick Costello, interviewed 2004: 3.

44. Ibid., 3.

45. Ibid., 4.

46. Edward Guinness, *The Guinness Book of Guinness 1935–1985: An Anthology Based on the First 50 Years of The Park Royal Brewery and Its Connections* (London: Guinness Publishing, 1988), 111.

47. Ibid., 112.

48. Ibid., 113. There is a real "Ealing comedy" feel to this account, reflecting Ealing's more conservative period of the 1950s where trade unionism is seen as something other, foreign and

ideological—somehow un-English. Ealing had made a film about a small brewery just before the Second World War broke out called *Cheer Boys Cheer*. For a short but fascinating account of how this film fits into the Ealing genre, see Charles Barr, *Ealing Studios* (London: Studio Vista, 1993), 5–6.

49. While working in the archives in Dublin in 2009, I was traveling to the storehouse where the archives are located in the city and got into a discussion on a tram with the wife of a former worker who, unbidden, emphasized the high reputation for social welfare Guinness had.

50. Guinness, *Guinness Book of Guinness*, 114.

51. This clearly has marked similarities and differences from welfare capitalism as practiced elsewhere; see, for example, Sanford Jacoby, *Modern Manors: Welfare Capitalism since the New Deal* (Princeton, NJ: Princeton University Press, 1997).

52. Using his figures, these would have occurred in 1969, 1965, 1961, and 1955. However, it is clear that the first strike occurred at the plant in 1947. This may have been the earliest that Glendon is referring to and so is an interesting illustration of how official and unofficial documentation contradict and complement each other. Ian Glendon, "The Participant Observer and Groups in Conflict: A Case Study from Industry" (unpublished PhD thesis, London School of Economics/University of London, 1977), 102–4.

53. There were approximately 150 craft workers on site at that time, giving roughly twenty members per craft union; Glendon, "Participant Observer," 279. Glendon's study captures the brewery at a particular moment of industrial relations. He reflects well the tensions at the site, but these are less marked by vertical conflict between management and workers than between and within the unions and between shop floor workers and their representatives. As Glendon notes, "Inter-union relations within the Firm left much to be desired. There was enmity between the Inside and Road branches of the Majority Union [TGWU], expressed most forcefully between their senior representatives. There was friction between the Inside Branch and the Minority Unions [craft], exhibiting itself in much the same way" (p. 23).

In one of his field notes, Glendon relates attending a stewards' meeting: "The meeting was volatile, and my impression was one of militancy which seemed to hang in the oily atmosphere of the shop. I was introduced by a heavily-spoken man as: 'someone they all knew about', and the meeting went ahead. Suspicious glances were cast at me, and I felt conspicuous in the overall-clad setting." Glendon, "Participant Observer," 38.

54. These figures use comparative statistics from the *Employment and Productivity Gazette* during 1969–1970; Glendon, "Participant Observer," 16.

55. Strangleman, *Work Identity at the End of the Line?*, 93. It is fascinating to see the way oral histories mirror the statistical reality of the job market. Both railway and brewery workers reported experience of tight labor markets at this time and the way it afforded them choice and to some extent power.

56. Terry Aldridge, interviewed 2015: 23.

57. Ibid., 23–24.

58. Glendon, "Participant Observer," 23.

59. Henry Dawson, interviewed 2015: 11.

60. Terry Aldridge, interviewed 2015: 24.

61. Dave Bathurst, interviewed 2004: 6.

62. Alan Mudie, interviewed 2004: 5.

63. David Hughes, interviewed 2009: 9.

64. Ibid., 10.

65. Barry Hubbard, interviewed 2004: 2–3.

66. Mike Thomas, interviewed 2015: 6–7.

67. This refers to the figures collected for tax purposes on the relative strength of the beer brewed; the stronger the beer, the higher the tax.

68. Terry Aldridge, interviewed 2015: 37–38.

69. David Hughes, interviewed 2009: 8–9.

70. Ibid., 9.

71. Graham Bayford, interviewed 2004: 2.

72. Ray Snook, interviewed 2004: 5.
73. Henry Dawson, interviewed 2015: 24.
74. Terry Aldridge, interviewed 2015: 13–14.
75. Ibid., 25–26.
76. Ibid., 27.
77. David Hughes, interviewed 2009: 31.
78. Anonymous, interview, 2005: 6.
79. Anonymous, interview, 2005: 8.
80. David Hughes, *A Bottle of Guinness Please: The Colourful History of Guinness* (Wokingham, UK: Phimboy, 2006), 5.
81. Ibid.
82. The term *embeddedness* comes from Karl Polanyi's *The Great Transformation*, itself a statement about the need to socialize the market made at the end of the Second World War. Essentially, Polanyi recorded attempts across time to disembed economic structures from social relationships. Polanyi always saw this as an impossible task, but it is one that those advocating an extreme form of market liberalism never ceased to push. Karl Polanyi, *The Great Transformation, The Political and Economic Origins of Our Time* (Boston: Beacon Books, 1992).
83. As Spanish sociologist of work Juan Castillo says:

    Recovering the collective and historic memory requires then struggling to identify the different forms that memory has adopted in time and space. Not just recovering and integrating in a work and production process the material vestiges, but also the marks left in persons and institutions. This "industrial atmosphere" as Alfred Marshall called it". Juan Castillo, "The Memory of Work and the Future of Industrial Heritage," *Forum: Qualitative Social Research* 12, no. 3 (2011): 1–14, 7.

84. For an account of the idea of a structure of feeling, see Raymond Williams, *The Country and the City* (Oxford: Oxford University Press, 1973) and Raymond Williams, *Marxism and Literature* (Oxford: Oxford University Press, 1977). For more on industrial culture, see David Byrne, "Industrial Culture in a Post-Industrial World: The Case of the North East of England," *City* 6, no. 3 (2002): 279–89. See also David Byrne and Aiden Doyle, "The Visual and the Verbal," in *Picturing the Social Landscape: Visual Methods and the Sociological Imagination*, ed. Caroline Knowles and Paul Sweetman (London: Routledge, 2004), 166–77.
85. In his fascinating account of redundant workers, Douglas Ezzy uses the work of ethnomethodologist Harold Garfinkel and in particular his notion of the "breaching experiment," wherein established norms and values are deliberately violated in order to expose the taken-for-granted assumptions and patterns underlying everyday life. Ezzy says that unemployment similarly disrupts and reveals the taken-for-granted feelings we have about work. Harold Garfinkel, *Studies in Ethnomethodology* (Englewood Cliffs, NJ: Prentice Hall, 1967). See also the way Ezzy uses this notion in terms of individual experience of unemployment in Douglas Ezzy, *Narrating Unemployment* (Aldershot, UK: Ashgate, 2001).
86. Émile Durkheim, *Professional Ethics and Civic Morals* (London: Routledge, 1992; first published 1957), 6–7.
87. Edward Palmer Thompson, *The Making of the English Working Class* (London: Penguin, 1963), 12.

Chapter 5

1. In fact, the people posing in the poster were young members of the Hendon Conservative Association; they were photographed numerous times in different clothing. The poster has come to be seen as important because it represents the importation into British politics of American political techniques. See http://www.campaignlive.co.uk/article/history-advertising-no-90-labour-isnt-working-poster/1281255 (accessed January 4, 2016).
2. Over the past decade, there have been many popular histories of the 1970s; they sometimes reinforce but mostly disrupt the more settled narrative of the era. See Andy Beckett, *When the Lights Went Out: Britain in the Seventies* (London: Faber and Faber, 2009);

Francis Wheen, *Strange Days Indeed: The Golden Age of Paranoia* (London: Fourth Estate, 2009); Dominic Sandbrook, *State of Emergency: The Way We Were: Britain 1970–1974* (London: Penguin, 2010); Dominic Sandbrook, *Seasons in the Sun: The Battle for Britain 1974–1979* (London: Penguin, 2012).

3. Like the historiography of the 1970s, the 1980s has quickly caught up as a decade worthy of popular focus. In addition to Alwyn W. Turner, *Rejoice! Rejoice! Britain in the 1980s* (London: Aurum Press, 2010), see Andy McSmith, *No Such Thing as Society: A History of Britain in the 1980s* (London: Constable, 2011); Andy Beckett, *Promised You a Miracle: UK 80–82* (London: Allen Lane, 2015); Dylan Jones, *The Eighties: One Day, One Decade* (London: Windmill, 2013); Graham Stewart, *Bang! A History of Britain in the 1980s* (London: Atlantic Books, 2013).

4. A fuller and more detailed sociological account of the period can be found in Colin Hay, "Narrating the Crisis: The Discursive Construction of the 'Winter of Discontent,'" *Sociology* 30, no. 2 (1996): 253–77.

5. As brewing industry historians Gourvish and Wilson say: "At first sight, we might be tempted to conclude that the industry was the exemplar of everything that has been considered defective or, at the very least, inhibiting in British manufacturing since the late nineteenth century. A strong family orientation and a cosy, amateur style, reflected in a 'club' atmosphere in the boardroom, was characteristic of most, if not all, breweries in the first half of the twentieth century, as it had been in the second half of the nineteenth." Terence R Gourvish and Richard G Wilson, *The British Brewing Industry 1830–1980* (Cambridge, UK: Cambridge University Press, 1994), 373.

6. *The Economist*, September 19, 1964, cited in ibid., 374.

7. Ibid., 378.

8. Ibid., 451–52.

9. The "tie" refers here to the ownership by brewers of public houses. This meant that landlords or landladies had to source their beer largely, and often exclusively, from the owning brewer.

10. John Spicer, Chris Thurman, John Walters, and Simon Ward, *Intervention in the Modern UK Brewing Industry* (Basingstoke, UK: Palgrave, 2012), 1.

11. Gourvish and Wilson, *British Brewing Industry*, 472.

12. Spicer et al., *Intervention in the Modern UK Brewing Industry*, 4.

13. Gourvish and Wilson, *British Brewing Industry*, 479.

14. Spicer et al., *Intervention in the Modern UK Brewing Industry*, 34–35. By measures of nominal capital, Guinness was by far the smallest of the big brewers—£26.5 million compared to £157.7 million for Allied, the largest. However, its market value in 1970 was £134.0 million; see Gourvish and Wilson, *British Brewing Industry*, 472.

15. For the definitive history of bottled Guinness, see David Hughes, *"A Bottle of Guinness Please": The Colourful History of Guinness* (Wokingham, UK: Phimboy, 2006).

16. Gourvish and Wilson, *British Brewing Industry*, 480–81.

17. Jonathan Guinness, *Requiem for a Family Business* (London: Pan, 1997), 88.

18. Ibid.

19. Gourvish and Wilson, *British Brewing Industry*, 562–63. For an account of Guinness advertising history, see Jim Davies, *The Book of Guinness Advertising* (London: Guinness Publishing, 1998).

20. To Guinness purists, the bottled stout is far superior to the draught beer; see Hughes, *"A Bottle of Guinness Please."*

21. Spicer et al., *Intervention in the Modern UK Brewing Industry*, 38.

22. See K Bhaskar, "Three Case Studies—Guinness, Spillers and Nestles," in *Reading on Mergers and Takeovers*, ed. John Malcolm Samuels (London: Paul Elek Books, 1972), 97–122.

23. Guinness, *Requiem*, 87.

24. A number of books were published quickly during or just after the "Guinness affair." See, for example, Guinness, *Requiem*; Edward Guinness, *A Brewer's Tale: Memoirs of Edward Guinness CVO* (Croydon, UK: CPI Group, 2014); Michele Guinness, *The Guinness Spirit: Brewers and Bankers, Ministers and Missionaries* (London: Hodder and Stoughton, 1999); James Saunders,

Nightmare: The Ernest Saunders Story (London: Hutchinson, 1989). This book has the interesting convention of using Saunders's first name, Ernest, in quotes, hence the slightly strange feel to the quotations that follow. See also Nick Kochan and Hugh Pym, *The Guinness Affair: Anatomy of a Scandal* (London: Christopher Helm, 1987); Peter Pugh, *Is Guinness Good For You? The Bid for Distillers—The Inside Story* (London: Financial Training, 1987). See also Ivan Fallon and James Srodes, *Takeovers* (London: Hamish Hamilton, 1987), for extensive coverage of Guinness and the Guinness affair and a near-contemporaneous account of 1980s mergers and acquisitions and their roots in the 1970s.

25. Saunders, *Nightmare*, xii.

26. Ibid., 55. Tony Purcell was the managing director of Guinness at the time of Saunders's appointment.

27. I stumbled across this file in the Guinness archive in Scotland but did not realize its purpose until reading *Nightmare* sometime later. There were no notes to contextualize the aim of the file, and it was randomly filed along with other material of the era in no particular order.

28. Guinness had been floated on the London Stock Exchange in 1886; see chapter 1 for more details.

29. Saunders, *Nightmare*, 57.

30. Ibid., 62.

31. Ibid., 58.

32. Ibid., 66.

33. Pugh, *Is Guinness Good For You?*, 24.

34. Ibid., 23–24.

35. Kochan and Pym note: "Upwards of one thousand jobs were quickly lost, but investment in plant to the tune of £100 million was planned to stretch to the end of the decade. He had to tackle the unions in a company whose industrial relations were good, and apparently they [the unions] admired his unflinching determination and toughness." Kochan and Pym, *The Guinness Affair*, 23.

36. Saunders, *Nightmare*, 82.

37. Ibid., 82.

38. Ibid., 83.

39. Ibid., 102.

40. For an account of the Bells acquisition see ibid., 117–34; Kochan and Hugh Pym, *The Guinness Affair* chapters 3 and 4; Pugh, *Is Guinness Good For You?*, chapter 3.

41. See Kochan and Hugh Pym, *The Guinness Affair*, chapters 5–12; Pugh, *Is Guinness Good For You?*, chapters 4–8. For more details of the trial, see Guinness, *Requiem*, chapter 19.

42. For example, it takes center stage in Fallon and Srodes, *Takeovers*.

43. For a flavor of the debate about British or English industrial decline and the failure of management, see Martin J. Wiener, *English Culture and the Decline of the Industrial Spirit 1850–1980* (Cambridge, UK: Cambridge University Press, 1981); Bruce Collines and Keith Robbins, eds., *British Culture and Economic Decline* (London: Weidenfeld and Nicolson, 1990).

44. Diageo was formed in 1997 as a merger between Grand Metropolitan and Guinness.

45. Edward Guinness, interviewed 2013: 15.

46. Ibid., 18–19.

47. In his autobiography, Edward Guinness devotes a lot of space to the role he played within the trade and industry bodies, committees, and charities. It is clear that Saunders saw Edward Guinness's role as smoothing ruffled feathers in the industry, maintaining relationships, or repairing the damage caused by Saunders's methods. Guinness, *A Brewer's Tale*, chapter 11.

48. Edward Guinness, interviewed 2013: 20.

49. Ibid., 18.

50. Guinness, *Brewer's Tale*, 392.

51. See, for example, Peter Pagnamenta and Richard Overy, *All Our Working Lives* (London: BBC Books, 1984); Chris Smith, John Child, and Michael Rowlinson, *Reshaping Work: The Cadbury Experience* (Cambridge, UK: Cambridge University Press); Margret Williamson, *Life at the*

ICI: Memories of Working at ICI Billingham (Hartlepool, UK: Teesside Industrial Memories Project, 2008).

52. For examples in the United States, see Bennett Harrison and Barry Bluestone, *The Great U-Turn: Corporate Restructuring and the Polarizing of America* (New York: Basic Books, 1988). For the United Kingdom, see John MacInnes, *Thatcherism at Work: Industrial Relations and Economic Change* (Milton Keynes, UK: Open University Press, 1987); John Eldridge, Peter Cressey, and John MacInnes, *Industrial Sociology and Economic Crisis* (New York: Harvester Wheatsheaf, 1991).

53. See David Harvey, *The Condition of Postmodernity: An Enquiry into the Origins of Cultural Change* (Oxford: Blackwell, 1989), part 2; David Beale, *Driven by Nissan: A Critical Guide to New Management Techniques* (London: Lawrence and Wishart, 1994). For a critical summary of these labor strategies, see Anna Pollert, "The 'Flexible Firm': Fixation or Fact?," *Work, Employment and Society* 2, no. 3 (1988): 281–316.

54. William Lazonick and Mary O'Sullivan, "Maximizing Shareholder Value: A New Ideology for Corporate Governance," *Economy and Society* 29, no. 1 (2000): 13–35, 18.

55. For a broader discussion of the nature of this period, see Jefferson Cowie, *The Great Exception: The New Deal and the Limits of American Politics* (Princeton, NJ: Princeton University Press, 2016). See also Christian Olaf Christiansen, *Progressive Business: An Intellectual History of the Role of Business in American Society* (Oxford: Oxford University Press, 2015).

56. For more on the ideology of shareholder value, see Karel Williams, "From Shareholder Value to Present-Day Capitalism," *Economy and Society* 29, no. 1 (2000): 1–12; Julie Froud, Colin Haslam, Sukhdev Johal, and Karel Williams, "Shareholder Value and Financialization: Consultancy Promises, Management Moves," *Economy and Society* 29, no. 1 (2000): 80–110.

57. David Weil, *Fissured Workplace: Why Work Became So Bad for So Many and What Can Be Done to Improve It* (Cambridge, MA: Harvard University Press, 2014).

58. Henry Dawson, interviewed 2015: 13.

59. Ibid., 13–14.

60. Barry Hubbard, interviewed 2005: 7–8.

61. David Hughes, interviewed 2009: 2.

62. Ibid., 10.

63. Ibid.

64. Ibid.

65. Ibid.

66. Ibid., 15.

67. Ray Snook, interviewed 2004: 5–6.

68. Ibid., 6.

69. Henry Dawson, interviewed 2015: 13.

70. Alan Mudie, interviewed 2004: 6.

71. John Woodgate, interviewed 2004: 6.

72. Dave Bathurst, interviewed 2004: 7.

73. For accounts of the contemporaneous industrial relations context in the United Kingdom, see MacInnes, *Thatcherism at Work*; Eldridge et al., *Industrial Sociology and Economic Crisis*; Doreen Massey and Richard Meegan, *The Anatomy of Job Loss: The How, Why and Where of Employment Decline* (London: Methuen, 1982).

74. Terry Aldridge, interviewed 2015: part 1, 10.

75. Ibid., part 2, 12.

76. Ibid., part 2, 14–15.

77. Mick Costello, interviewed 2004: 4.

78. Ibid., 5.

79. Barry Hubbard, interviewed 2004: 8.

80. Dave Bathurst, interviewed 2004: 2.

81. On the point about companies using comparisons between plants to leverage change, see Huw Beynon, *Working for Ford* (London: Penguin, 1973), 291. See also Jefferson Cowie, *Capital Moves: RCA's 70-Year Quest for Cheap Labor* (Ithaca, NY: Cornell University Press, 1999).

82. Dave Bathurst, interviewed 2004: 2.
83. Ibid., 7–8.
84. Ibid., 8.
85. John Woodgate, interviewed 2004: 3.
86. Ibid., 5.
87. Ray Snook, interviewed 2004: 6.
88. Edward Palmer Thompson, "Peculiarities of the English," in *The Socialist Register*, eds. Ralph Miliband and John Saville (London: Merlin, 1965), 311–62.

Chapter 6

1. Stephen Poliakoff, *Friends and Crocodiles and Gideon's Daughter: Screenplays* (London: Methuen, 2005), 97.
2. Ibid., 99.
3. Ibid., xxiii.
4. Nicholas Comfort, *Surrender: How British Industry Gave Up the Ghost 1952–2012* (London: Biteback Publishing, 2012), 1–2; see also Jim Tomlinson, "De-industrialization Not Decline: A New Meta-narrative for Post-War British History," *Twentieth Century British History* 27, no. 1 (2016): 76–99.
5. Martin Wiener, *English Culture and the Decline of the Industrial Spirit 1850–1980* (Cambridge, UK: Cambridge University Press, 1981); Bruce Collins and Keith Robbins, eds., *British Culture and Economic Decline* (London: Weidenfeld and Nicolson, 1990).
6. For the United Kingdom, see Frank Blackaby, ed., *De-Industrialisation* (London: Heinemann, 1978); Johnathan Gershuny, *After Industrial Society? The Emerging Self-service Economy* (London: Macmillan, 1978). For the United States, see Barry Bluestone and Bennett Harrison, *The Deindustrialization of America: Plant Closing, Community Abandonment, and the Dismantling of Basic Industry* (New York: Basic Books, 1982). For an overview, see Tim Strangleman and James Rhodes, "The 'New' Sociology of Deindustrialisation? Understanding Industrial Change," *Sociology Compass* 8, no. 4 (2014): 411–21.
7. A whole series of films and TV dramas were filmed at Park Royal, including *Basic Instinct 2*, *Bat Man Begins*, *Messiah*, and the political comedy *The Thick of It*.
8. Jefferson Cowie and Joseph Heathcott, eds., *Beyond the Ruins: The Meanings of Deindustrialization* (Ithaca, NY: Cornell University Press, 2003).
9. See David Bensman and Roberta Lynch, *Rusted Dreams: Hard Times in a Steel Community* (New York: McGraw-Hill, 1987); Bluestone and Harrison, *Deindustrialization of America*; Christine Walley, *Exit Zero: Family and Class in Postindustrial Chicago* (Chicago: Chicago University Press, 2013); Bill Bamberger and Cathy Davidson, *Closing: The Life and Death of an American Factory* (New York: Norton, 1998); Tom Juravich, *At the Altar of the Bottom Line: The Degradation of Work in the 21st Century* (Amherst: University of Massachusetts Press, 2009), chapter 4; Kate Dudley, *End of the Line: Lost Jobs, New Lives in Postindustrial America* (Chicago: Chicago University Press, 1994); Ian Roberts, *Craft, Class and Control: The Sociology of a Shipbuilding Community* (Edinburgh: Edinburgh University Press, 1993).
10. Ruth Milkman, *Farewell to the Factory: Auto Workers in the Late Twentieth Century* (Berkeley: University of California Press, 1997). The other side of this attitude to layoffs in the auto industry can be found in Victor Chen's recent book, which compares and contrasts laid-off workers in the United States and Canada In a number of cases, Chen emphasizes the liberatory effects of such work for women seeking financial independence from abusive partners. Victor Tan Chen, *Cut Loose: Jobless and Hopeless in an Unfair Economy* (Oakland: University of California Press, 2015).
11. *The Guardian*, April 16, 2004.
12. While beer sales fell during this period, wine sales went from 18 percent to 32 percent of total alcohol consumed, with cider rising from 3 percent to 9 percent. Guinness sales were further squeezed by the long-term trend away from ales and stout and the rise of lager. For a fascinating and comprehensive overview of the United Kingdom industry, see John Spicer, Chris Thurman, John Walters, and Simon Ward, *Intervention in the Modern UK Brewing Industry* (Basingstoke, UK: Palgrave, 2012).

13. Economic geographer Andy Pike, who studies the brewing sector, has talked about both the geographical entanglement in place of products and brands and how the way commodification, marketization, and financialization tend to loosen up and disembed social relationships. The decision to close Park Royal rather than its sister plant in Ireland was made taking into consideration a whole series of factors—historical, spatial, political, economic, and financial. As Pike argues, "Finance-driven capitalism may be more autonomous from the 'real' economy, but it cannot escape its inherently geographical foundations . . . National 'varieties of capitalism' with distinctive material and social characteristics guide company behavior and mediate financialization and shareholder value in particular ways." Andy Pike, "'Shareholder Value' Versus the Regions: The Closure of the Vaux Brewery in Sunderland," *Journal of Economic Geography* 6, no. 2 (2006): 201–22, 205.

14. Graham Bayford, interviewed 2005: 5.

15. Dave Bathurst, interviewed 2004: 8.

16. Barry Hubbard, interviewed 2004: 10.

17. Les Woodgate, interviewed 2004: 7.

18. Simon Basketter, *Socialist Worker Online*, April 24, 2004. The piece went on to note that Irish corporation tax was 12.5 percent compared to the UK figure of 30 percent.

19. Les Woodgate, interviewed 2004: 8.

20. Anonymous interview, 2005: 21.

21. Graham Bayford, interviewed 2005: 6.

22. Barry Hubbard, interviewed 2004: 10.

23. Ray Snook, interviewed 2004: 8.

24. Dave Bathurst, interviewed 2004: 9.

25. Ibid. It is worth contrasting the situations of laid-off UK and US workers. The Guinness workers had a relatively good company pension plan, plus a good severance package linked to seniority. They also were covered by Britain's national health care. In the United States, laid-off workers are left with much less of a safety net, leading to sometimes brutal circumstances.

26. See Tim Strangleman, *Work Identity at the End of the Line? Privatisation and Culture Change in the UK Rail Industry* (Basingstoke, UK: Palgrave, 2004a). See also Tim Strangleman and Ian Roberts, "Looking through the Window of Opportunity: The Cultural Cleansing of Workplace Identity," *Sociology* 33, no. 1 (1999): 47–67.

27. Dave Bathurst, interviewed 2004: 11.

28. Ibid.

29. Anonymous interview, 2004: 15.

30. Ibid.

31. Richard Sennett, *The Corrosion of Character: The Personal Consequences of Work in the New Capitalism* (New York: Norton, 1998), 147

32. See Wendy Loretto and Sarah Vickerstaff, "Gender, Age and Flexible Working in Later Life," *Work, Employment and Society* 29, no. 2 (2015): 233–49.

33. Ray Snook, interviewed 2004: 10.

34. Graham Bayford, interviewed 2005: 9.

35. Dave Bathurst, interviewed 2004: 9.

36. Ibid., 14.

37. Anonymous interview, 2005: 9–10.

38. Les Woodgate, interviewed 2004: 9.

39. For an insight into the historical roots of this delineation, see Alasdair Clayre, *Work and Play: Ideas and Experience of Work and Leisure* (London: Weidenfeld and Nicolson, 1974).

40. Les Woodgate, interviewed 2004: 11.

41. Ibid., 11–12.

42. Dave Bathurst, interviewed 2004: 12–13.

43. Ibid., 13.

44. Sennett, *Corrosion of Character*, 99.

45. Mick Costello, interviewed 2005: 12.

46. Ibid., 12.

47. Ray Snook, interviewed 2004: 11.
48. Mick Costello, interviewed 2005: 4.
49. Ibid., 11.
50. Anonymous interview, 2005: 18.
51. Henry Dawson, interviewed 2005: 12.
52. Ibid.
53. Edward Guinness, *A Brewer's Tale: Memoirs of Edward Guinness CVO* (Croydon, UK: CPI Group, 2014): 442–43.
54. Ruth Milkman, *Farewell to the Factory: Auto Workers in the Late Twentieth Century* (Berkeley: University of California Press, 1997).

Chapter 7

1. Owen Hatherley, *A Guide to the New Ruins of Great Britain* (London: Verso, 2010): xxxiv–xxxv.
2. Kate Dudley quotes one of her interviewees, Donna Clausen, saying, "You know, tell them that it was a place where we worked, and that when they tore the building down, Grandma went and got herself a brick. For all that I put in there, I figure I at least deserve a brick." Kathryn Marie Dudley, *The End of the Line: Lost Jobs, New Lives in Postindustrial America* (Chicago: University of Chicago Press, 1994), 173.
3. Steven High and David Lewis, *Corporate Wasteland: The Landscape and Memory of Deindustrialization* (Ithaca, NY: Cornell University Press, 2007): 23–24.
4. Bradley L. Garrett, "Assaying History: Creating Temporal Junctions through Urban Exploration," *Environment and Planning D: Society and Space* 29, no. 6 (2011): 1048–67, 1049; see also Bradley L. Garrett, *Explore Everything: Place-Hacking the City* (London: Verso, 2013); Ninjalicious, *Access All Areas: A User's Guide to the Art of Urban Exploration* (Toronto: Infiltration, 2005).
5. See, for example, Byron Olsen and Joseph Cabadas, *The American Auto Factory* (St. Paul, MN: Motor Books, 2009); Joseph Cabadas, *River Rouge: Ford's Industrial Colossus* (St. Paul, MN: Motor Books, 2004); Ford R. Bryan, *Rouge: Pictured in Its Prime* (Dearborn, MI: Motor Books, 2003); Michael W. R. Davis, *Chrysler Heritage: A Photographic History* (Chicago: Tempus, 2001); Klaus Tenfelde, ed., *Pictures of Krupp: Photography and History in the Industrial Age* (London: Philip Wilson, 2005). See also Gillian Bardsley and Colin Corke, *Making Cars at Longbridge: 100 Years in the Life of a Factory* (Stroud, UK: Alan Sutton, 2006); Julian Germain, *Steelworks: Consett, from Steel to Tortilla Chips* (London: Why Not Publishing, 1990); Stuart Whipps, *Ming Jue: Photographs of Longbridge and Nanjing* (Walsall, UK: New Art Gallery Walsall, 2008); François Bon and Antoine Stéphani, *Billancourt* (Paris: Éditions Cercle d'Art, 2003).
6. Steven High, "'The Wounds of Class': A Historical Reflection on the Study of Deindustrialization, 1973–2013," *History Compass* 11, no. 11 (2013): 994–1007, 999. See also Steven High, "Beyond Aesthetics: Visibility and Invisibility in the Aftermath of Deindustrialization," *International Labor and Working-Class History* 84 (Winter 2013): 140–53. For a broader consideration of nostalgia and the aesthetics of industrial ruins, see Tim Strangleman, "'Smokestack Nostalgia,' 'Ruin Porn' or Working-Class Obituary: The Role and Meaning of Deindustrial Representation," *International Labor and Working-Class History* 84 (Winter 2013a): 23–37. See also Dora Apel, *Beautiful Terrible Ruins: Detroit and the Anxiety of Decline* (New Brunswick, NJ: Rutgers University Press, 2015). For more abstract academic accounts of the meanings of ruins, see Dylan Trigg, *The Aesthetics of Decay* (New York: Peter Lang, 2006); Robert Harbison, *Ruins and Fragments: Tales of Loss and Rediscovery* (London: Reaktion, 2015); Julia Hell and Andreas Schönle, eds., *Ruins of Modernity* (Durham, NC: Duke University Press, 2010).
7. See Edward Platt, *Leadville: A Biography of the A40* (London: Picador, 2000); Raphael Samuel, *Theatres of Memory: Volume 1: Past and Present in Contemporary Culture* (London: Verso, 1994), 305.
8. *Park Royal London* (Spring 1998): 9. This is the magazine of the Park Royal Partnership.
9. "Listing" refers to the registration of historic buildings in the United Kingdom. Listed buildings fall into three categories, 1, 2*, and 2. All but 3.2 percent of listed buildings predate

the twentieth century. See https://historicengland.org.uk/listing/what-is-designation/listed-buildings/ (accessed August 2, 2016).

10. Letter from Bronwin Edwards, Twentieth Century Society, to Department of Culture, Media and Sport, February 18, 1998.

11. The local council for the area in which the brewery was located.

12. Letter from Kenneth Powell, Twentieth Century Society to Planning Officer at Brent Council, November 3, 1998.

13. Ibid.

14. "Guinness Turns Developer to Build £500m HQ," *Financial Times* (2000), http://www.davidlawson.co.uk/Files/GUIN-FT_FE0.htm (accessed July 26, 2016).

15. "End of Era for Work of Pure Genius; Plans to Demolish Brewery That Is Hailed as Modern Masterpiece," *The Guardian*, June 7, 2005.

16. Gavin Stamp, *Anti-Ugly: Excursions in English Architecture and Design* (London: Aurum, 2013), 30.

17. Ibid., 33.

18. Rob Sharp, "Brewery Heritage Denied," *Architects' Journal*, June 9, 2005: 11.

19. Ibid.

20. Ibid.

21. Cartoon by Louis Hellman, *Architects' Journal*, June 9: 22.

22. Gavin Stamp, interviewed 2009: 1.

23. Ibid., 1.

24. Ibid., 10.

25. Peter Maher, interviewed 2005: 13.

26. Ibid., 13.

27. Ibid., 14.

28. Ibid., 15.

29. Henry Dawson, interviewed 2005: 13.

30. Ibid.

31. Bankside was the former oil-fired power station designed by Giles Gilbert Scott in 1947. It opened in 1952 and generated electricity until 1981, after which it was converted into Tate Modern art gallery. It shared many of the features of Gilbert Scott's treatment of the Guinness brewery.

32. Dave Bathurst, interviewed 2004: 19.

33. Ibid., 19.

34. Ibid., 19–20.

35. Adrian Sturgess, interviewed 2009: 8.

36. Ibid., 10.

37. Ibid., 10.

38. Ibid., 11.

39. Ibid., 40.

40. Ibid., 23.

41. Ibid., 25.

42. Ibid., 32.

43. Terry Aldridge, interviewed 2015: 26.

44. Ibid., 26.

45. Ibid., 26–27.

46. Henry Dawson, interviewed 2015: 22.

47. Ibid.

48. Sylvain Margaine, Forbidden Places website, http://www.forbidden-places.net/urban-exploration-park-royal-guinness-brewery#1 (accessed July 28, 2016).

49. Comments posted on Forbidden Places website, http://www.forbidden-places.net/urban-exploration-park-royal-guinness-brewery#23 (accessed July 28, 2016).

50. Bridget Fowler, *The Obituary as Collective Memory* (London: Routledge, 2007), 8.

51. Avery Gordon, *Ghostly Matters: Haunting and the Sociological Imagination* (Minneapolis: University of Minnesota Press, 2008).

Conclusion

1. http://www.doctorwholocations.net/locations/diageoparkroyal (accessed September 7, 2016).

2. See, for example, John Lancaster, Brexit Blues, *London Review of Books* 38, no. 15 (July 2016): 3–6.

3. Jefferson Cowie, *The Great Exception: The New Deal and the Limits of American Politics* (Princeton, NJ: Princeton University Press, 2016).

4. Tony Blair, speech to the 2005 Labour Party Conference, quoted in John Harris, "Does the Left Have a Future?," *The Guardian*, September 6, 2016.

Bibliography

Addison, Paul. *The Road to 1945: British Politics and the Second World War.* 2nd ed. London: Pimlico, 1994.

Apel, Dora 2015. *Beautiful Terrible Ruins: Detroit and the Anxiety of Decline.* New Brunswick, NJ: Rutgers University Press, 2015.

Baldwin, Stanley. *On England and Other Addresses.* London: Penguin, 1937.

Bamberger, Bill, and Cathy Davidson *Closing: The Life and Death of an American Factory.* New York: Norton, 1999.

Bardsley, Gillian, and Colin Corke. *Making Cars at Longbridge: 100 Years in the Life of a Factory.* Stroud, UK: Alan Sutton, 2006.

Barr, Charles. *Ealing Studios.* London: Studio Vista, 1993.

Bauman, Zygmunt. *Work, Consumerism and the New Poor.* Buckingham, UK: Open University Press, 2000.

Baxendale, John, and Christopher Pawling. *Narrating the Thirties: A Decade in the Making: 1930 to the Present.* Basingstoke, UK: MacMillan, 1996.

Beale, David. *Driven by Nissan: A Critical Guide to New Management Techniques.* London: Lawrence and Wishart, 1994.

Beck, Ulrich *The Brave New World of Work.* Cambridge, UK: Polity, 2000.

Beckett, Andy. *Promised You a Miracle: UK 80–82.* London: Allen Lane, 2015.

Beckett, Andy, *When the Lights Went Out: Britain in the Seventies.* London: Faber and Faber, 2009.

Bensman, David, and Roberta Lynch *Rusted Dreams. Hard Times in a Steel Community* New York: McGraw-Hill, 1987.

Betjeman, John *Coming Home: An Anthology of Prose.* London: Vintage, 1997.

Betjeman, John *London's Historic Railway Stations.* London: John Murray, 1972.

Beynon, Huw. *Working for Ford.* London: Penguin, 1973.

Bhaskar, K "Three Case Studies—Guinness, Spillers and Nestles." In *Reading on Mergers and Takeovers*, edited by John Malcolm Samuels. London: Paul Elek Books, 1972.

Blackaby, Frank, ed. *De-Industrialisation.* London: Heinemann, 1978.

Bluestone, Barry, and Bennett Harrison *The Deindustrialization of America: Plant Closings, Community Abandonment, and the Dismantling of Basic Industry.* New York: Basic Books, 1982.

Blythe, Ronald. *The Age of Illusion: Some Glimpses of Britain between the Wars 1919–1940.* Oxford: Oxford University Press, 1983.

Bon, François, and Antoine Stéphani. *Billancourt.* Paris: Éditions Cercle d'Art.

Bonnett, Alastair. 2010. *Left in the Past: Radicalism and the Politics of Nostalgia.* London: Continuum, 2003.

Boyes, Georgina *The Imagined Village Culture, Ideology and the English Folk Revival.* Manchester, UK: Manchester University Press, 1993.

Broomfield, Maurice. *Maurice Broomfield Photographs.* London: Foto8, 2009.

Brown, Elizabeth *The Corporate Eye: Photography and the Rationalization of American Commercial Culture, 1884–1929.* Baltimore, MD: Johns Hopkins University Press, 2005.

Brown, Richard K, and Peter Brannen "Social Relations and Social Perspectives amongst Shipbuilding Workers: A Preliminary Statement." *Sociology* 4, no. 1 (1970): 71–84.

Bryan, Ford R *Rouge: Pictured in Its Prime.* Dearborn, MI: Motor Books, 2003.

Burawoy, Michael. *Manufacturing Consent: Changes in the Labor Process under Monopoly Capitalism*. London: University of Chicago Press, 1982.

Byrne, David. "Industrial Culture in a Post-Industrial World: The Case of the North East of England." *City* 6, no. 3 (2002): 279–89.

Byrne, David, and Aiden Doyle. "The Visual and the Verbal." In *Picturing the Social Landscape: Visual Methods and the Sociological Imagination*, edited by Caroline Knowles and Paul Sweetman, 166–77. London: Routledge, 2004.

Cabadas, Joseph. *River Rouge: Ford's Industrial Colossus*. St. Paul, MN: Motorbooks International, 2004.

Castillo, Juan. "The Memory of Work and the Future of Industrial Heritage." *Forum: Qualitative Social Research* 12, no. 3 (2011): 1–14.

Chance, Helena. "The Angel in the Garden Suburb: Arcadian Allegory in the 'Girls' Grounds' at the Cadbury Factory, Bournville, England, 1880–1930." *Studies in the History of Gardens and Designed Landscapes* 27, no. 3 (2007): 197–216.

Chase, Malcolm. "'Nothing Less than a Revolution'?: Labour's Agricultural Policy." In *Labour's High Noon: The Government and the Economy 1945–51*, edited by Jim Firth, 78–95. London: Lawrence and Whishart, 1993.

Chen, Victor Tan. *Cut Loose: Jobless and Hopeless in an Unfair Economy*. Oakland, CA: University of California Press, 2015.

Christiansen, Christian Olaf. *Progressive Business: An Intellectual History of the Role of Business in American Society*. Oxford: Oxford University Press, 2015.

Clayre, Alasdair. *Work and Play: Ideas and Experience of Work and Leisure*. London: Weidenfeld and Nicolson, 1974.

Clemens, Paul. *Punching Out: One Year in a Closing Auto Plant*. New York: Doubleday, 2011.

Coates, Ken, and Richard Silburn. *Poverty: The Forgotten Englishmen*. London: Penguin Books, 1970.

Cohen, Lizabeth. "What Kind of World Have We Lost? Workers' Lives and Deindustrialization in the Museum." *American Quarterly* 41, no. 4 (1989): 670–81.

Collins, Bruce, and Keith Robbins, eds. *Debates in Modern History: British Culture and Economic Decline*. London: Weidenfeld and Nicolson, 1990.

Collis, Robert. *Identity of England*. Oxford: Oxford University Press, 2002.

Comfort, Nicholas. *Surrender: How British Industry Gave up the Ghost 1952–2012*. London: Biteback Publishing, 2012.

Conway, Martin. *Autobiographical Memory: An Introduction*. Milton Keynes, UK: Open University Press, 1990.

Cowie, Jefferson. *Capital Moves: RCA's 70-Year Quest for Cheap Labor*. Ithaca, NY: Cornell University Press, 1999.

Cowie, Jefferson. *The Great Exception: The New Deal and the Limits of American Politics*. Princeton, NJ: Princeton University Press, 2016.

Cowie, Jefferson. *Stayin' Alive: The 1970s and the Last Days of the Working Class*. New York: The New Press, 2010.

Cowie, Jefferson, and Joseph Heathcott, eds. *Beyond the Ruins: The Meanings of Deindustrialization*. Ithaca, NY: Cornell University Press, 2003.

Cowie, Jefferson, and Nick Salvatore. "The Long Exception: Rethinking the New Deal in American History." *International Labor and Working-Class History* 74 (Winter 2008): 3–32.

Cuneo, Terence. *The Mouse and His Master: The Life and Work of Terence Cuneo*. London: New Cavendish, 1977.

D'Arazien, Arthur. *Big Picture: The Artistry of D'Arazien*. Kent, OH: Kent State University Press, 2002.

Darley, Gillian. *Factory*. London: Reaktion, 2003.

Davies, Jim. *The Book of Guinness Advertising*. London: Guinness Publishing, 1998.

Davis, Fred. *Yearning for Yesterday: A Sociology of Nostalgia*. New York: The Free Press, 1979.

Davis, Michael W. R. *Chrysler Heritage: A Photographic History*. Chicago: Tempus, 2001.

Dawson, Christopher J. *Steel Remembered: Photographs from the LTV Steel Collection*. Kent, OH: Kent State University Press, 2008.

Dennison, S. R, and Oliver MacDonagh. *Guinness 1886–1939: From Incorporation to the Second World War*. Cork: University of Cork Press, 1998.

Dicks, Bella *Heritage, Place and Community*. Cardiff: University of Wales Press, 2000.

Dorling, Daniel. *Injustice: Why Social Inequality Persists*. Bristol: Policy Press, 2011.

Dublin, Thomas, and Walter Light. *The Face of Decline: The Pennsylvania Anthracite Region in the Twentieth Century*. Ithaca, NY: Cornell University Press, 2005.

Dudley, Kathryn Marie. *End of the Line: New Lives in Postindustrial America*. Chicago: Chicago University Press, 1994.

Durkheim, Émile. *The Division of Labour in Society*. New York: The Free Press, 1964 [First published 1893].

Durkheim, Émile. *Professional Ethics and Civic Morals*. London: Routledge, 1992 [First published 1957].

Edensor, Tim. *Industrial Ruins: Space, Aesthetics and Materiality*. Oxford: Berg, 2005.

Eldridge, John E. T. *Industrial Disputes: Essays in the Sociology of Industrial Relations*. London: Routledge and Kegan Paul, 1968.

Eldridge, John, Peter Cressey, and John MacInnes. *Industrial Sociology and Economic Crisis*. New York: Harvester Wheatsheaf, 1991.

Ezzy, Douglas. *Narrating Unemployment*. Aldershot, UK: Ashgate, 2001.

Fallon, Ivan, and James Srodes. *Takeovers*. London: Hamish Hamilton, 1987.

Fine, Linda *The Story of Reo Joe: Work, Kin, and Community in Autotown, USA*. Philadelphia: Temple University Press, 2004.

Fones-Wolf, Elizabeth *Selling Free Enterprise: The Business Assault on Labor and Liberalism 1945– 60*. Chicago: University of Illinois, 1994.

Foster, Roy. *Modern Ireland 1600–1972*. London: Penguin, 1988.

Fowler, Bridget. *The Obituary as Collective Memory*. London: Routledge, 2007.

Fox, Alan *History and Heritage: The Social Origins of the British Industrial Relations System*. London: Allen and Unwin, 1985.

Frayn, Michael. "Festival." In *Age of Austerity*, edited by Michael Sissons and Philip French, 305–26. Oxford: Oxford University Press, 1963.

Froud, Julie, Colin Haslam, Sukhdev Johal, and Karel Williams. "Shareholder Value and Financialization: Consultancy Promises, Management Moves." *Economy and Society* 29, no. 1 (2000): 80–110.

Gardiner, Juliet *Picture Post Women*. London: Collins and Brown, 1993.

Garfinkel, Harold. *Studies in Ethnomethodology*. Englewood Cliffs, NJ: Prentice-Hall, 1967.

Germain, Julian *Steelworks: Consett, from Steel to Tortilla Chips*. London: Why Not Publishing, 1990.

Garrett, Bradley L "Assaying History: Creating Temporal Junctions through Urban Exploration." *Environment and Planning D: Society and Space* 29, no. 6 (2011): 1048–67.

Garrett, Bradley L *Explore Everything: Place-Hacking the City*. London: Verso, 2013.

Gershuny, Johnathan *After Industrial Society? The Emerging Self-Service Economy*. London: Macmillan, 1978.

Glucksmann, Miriam *Women Assemble: Women Workers and the "New Industries" in Inter-War Britain*. London: Routledge, 1990.

Goldthorpe, John, David Lockwood, Frank Bechhofer, and Jenifer Platt. *The Affluent Worker: Industrial Attitudes and Behaviour*. Cambridge, UK: Cambridge University Press, 1968.

Gordon, Avery. *Ghostly Matters: Haunting and the Sociological Imagination*. Minneapolis: University of Minnesota Press, 2008.

Gorz, André *Reclaiming Work: Beyond the Wage-Based Society*. Cambridge, UK: Polity, 1999.

Gourvish, Terence R, and Richard G Wilson *The British Brewing Industry 1830–1980*. Cambridge, UK: Cambridge University Press, 1994.

Guinness, Edward. *A Brewer's Tale: Memoirs of Edward Guinness CVO*. Croydon, UK: CPI Group, 2014.

Guinness, Edward. *The Guinness Book of Guinness 1935–1985: An Anthology Based on the First 50 Years of The Park Royal Brewery and Its Connections*. London: Guinness Publishing, 1988.

Guinness, Jonathan *Requiem for a Family Business*. Basingstoke, UK: Pan Books, 1997.

Guinness, Michele. *The Guinness Spirit: Brewers and Bankers, Ministers and Missionaries.* London: Hodder and Stoughton, 1999.

Hall, David. *Working Lives: The Forgotten Voices of Britain's Post-War Working Class.* London: Bantam Press, 2012.

Hampton, Janie. *The Austerity Olympics: When the Games Came to London in 1948.* London: Aurum, 2008.

Harbison, Robert. *Ruins and Fragments: Tales of Loss and Rediscovery.* London: Reaktion Books, 2015.

Harrison, Godfrey. *Alexander Gibb: The Story of an Engineer.* London: Geoffery Bles, 1950.

Harvey, David. *The Condition of Postmodernity: An Enquiry into the Origins of Cultural Change.* Oxford: Blackwell, 1989.

Hatherley, Owen. *A Guide to the New Ruins of Great Britain.* London: Verso, 2010.

Hay, Colin. "Narrating the Crisis: The Discursive Construction of the 'Winter of Discontent'." *Sociology* 30, no. 2 (1996): 253–77.

Hell, Julia, and Andreas Schönle, eds. *Ruins of Modernity.* Durham, NC: Duke University Press, 2010.

Heller, Michael. "Editorial Introduction Company Magazines 1880–1940: An Overview." *Management and Organizational History* 3 (2008): 3–4.

Higgins, James J. *Images of the Rust Belt.* Kent, OH: Kent State University Press, 1999.

High, Steven. "Beyond Aesthetics: Visibility and Invisibility in the Aftermath of Deindustrialization." *International Labor and Working-Class History* 84 (Winter 2013): 140–53.

High, Steven. *Industrial Sunset: The Making of North America's Rust Belt, 1969–1984.* Toronto: University of Toronto Press, 2003.

High, Steven. "'The Wounds of Class': A Historical Reflection on the Study of Deindustrialization, 1973–2013." *History Compass* 11, no. 11 (2013): 994–1007.

High, Steven, and David Lewis. *Corporate Wasteland: The Landscape and Memory of Deindustrialization.* Ithaca, NY: Cornell University Press, 2007.

Hoggart, Richard. *The Uses of Literacy.* London: Penguin, 1957.

Hoskins, William George. *The Making of the English Landscape.* London: Penguin, 1955.

Howarth, Ken. *Oral History: A Handbook.* Stroud, UK: Alan Sutton, 1998.

Howell, Owen Bulmer. *The Park Royal Development Company Ltd.* London: Guinness, 1959.

Howkins, Alun. *The Death of Rural England: A Social History of the Countryside since 1900.* London: Routledge, 2003.

Hughes, David. *A Bottle of Guinness Please: The Colourful History of Guinness.* Wokingham, UK: Phimboy, 2006.

Hughes, David. *Gilroy Was Good for Guinness.* Dublin: Liberties Press, 2013.

Huxley, Aldous. *Brave New World.* London: Grafton, 1932.

Hyman, Richard. "Praetorians and Proletarians: Unions and Industrial Relations." In *Labour's High Noon: The Government and the Economy 1945–51,* edited by Jim Firth, 165–195. London: Lawrence and Whishart, 1993.

Jackson, Kevin. *Humphrey Jennings.* Basingstoke, UK: Picador, 2004.

Jacoby, Sanford. *Modern Manors: Welfare Capitalism since the New Deal.* Princeton, NJ: Princeton University Press, 1997.

Jellicoe, Geoffrey. *Studies in Landscape Design.* Oxford: Oxford University Press, 1960.

Jellicoe, Geoffrey, and Susan Jellicoe. *The Landscape of Man: Shaping the Environment from Prehistory to the Present Day.* 3rd ed. London: Thames and Hudson, 1995.

Jennings, Humphrey. *Pandaemonium: The Coming of the Machine as Seen by Contemporary Observers.* London: Picador, 1985.

Jones, Dylan. *The Eighties: One Day, One Decade.* London: Windmill, 2013.

Juravich, Tom. *At the Altar of the Bottom Line: The Degradation of Work in the 21st Century.* Amherst: University of Massachusetts Press, 2009.

Kochan, Nick, and Hugh Pym. *The Guinness Affair: Anatomy of a Scandal.* London: Christopher Helm, 1987.

K'Meyer, Tracey, and Joy L Hart. *I Saw It Coming: Worker Narratives of Plant Closing and Job Loss.* Basingstoke, UK: Palgrave, 2011.

Lancaster, John. "Brexit Blues." *London Review of Books* 38, no. 15 (July 2016): 3–6.

Lane, Carrie M. *A Company of One: Insecurity, Independence, and the New World of White-Collar Unemployment*. Ithaca, NY: Cornell University Press, 2011.

Lazonick, William, and Mary O'Sullivan. "Maximizing Shareholder Value: A New Ideology for Corporate Governance." *Economy and Society* 29, no. 1 (2000): 13–35.

Linehan, Denis. "An Archaeology of Dereliction: Poetics and Policy in the Governing of Depressed Industrial Districts in Interwar England and Wales." *Journal of Historical Geography* 26, no. 1 (2000): 99–113.

Linehan, Denis. "Regional Survey and the Economic Geographies of Britain 1930–1939." *Transactions of the Institute of British Geographers*, New Series, 28, no. 1 (2003): 96–122.

Linkon, Sherry Lee. "Navigating Past and Present in the Deindustrial Landscape: Contemporary Writers on Detroit and Youngstown." *International Labor and Working-Class History* 84 (Winter 2013): 38–54.

Linkon, Sherry Lee, and John Russo. *Steeltown USA: Work and Memory in Youngstown*. Lawrence: University of Kansas Press, 2002.

Logan, Philip C. *Humphrey Jennings and the British Documentary Film: A Re-Assessment*. Farnham, UK: Ashgate, 2011.

Loretto, Wendy, and Sarah Vickerstaff. "Gender, Age and Flexible Working in Later Life." *Work, Employment and Society* 29, no. 2 (2015): 233–49.

Lummis, Trevor. "Structure and Validity in Oral Evidence." In *The Oral History Reader*, 2nd ed., edited by Robert Perks and Alistair Thomson, 255–60. London: Routledge, 1998.

Lynch, Patrick, and John Vaizey. *Guinness's Brewery in the Irish Economy 1759–1876*. Cambridge, UK: Cambridge University Press, 1960.

Lyons, F. S. L. *Ireland since the Famine*. London: Fontana, 1971.

MacInnes, John. *Thatcherism at Work: Industrial Relations and Economic Change*. Milton Keynes, UK: Open University Press, 1987.

Maharidge, Dale, and Michael Williamson. *Journey to Nowhere: The Saga of the New Underclass*. New York: Hyperion, 1985.

Maharidge, Dale, and Michael Williamson. *Someplace like America: Tales from the New Great Depression*. Berkeley: University of California Press, 2011.

Marchand, Roland. *Creating the Corporate Soul: The Rise of Public Relations and Corporate Imagery in American Big Business*. Berkeley: University of California Press, 1998.

Marglin, Stephen. "The Origins and Functions of Hierarchy in Capitalist Production." In *Capital and Labour: A Marxist Primer*, edited by Theo Nichols, 237–54. London: Fontana, 1980.

Marshall, T. H. *Citizenship and Social Class*. London: Pluto, 1992 [First Published 1950].

Marx, Leo. *The Machine in the Garden: Technology and the Pastoral Ideal in America*. Oxford: Oxford University Press, 1964.

Massey, Doreen, and Richard Meegan. *The Anatomy of Job Loss: The How, Why and Where of Employment Decline*. London: Methuen, 1982.

Matless, David. *Landscape and Englishness*. London: Reaktion, 1998.

McGlade, Fred. *The History of the British Army Film and Photographic Unit in the Second World War*. Solihull, UK: Helion, 2010.

McSmith, Andy. *No Such Thing as Society: A History of Britain in the 1980s*. London: Constable, 2011.

Merriman, Peter. *Driving Spaces: A Cultural-Historical Geography of England's M1 Motorway*. Oxford: Blackwell, 2007.

Milkman, Ruth. *Farewell to the Factory: Auto Workers in the Late Twentieth Century*. Berkeley: University of California Press, 1997.

Miller, Daniel. *The Comfort of Things*. Cambridge, UK: Polity Press, 2008.

Mills, Edward. *The Modern Factory*. London: The Architectural Press, 1951.

Modell, Judith, and Charlee Brodsky. *A Town without Steel: Envisioning Homestead*. Pittsburgh: University of Pittsburgh Press, 1998.

Moodley, Kiran. "Thatcher's Greatest Legacy: The Rewriting of the Seventies." *New Statesman*, April 16, 2013.

Mortimer, Jim. "The Changing Mood of Working People." In *Labour's High Noon: The Government and the Economy 1945–51*, edited by Jim Firth, 243–54. London: Lawrence and Wishart, 1993.

Mozingo, Louise. *Pastoral Capitalism: A History of Suburban Corporate Landscapes*. Cambridge, MA: MIT Press, 2011.

Muggeridge, Malcolm *The Thirties: 1930–1940 in Great Britain*. London: Fontana, 1967.

Nadel-Klein, Jane. *Fishing for Heritage: Modernity and Loss along the Scottish Coast*. Oxford: Berg, 2003.

Newby, Howard. *The Deferential Worker*. London: Penguin, 1977.

Nichols, Theo. *The British Worker Question: A New Look at Workers and Productivity in Manufacturing*. London: Routledge and Kegan Paul, 1986.

Ninjalicious. *Access All Areas: A User's Guide to the Art of Urban Exploration*. Toronto: Infiltration, 2005.

Nye, David. *America as Second Creation: Technology and Narratives of New Beginnings*. Cambridge: MIT Press, 2003.

Nye, David. *American Technological Sublime*. Cambridge, MA: MIT Press, 1994.

Nye, David. *Image Worlds: Corporate Identity at General Electric*. Cambridge, MA: MIT Press, 1985.

Nye, David. *Narratives and Spaces: Technology and the Construction of American Culture*. Exeter, UK: University of Exeter Press, 1997.

Offer, Avner. "British Manual Workers: From Producers to Consumers, c. 1950–2000." *Contemporary British History* 22, no. 4 (2008): 537–71.

O'Hara, S. Paul. *Gary: The Most American of All American Cities*. Bloomington: Indiana University Press, 2011.

Olsen, Byron, and Joseph Cabadas. *The American Auto Factory*. St. Paul, MN: Motor Books, 2009.

Orwell, George. *The Road to Wigan Pier*. London: Penguin, 1937.

Overy, Richard. *The Morbid Age: Britain and the Crisis of Civilization, 1919–1939*. London: Penguin, 2009.

Pagnamenta, Peter, and Richard Overy. *All Our Working Lives*. London: BBC Books, 1984.

Pahl, Ray. *Divisions of Labour*. Oxford: Blackwell, 1984.

Parker, Julia *Citizenship, Work and Welfare: Searching for the Good Society*. Basingstoke, UK: Palgrave, 1998.

Pike, Andy. "'Shareholder Value' Versus the Regions: The Closure of the Vaux Brewery in Sunderland." *Journal of Economic Geography* 6, no. 2 (2006): 201–22.

Piketty, Thomas. *Capital in the Twenty-First Century*. Cambridge, UK: Harvard University Press, 2014.

Platt, Edward. *Leadville: A Biography of the A40*. London: Picador, 2000.

Poliakoff, Stephen *Friends and Crocodiles and Gideon's Daughter: Screenplays*. London: Methuen, 2005.

Pollert, Anna "The 'Flexible Firm': Fixation or Fact?" *Work, Employment and Society* 2, no. 3 (1988): 281–316.

Portelli, Alessandro *The Death of Luigi Trastulli and Other Stories: Form and Meaning in Oral History*. Albany: SUNY Press, 2001.

Portelli, Alessandro "What Makes Oral History Different." In *The Oral History Reader*, 2nd ed., edited by Robert Perks and Alistair Thomson, 32–42. London: Routledge, 1998.

Priestley, J. B. *English Journey*. London: Penguin, 1934.

Pugh, Peter. *Is Guinness Good for You? The Bid for Distillers—The Inside Story*. London: Financial Training, 1987.

Quirke, Carol. *Eyes on Labor: News Photography and America's Working Class*. Oxford: Oxford University Press, 2012.

Roberts, Ian *Craft, Class and Control*. Edinburgh: Edinburgh University Press, 1993.

Rolt, L. T. C. *High Horse Riderless*. Bideford, UK: Green Books, 1947 [republished 1988].

Rosanvallon, Pierre. *The Society of Equals*. Cambridge, UK: Harvard University Press, 2013.

Rose, Gillian *Visual Methodologies: An Introduction to the Interpretation of Visual Materials*. 3rd ed. London: Sage, 2012.

Rosen, Harold. *Speaking from Memory: The Study of Autobiographical Discourse*. Stoke-on-Trent, UK: Trentham Books, 1998.

Rosenblum, Barbara *Photographers at Work: A Sociology of Photographic Styles*. New York: Holmes and Meier, 1978.

Russell, Dave. *Looking North: Northern England and the National Imagination*. Manchester, UK: Manchester University Press, 2004.

Russell, Patrick, and James Piers Taylor, eds. *Shadows of Progress: Documentary Films in Post-War Britain*. London: BFI/Palgrave, 2010.

Saler, Michael. *As If: Modern Enchantment and the Literary Prehistory of Virtual Reality*. Oxford: Oxford University Press, 2012.

Saler, Michael. *The Avant-Garde in Interwar England: Medieval Modernism and the London Underground*. Oxford: Oxford University Press, 1999.

Sampsell-Willmann, Kate. *Lewis Hine as Social Critic*. Jackson: University Press of Mississippi, 2009.

Samuel, Raphael. *Theatres of Memory*. Vol. 1, *Past and Present in Contemporary Culture*. London: Verso, 1994.

Samuel, Raphael, and Paul Thompson *The Myths We Live By*. London: Routledge, 1990.

Sandbrook, Dominic. *Seasons in the Sun: The Battle for Britain 1974–1979*. London: Penguin, 2012.

Sandbrook, Dominic. *State of Emergency: The Way We Were: Britain 1970–1974*. London: Penguin, 2010.

Saunders, James. *Nightmare: The Ernest Saunders Story*. London: Hutchinson, 1989.

Savage, Mike. *Identities and Social Change in Britain since 1940: The Politics of Method*. Oxford: Oxford University Press, 2010.

Scott, Peter. "Women, Other 'Fresh' Workers, and the New Manufacturing Workforce of Interwar Britain." *International Review of Social History* 45, no. 3 (2000): 449–74.

Sekula, Allan. "Photography between Labour and Capital." In *Mining Photographs and Other Pictures: A Selection from the Negative Archives of Shedden Studio, Glace Bay, Cape Breton 1948–1968*, 193–268. Glace Bay, Nova Scotia: NSCAD/UCCB Press, 2000.

Sennett, Richard. *The Corrosion of Character: The Personal Consequences of Work in the New Capitalism*. London: Norton, 1998.

Sidorick, Daniel. *Condensed Capitalism: Campbell Soup and the Pursuit of Cheap Production in the Twentieth Century*. Ithaca, NY: Cornell University Press, 2009.

Skinner, Joan *Form and Fancy: Factories and Factory Buildings by Wallis, Gilbert and Partners, 1916–1939*. Liverpool, UK: Liverpool University Press, 1997.

Smith, Chris, John Child, and Michael Rowlinson *Reshaping Work: The Cadbury Experience*. Cambridge, UK: Cambridge University Press, 1990.

Spens, Michael. *Gardens of the Mind: The Genius of Geoffrey Jellicoe*. Woodbridge, UK: Antique Collectors' Club, 1992.

Spicer, John, Chris Thurman, John Walters, and Simon Ward. *Intervention in the Modern UK Brewing Industry*. Basingstoke, UK: Palgrave, 2012.

Stamp, Gavin *Anti-Ugly: Excursions in English Architecture and Design*. London: Aurum, 2013.

Stamp, Gavin "Giles Gilbert Scott and the Problem of Modernism." *Architectural Design* 10–11 (1979): 72–83.

Standing, Guy. *The Precariat: The New Dangerous Class*. London: Bloomsbury, 2011.

Stasz, Clarice. "The Early History of Visual Sociology." In *Images of Information: Still Photography in the Social Sciences*, edited by John Wagner, 119–137. London: Sage, 1979.

Stebbing, Peter. "Industrial Image 1918 to 1986." In *Industrial Image; British Industrial Photography 1843 to 1986*, edited by Sue Davies and Caroline Collier, 37–65. London: Photographers' Gallery, 1986.

Stewart, Graham *Bang! A History of Britain in the 1980s*. London: Atlantic Books, 2013.

Strangleman, Tim. "Networks, Place and Identities in Post-Industrial Mining Communities." *International Journal of Urban and Regional Research* 25, no. 2 (2001): 253–67.

Strangleman, Tim. "The Nostalgia for Permanence at Work? The End of Work and Its Commentators." *Sociological Review* 55, no. 1 (2007): 81–103.

Strangleman, Tim. "Representations of Labour: Visual Sociology and Work." *Sociological Compass* 2, no. 4 (2008): 1491–505.

Strangleman, Tim. "'Smokestack Nostalgia,' 'Ruin Porn,' or Working-Class Obituary: The Role and Meaning of Deindustrial Representation." *International Labor and Working-Class History* 84 (Winter 2013): 23–37.

Strangleman, Tim. "Visual Sociology and Work Organization: An Historical Approach." In *The Routledge Companion to Visual Organization*, edited by Emma Bell, Samantha Warren, and Jonathan E. Schroeder. London: Taylor and Francis, 2013.

Strangleman, Tim. "Ways of (Not) Seeing Work: The Visual as a Blind Spot in WES?" *Work, Employment and Society* 18, no. 1 (2004): 179–92.

Strangleman, Tim. *Work Identity at the End of the Line? Privatisation and Culture Change in the UK Rail Industry*. Basingstoke, UK: Palgrave, 2004.

Strangleman, Tim. "Work Identity in Crisis? Rethinking the Problem of Attachment and Loss at Work." *Sociology* 46, no. 3 (2012): 411–25.

Strangleman, Tim, Emma Hollywood, Huw Beynon, Ray Hudson, and Katy Bennett. "Heritage Work: Re-representing the Work Ethic in the Coalfields." *Sociological Research Online* 4, no. 1 (1999).

Strangleman, Tim, and James Rhodes. "The 'New' Sociology of Deindustrialisation? Understanding Industrial Change." *Sociology Compass* 8, no. 4 (2014): 411–21.

Swann, Paul. *The British Documentary Film Movement 1926–1946*. Cambridge, UK: Cambridge University Press, 1989.

Symons, Julian. *The Thirties: A Dream Revolved*. London: Cresset Press, 1960.

Tenfelde, Klaus, ed. *Pictures of Krupp: Photography and History in the Industrial Age*. London: Philip Wilson Publishers, 2005.

Terkel, Studs. *Working: People Talk about What They Do All Day and How They Feel about What They Do*. New York: Pantheon Books, 1972.

Thompson, Edward Palmer. *The Making of the English Working Class*. London: Penguin, 1963.

Thompson, Edward Palmer. "Peculiarities of the English." In *The Socialist Register*, edited by Ralph Miliband and John Saville, 311–362. London: Merlin, 1965.

Todd, Selina. "Affluence, Class and Crown Street: Reinvestigating the Post-War Working Class." *Contemporary British History* 22, no. 4 (2008): 501–18.

Tomlinson, Jim. "De-industrialization Not Decline: A New Meta-narrative for Post-War British History." *Twentieth Century British History* 27, no. 1 (2016): 76–99.

Trigg, Dylan. *The Aesthetics of Decay: Nothingness, Nostalgia, and the Absence of Reason*. New York: Peter Lang, 2006.

Turner, Alwyn W. *Rejoice! Rejoice! Britain in the 1980s*. London: Aurum Press, 2010.

Walley, Christine. *Exit Zero: Family and Class in Postindustrial Chicago*. Chicago: Chicago University Press, 2013.

Ward, John. "The Walter Nurnberg Photograph Collection at the National Museum of Photography, Film and Television, Bradford." In *Presenting Pictures*, edited by Bernard Finn, 146–56. London: Science Museum, 2004.

Watkins, Charles. *Trees, Woods and Forests: A Social and Cultural History*. London: Reaktion, 2014.

Weber, Max. "Capitalism and Rural Society in Germany." In *From Max Weber: Essays in Sociology*, edited by Hans H. Gerth and C. Wright Mills, 363–85. London: Routledge, 1970.

Weil, David. *Fissured Workplace: Why Work Became So Bad for So Many and What Can Be Done to Improve It*. Cambridge, MA: Harvard University Press, 2014.

Wheen, Francis. *Strange Days Indeed: The Golden Age of Paranoia*. London: Fourth Estate, 2009.

Whipps, Stuart. *Ming Jue: Photographs of Longbridge and Nanjing*. Walsall, UK: The New Art Gallery Walsall, 2008.

Whiting, Richard. "Affluence and Industrial Relations in Post-War Britain." *Contemporary British History* 22, no. 4 (2008): 519–36.

Wiener, Martin. *English Culture and the Decline of the Industrial Spirit 1850–1980*. Cambridge, UK: Cambridge University Press, 1981.

Wiesen, S. Jonathan. *West German Industry and the Challenge of the Nazi Past, 1945–1955*. Chapel Hill: University of North Carolina Press, 2001.

Williams, Karel. "From Shareholder Value to Present-Day Capitalism." *Economy and Society* 29 (2000): 1–12.

Williams, Raymond. *The Country and the City*. Oxford: Oxford University Press, 1973.

Williams, Raymond. *Marxism and Literature*. Oxford: Oxford University Press, 1977.

Williamson, Margret. *Life at the ICI: Memories of Working at ICI Billingham.* Hartlepool, UK: Teesside Industrial Memories Project, 2008.

Williamson, Philip. *National Crisis and National Government: British Politics, the Economy and Empire, 1926–1932.* Cambridge, UK: Cambridge University Press, 2003.

Wilson, Derek. *Dark and Light: The Story of the Guinness Family.* London: Orion Books, 1998.

Wollman, David H., and Donald R. Inman. *Portraits in Steel: An Illustrated History of Jones and Laughlin Steel Corporation.* Kent, OH: Kent State University Press, 1999.

Yates, JoAnne. *Control through Communication: Rise of System in American Management.* Baltimore, MD: Johns Hopkins University Press, 1993.

Yenne, Bill. *Guinness: The 250-Year Quest for the Perfect Pint.* Hoboken, NJ: John Wiley, 2007.

Yow, Valerie. *Recording Oral History: A Guide for the Humanities and Social Sciences.* Plymouth, UK: Altamira Press, 2005.

Zadoorian, Michael. *The Lost Tiki Palaces of Detroit.* Detroit: Wayne State University Press, 2009.

Index

THE OXFORD ORAL HISTORY SERIES

J. TODD MOYE (University of North Texas)
KATHRYN NASSTROM (University of San Francisco), and
ROBERT PERKS (The British Library), *Series Editors*
DONALD A RITCHIE, *Senior Advisor*